Dyslexia at College

Increasing numbers of dyslexic students are now attending colleges and universities, yet tutors still tend to have very little specific training to help them deal with the needs of these students. This can cause problems for both student and teacher.

Through their wide experience of working with students with dyslexia, Dorothy Gilroy and Tim Miles are able to offer useful and practical advice to students about how to get the most from their college experience and the kinds of support which are available. They also provide teachers with the information they require in order to meet the needs of those students more effectively.

In this new edition of their well-known text, they have thoroughly up-dated and expanded their original material. In accordance with recent thinking, the book emphasises not just the the weaknesses of dyslexics, but their special talents. Many more dyslexics now go to college or university compared with previously; and the book gives advice not only to students but also to tutors and those concerned with setting up support services. There is also a chapter on the use of new technology.

Dorothy Gilroy and **Tim Miles** both work in the Dyslexia Unit at the University of Wales at Bangor. They have extensive experience of working with dyslexic students and their teachers. Dorothy Gilroy is the author of *Dyslexia and Higher Education* and Tim Miles is the co-author (with Elaine Miles) of *Help for Dyslexic Children* and co-editor of *Dyslexia and Mathematics*.

Dyslexia at College

Second edition

D.E. Gilroy and T.R. Miles
with contributions from C.R. Wilsher,
A.B. Bullock, S.J. Martin, S. Batty and
F. Zinovieff

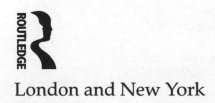

London and New York

First edition published 1986
by Methuen & Co. Ltd.

Reprinted 1992
by Routledge
11 New Fetter Lane, London EC4P 4EE

Second edition published 1996
by Routledge

Simultaneously published in the USA and Canada
by Routledge
29 West 35th Street, New York, NY 10001

© 1996 D.E. Gilroy and T.R. Miles

Text designed by Mark Mitchell

Typeset in Palatino by
Ponting–Green Publishing Services, Chesham, Bucks
Printed and bound in Great Britain by
Clays Ltd, St Ives plc

British Library Cataloguing in Publication Data
A catalogue record for this book is available from the
British Library

Library of Congress Cataloguing in Publication Data
A catalogue record for this book has been requested

ISBN 0–415–12778–5

Contents

Foreword

This book is intended for dyslexic students of all ages, and for their teachers and advisors. It deals in particular with the needs of those who have entered, or hope to enter, some form of tertiary education, whether at Art College, Sixth Form College, College of Higher Education, or University. We shall use the word 'college' to refer in general to these different institutions and the word 'student' to refer to anyone taking such courses.

Since the book was first published in 1986 the number of dyslexics who are entering Higher Education has increased dramatically (for detailed statistics see Chapter 3, note 3.15). This is due partly to the greater public awareness of dyslexia since the 1981 Education Act, the improvement of examination provisions, and the increasing support given to their members by local Dyslexia Associations; it is also now much more feasible for dyslexic students to enter Higher Education through routes such as BTEC (Business and Technology Education Council) and GNVQ (General National Vocational Qualifications) which emphasize vocational and practical as well as theoretical skills. ACCESS courses have opened up opportunities for people in their thirties and forties (and occasionally for those who are even older), many of whom did not realize in their younger days that they were dyslexic but who now recognize that they have many more talents than they originally supposed.

As a result of growing numbers, support services for dyslexic students in Higher Education have begun to develop in many institutions. These have been enhanced by funding from HEFC (the Higher Education Funding Council) in 1993–4 and 1994–5. The need, therefore, for understanding on the part of the tutors and for self-understanding on the part of dyslexics has become even greater than when this book first appeared.

Many of our suggestions are simple matters of common sense, and we do not doubt that plenty of 'sound practice' already exists among both tutors and students. Moreover some of the points which we make, for example those concerned with study skills and essay writing, may be of help to non-dyslexic students also. It is important, however, that those working with dyslexics, and indeed the dyslexics themselves, should have a clear understanding of what their distinctive needs are. It is widely agreed that departures from 'sound practice' are more damaging to dyslexics than they are to non-dyslexics.

The main changes in the 1996 edition are as follows. (1) The research information in Chapter 1 has been up-dated, and attention is called to the evidence that because of their unusual balance of skills dyslexics may well have quite unusual talents in certain areas. There is less tendency now than there was ten years ago to think of dyslexia as a 'handicap', and we have tried to reflect this point in the book as a whole. (2) There is a new Chapter 2 which is entitled 'Understanding your assessment'. Most dyslexics nowadays will at some stage of their lives have had an assessment, and we believe that some of them will need help in putting what they have been told to best use. (3) The previous Chapter 2, now Chapter 3, has been up-dated to take account of the many different routes to Higher Education which are now possible. (4) Chapters 4 to 12 and Chapters 16 to 18 (Chapters 3 to 10 of the 1986 edition) have been added to and modified to take account of the experience which both authors, particularly DEG, have gained since the first edition was published. (5) Chapters 13, 14, and 15 are new. In Chapter 13 we thought that it would be appropriate to try to remove some of the worry experienced by a number of dyslexic students over mathematics and statistics; Chapter 14 discusses the many recent advances in information technology, while Chapter 15 indicates the extent to which special examination provision has become available for dyslexics in the last few years. DEG is now named as first author, since her work contributed to a much larger share of the second edition.

Where appropriate, documentation of the claims made in the main text has been included in the form of notes to each chapter, along with extra comments which would have interrupted the flow of the argument in the main text. These are available for consultation if the reader so wishes. Recommended books on study skills and related topics are given in a separate section at the end.

We have used 'he' and 'she' interchangeably on the grounds that students and tutors can be of either sex! Readers should make the necessary adjustments.

We should like to express our gratitude to all those dyslexic students – too numerous to name individually – who have talked to us about their personal needs and thus contributed to the writing of this book. We should also like to thank the five ex-students who have written appendices – Colin Wilsher, Andrew Bullock, Stephen Martin, Simon Batty, and Fiona Zinovieff. Finally we should like to thank Neil Browning and Bethan Henderson, both of the School of Psychology, University of Wales, Bangor, for all their help with the copying of material on to the appropriate disks.

D.E. GILROY
T.R. MILES
Bangor, 1995

Authors' note

You are strongly advised to read this book only *in small 'doses'*. We suggest you select from the table of contents those sections which are *relevant* to your needs on a particular occasion – do *not* try to read the book *all at once!*

Chapter 1

The dyslexic's strengths and weaknesses

WHAT IS DYSLEXIA?

By the time they have reached the age of 16 the great majority of diagnosed dyslexics will almost certainly be clear in their own minds where their main strengths and weaknesses lie. For the benefit of tutors and counsellors, however, and perhaps also for the benefit of those dyslexic students who have not had their difficulties fully explained to them, we thought it would be helpful in this first chapter to indicate briefly what dyslexia is and, in particular, how it affects those young adults who are taking (or who are interested in taking) courses of an academic kind.

Perhaps the simplest thing to say is that dyslexia involves a distinctive balance of skills. As will be seen in more detail later, dyslexics may often be very creative: they may have special gifts in engineering, computer programming, art, modelling, and the like; many of them have high reasoning powers, and some of them show a sensitive appreciation of literature and drama. The stumbling block is the written word. In almost all cases there will be a history of lateness in learning to read, while in almost all cases spelling is likely to remain very weak. Many have difficulty in learning new symbols and in memorizing lists of words, particularly if the individual items have to be put in the correct order. In addition, many cannot recite arithmetical tables and have idiosyncratic methods for doing subtraction. Some of them, when they speak, put words and syllables in the wrong order (for example, 'par cark', for 'car park') and many have difficulty in recalling auditory instructions or in 'taking in' written material if it is presented for only a very brief time (**see note 1.1**).

There is clear evidence that the condition runs in families, and it is possible that it is more common in boys than in girls, though in the last few years this has been called into question (**see note 1.2**). It is now established beyond doubt that it has an anatomical basis. Evidence for this is given below.

If during the dyslexic's school days teachers fail to understand the distinctive nature of his difficulties they may accuse him of pigheadedness ('How can he be so good at mending the television set yet so obstinate when it comes to reading and writing?'), of laziness, of lack of motivation, and the like. What can happen, of course, is that in an unsympathetic environment a dyslexic child may become discouraged. However, once he realizes – and his teachers realize – that the difficulties have arisen for some constitutional reason (or, to put the matter in simple terms, because that is how he is made) these feelings of discouragement are likely to be lessened. Indeed most dyslexics, when their difficulties are explained to them, experience an overwhelming sense of relief.

Occasionally, however, there are exceptions. Those who are diagnosed as dyslexic later in life sometimes worry at the thought of a long 'grind' ahead of them, and in some cases there is the fear that they may have passed the condition on to their children. To 'label' a condition does not, of course, make it any different, but those few individuals who are distressed by discovering that they are dyslexic may not always appreciate this. They can perhaps best be helped by a frank discussion of both their strengths and their weaknesses: a 'label' without such discussion is at best pointless, while at worst it can be demoralizing. This is why it is particularly irresponsible for any professional to 'throw' the label 'dyslexia' at someone without explanation. In the sections which follow we shall indicate how far the difficulties associated with dyslexia persist into adulthood.

READING, WRITING AND SPELLING

For most dyslexic adults, reading as such is not normally a major difficulty provided they are not under pressure of time and that the material is not too complicated. The main problems are that they are liable to be *slow* at reading and to be more than usually vulnerable when it comes to *mis*reading (**see note 1.3**).

With regard to slowness, it may take them longer than their non-dyslexic colleagues to read books or articles, to locate a word in a dictionary or a passage in a book or play, to find the right place in a mathematical table, to make sense of what has been written on the blackboard, or to check the times of buses or trains. Those dyslexics who can read reasonably adequately to themselves may nevertheless feel severely threatened when asked to read aloud (**see note 1.4**).

With regard to misreading, there are some quite serious risks which we shall need to consider more fully when we come to discuss examination techniques (Chapters 16 and 17). For instance, we know of a student in a physics examination who misread the direction of a vector line and wasted three-quarters of an hour before discovering his mistake. It is not that the adult dyslexic *cannot* read, but he needs to take extra care to avoid making mistakes which may seriously 'throw' him.

In addition, many dyslexics make errors in writing – including the omission of words or parts of words and the transposition of letters. One student, instead of writing 'correlated' wrote 'corelatated' and when told that he had made a mistake said that he could see nothing wrong (**see note 1.5**). A graduate student who had come to us for advice afterwards sent a cheque and explained in his letter that it was a small 'denotation' to the Dyslexia Unit.

Handwriting is sometimes difficult to read and may give the impression of being immature. Since relatively less attention is paid at school nowadays to spelling, one cannot pick out a dyslexic student from his spelling errors alone; but worry over correct spellings may sometimes cramp the dyslexic's style or lead to the substitution of a less effective word which is easier to spell in place of the word which he originally wanted.

SPOKEN LANGUAGE

Dyslexics are liable – more than others – to mispronounce words. The following mispronunciations were heard by one of us (DEG) at a student discussion group: 'arriteration' for 'reiteration', 'simpler' for 'similar', 'relieve' for 'believe', and 'up the ball' instead of 'up the wall'. Unless one is specially on the look out for them, errors of this kind are not always noticed in ordinary conversation. However, they may have repercussions on spelling and in some cases may give rise to confusion – as in the case of the psychology student who was unsure whether a particular piece of research had been carried out by Bradley or by Baddeley.

ESSAYS AND EXAMINATIONS

Planning and structuring of essays is often a problem, not, indeed, because the dyslexic student has too little to say – usually quite the opposite is the case – but because of a limitation of the amount of material that he can 'hold in mind' without writing it down. Even though he is fully capable of logical reasoning he may fail to appreciate that what has found its way to the paper does not adequately represent what he wanted to say. Essays written by dyslexic students, even though they may be full of good ideas, sometimes give the impression of lack of planning and structure. The same impression can also be given in their examination scripts, and, as we shall see in Chapter 18, this can give rise to problems of grading.

CALCULATION

Tutors should not be too surprised if some of their dyslexic students find difficulty over seemingly simple calculations. This can be true even in the case of those who can grasp highly complex mathematical ideas. For example, a university lecturer in physics has reported that he still does not know his six times table! 'I know that six sixes are thirty-six, but if you ask me what seven sixes are ... [counts laboriously upwards on his fingers] ... Forty-two; am I right?' (see note 1.6). By the age of 16 it is likely that most of those with a mathematical bent will have taught themselves compensatory strategies over calculation even though they may remain slow at it; nevertheless they may sometimes be caught unawares, particularly if they have at the same time to cope with advanced mathematical or statistical concepts. On a bad day things may simply 'go blank', and tutors unfamiliar with dyslexia can all too easily assume that the student is either very lazy or of very limited ability (see note 1.7). More will be said about mathematics in Chapter 13.

SOCIAL PROBLEMS

These can take many forms. For example, quite a number of students have told us of their embarrassment when they fail to remember someone's name. Several have found that learning to drive has highlighted their difficulties in following instructions over left and right. Recently, a student who was in the navy before coming to college said that a senior officer had sworn at him for confusing 'port' and 'starboard'. Some have told us that they avoid playing darts because, if they are asked to keep the score, they cannot carry out the calculations quickly enough. Some report that they mix up telephone numbers when dialling. Recently, a student confessed – perhaps not altogether seriously — that although most of his problems were behind him he was still the despair of his bank manager since the 'amount in words' on his cheques regularly failed to agree with the 'amount in figures'! (see note 1.8). Many dyslexic students can, indeed, laugh about their present difficulties and speak of their earlier struggles without bitterness, but it is important for tutors to remember that the scars may not have entirely healed.

SOME ENCOURAGING RESEARCH

As was mentioned earlier, dyslexics can sometimes be extremely gifted. They may well be strong on logic: thus many of them are good at evaluating arguments, weighing up evidence, and reaching appropriate decisions. Many are good at constructional tasks, for instance wiring up a circuit or mending the television set, at painting and modelling, at fashion design or at creating ingenious buildings from Lego and similar materials. Although we do not have exact statistics we think it highly likely that there is a relatively large proportion of dyslexic students on art and design courses.

It is now almost certain that the dyslexic's unusual balance of skills has a physiological basis. One of the most important pieces of recent research in this area has been that of Dr Albert Galaburda and his colleagues at Harvard University. By means of suitable techniques it was possible for Dr Galaburda to carry out post-mortem examinations on the brains of eight individuals known to have been dyslexic in their lifetime (**see note 1.9**). The research involved a special study of that part of the temporal lobe known as the *planum temporale*. Not only were there *ectopias* (intrusions of cells from one layer to another) which in themselves are evidence for unusual brain function; more importantly, it was found that in all eight cases, instead of the usual asymmetry which is found in 75 to 80 per cent of unselected brains, the two plana were approximately the same size. It is widely agreed by neurologists that in most people (though not everyone) the left half of the brain controls speech whereas the right half is concerned with visuo-spatial tasks and, in the words of Springer and Deutsch (**see note 1.10**), processes information 'simultaneously and holistically'. It therefore makes sense to suppose that in dyslexics there is an unusual balance between the functions of the two hemispheres: as a result they are weak at certain tasks involving rapid processing of language and at thinking in a 'linear' way but strong on creativity and 'lateral' thinking.

The findings of Dr Galaburda and his colleagues have recently been confirmed by studies of living brains (**see note 1.11**) and can therefore be regarded as firmly based.

A book which has developed this area of research in a particularly striking way is *In the Mind's Eye* by Thomas West (**see note 1.12**). West provides biographical sketches of a number of highly gifted and creative individuals – including Faraday, Einstein, and Thomas Alva Edison – who have nevertheless displayed the distinctive *balance* of skills characteristic of dyslexia. There is evidence that a number of them had highly chequered careers at school. West argues that many of the 'literacy' tasks at which they were weak can now be carried out by computer, and he thinks it likely that in the next few decades the creative skills of dyslexics will come into their own.

A POSSIBLE THEORY

There is no single agreed theory as to what causes dyslexia. However, one of the most important of current suggestions is that dyslexics have difficulty in coping adequately with stimuli which change too rapidly (**see note 1.13**).

Whether or not this is true in general, there is one very important – and familiar – situation where inability to cope at speed is a very severe disadvantage. This is the situation in which we need to listen to the sounds of speech. Although the experienced language user distinguishes separate words, speech from the physical point of view is a continuous and rapidly moving flow of energy changes; and what is relatively difficult for the dyslexic is to generate and reproduce the *spoken representations* of the things which he experiences. The difficulty is thus one of *verbal labelling*. A common description is to say that dyslexia involves a weakness at the *phonological* level (where phonology is the study of speech sounds in so far as they convey meaning). If a person's ability to deal with fast moving auditory stimuli is inadequate this will have some subtle effects whenever that person has to use language (**see note 1.14**). It is also likely that language skills in the dyslexic do not easily become automatic (**see note 1.15**).

It should be remembered, too, that if a stimulus has a spoken representation – for example 'CAT', '?', or 'x – 3' – then it is functioning as a *symbol*; and one aspect of dyslexia is therefore a difficulty in generating and recalling symbols (**see note 1.16**).

However, once the function of a given symbol has been understood, the dyslexic has no particular difficulty with comprehension. In general, the tasks at which dyslexics are likely to be successful are those which require good reasoning power and constructional ability but not the processing of symbols at speed.

CONCLUSIONS

From what has been said, it will be plain that there is no one sign by which a dyslexic person can be picked out. The manifestations of dyslexia are varied; to use the medical term, dyslexia is a 'syndrome', that is, a cluster or family of difficulties which regularly go together but which may take somewhat different forms in different individuals. By the age of 16 many dyslexics will have discovered ways of coping with most of these difficulties, and it is therefore possible for an unsympathetic tutor or examiner to say that he 'can't find anything wrong'. What one needs to look for is a combination of signs, any one of which would be insignificant on its own but which in conjunction add up to a meaningful picture of a person who is both gifted yet subtly handicapped. Many of us may have occasional uncertainties over left and right or may misdial a seven-figure telephone number without this being more than a temporary lapse. Similarly, a person may say 'laxadaisical' for 'lackadaisical' or write 'itinary' for 'itinerary' simply because he has not been taught to pay attention to the relevant differences. It is characteristic of the dyslexic, however, that he regularly makes mistakes which the rest of us make occasionally. If, in addition, there is a history of lateness in learning to read, poor spelling, and evidence of similar difficulties in other members of the family the pieces begin to fit together in such a way that a diagnosis of dyslexia becomes progressively more likely.

Perhaps the best advice that we can give to tutors is that they should be on the look-out for incongruities and that, if surprising mistakes or lapses occur, they should not immediately assume that the student is being lazy or 'difficult' or has lost interest in the course. It may even be that the time is right for some constructive words of encouragement.

Finally, if any student who has not so far been diagnosed as dyslexic has read this chapter and recognizes himself in some of the descriptions we strongly advise him to have himself assessed without delay (**see note 1.17**). It is possible he may be only a mild case, but whether this is so or not a positive diagnosis will almost certainly help him to make sense of some of the problems which he experienced earlier in life. It does not follow that he will have to make any appreciable changes in his lifestyle, and he need not be afraid that anyone will press him to do so. An increase in self-knowledge, however, is likely to be beneficial; and if there is a problem, however mild, it is not very sensible to 'shove it under the carpet' by denying its existence.

Chapter 2

Understanding your assessment

INTRODUCTION

In this chapter we offer some suggestions as to how the information obtained after an assessment can be put to best use. (If you have already been assessed and have no particular queries about the assessment or the psychologist's report we suggest you skip this chapter.)

Many dyslexic students nowadays before they reach college will have had assessments indicating that they are dyslexic and making recommendations. However this is not always true. We have come across plenty of students (particularly older ones) whose dyslexia has not been picked up until after the start of their college courses. In some cases tutors or lecturers have suspected dyslexia on the basis of their essays or other written work and in some cases they themselves have suspected that they are dyslexic and have come forward for assessment.

There may, of course, be students who for various reasons are poor spellers but who do not have the other typical signs associated with dyslexia. To deal with such cases many colleges operate a screening procedure: because a full assessment by a psychologist is expensive and there may be problems over funding it tutors at some colleges are asked to be as certain as possible that a student is dyslexic before sending him on to the psychologist.

THE DISABLED STUDENTS' ALLOWANCE

Now for some good news! Students who are on a maintenance grant and who are assessed as dyslexic can claim a Disabled Students' Allowance; this is an extra sum of money designed to help you through your course. (Do not, incidentally, be put off by the word 'disabled'. A dyslexic is not 'disabled' in any sense that need cause concern. It is simply that because you have special needs it is necessary for certain administrative purposes that you should be classified alongside those who are disabled.) (**See note 2.1.**)

It is a three-part allowance which consists of:

1 a general allowance intended to cover extra costs incurred by specific aspects of the disability which make it difficult for you to study (photocopying, for example);
2 an allowance for payment to non-medical helpers (for example those who provide special tutorial help);
3 a further allowance for major items of specialist equipment such as word processors (**see note 2.2**).

A formal assessment is, of course, essential for those who wish to claim special examination provision or to qualify for the Disabled Students' Allowance – those in charge of the money need to be satisfied that you are a genuine case!

As a result of the assessment the psychologist may make specific recommendations about your 'educational management'. For example, she may indicate the study support that you need, the type of computer equipment that you need, whether you should be given special examination provision, whether you would be helped by coloured filters or lenses (see Chapter 8), and so on.

You will be able to hand the whole of your report to your college staff, and the relevant section will indicate to them your needs, particularly with regard to special provision in examinations. If these needs are set out clearly it may then be possible for you to reclaim the cost of meeting them from the Disabled Students' Allowance. It will also be necessary for you to send the report to your Local Education Authority in support of your application for the payment.

During the assessment itself you will be asked to carry out a number of tasks or tests. The aim is to find out both your strong and your weak points. Even the word 'test' may be off-putting for some people, particularly if they have had unpleasant experiences of 'testing' in the past. However, in this case, there is no need to feel threatened. You are in no way being 'got at', and you will normally find that the psychologist who carries out the test is glad to talk to you about the results and willing to answer your questions.

READING AND SPELLING

The assessment will almost certainly include tests of reading and spelling. Your results on these tests will give an indication of the level of reading and spelling that you have reached. The key question you need to ask is whether this level is adequate for your needs. If it is not, then you would be wise to look for further help either before your course starts or, if you have already started it, as something additional to your existing studies.

The central aim of the assessment is to obtain an accurate indication both of your strengths and weaknesses. If you then decide that it is possible to do something about your weaknesses (as it certainly is in the case of poor reading and spelling) and that the effort is worth it then the assessment has helped you.

Your performance may be scored in terms of what are called 'percentiles'. If you are in, say, the 50th percentile this means that half of your fellow students will have scored higher than you on the test and half lower. If you are in the 95th percentile only 5 per cent of them will have scored higher; if you are in the 5th percentile only 5 per cent of them will have scored lower.

In all scores of this kind you are being compared with other people. Such comparisons can be useful *for some purposes*. However, there may also be times when it is more appropriate to compare your *present score* with the score which you yourself obtained on *an earlier occasion*, for example, if you want to know whether your reading performance has improved. In this connection some educationalists have found it helpful to distinguish *'norm based'* from *'criterion referenced'* tests. Let us suppose that you are told you have scored at the 50th percentile: this figure would be 'norm based' if the intention was to compare your result with that of other people, or in other words with the 'norm'. If, however, the issue is *whether you have reached a certain level* then the test is being used as a criterion referenced test; and in your case this is perhaps a more helpful way of using the results. The point can be illustrated by means of an example from a quite different field – that of taking your driving test. Here your examiner will not be very much interested in your performance relative to that of others; what concerns him is whether your driving is up to a particular standard. The driving test can therefore be regarded as a criterion referenced test.

It is possible (though this is less common nowadays) that your performance will be described in terms of a 'reading age' and of a 'spelling age'. If, for example, you have a 'reading age' of 11 years this means that your reading is on a level with that of a typical (non-dyslexic) 11-year-old. It does not, of course, mean that your mentality is in other ways like that of an 11-year-old! You should remember that most 11-year-olds are pretty adequate readers; and if you have a 'reading age' of 12 years and a 'spelling age' of 11½ years you should not have too much difficulty with college courses.

If you are interested you may like to talk to the person who did the testing about how the scores were obtained. Some reading tests involve the identification of single words whereas others involve making sense of a passage of prose – in which case there is a certain amount of scope for guessing from the context. In the case of single word reading the usual procedure is to award one point for each word correctly read; and it is worth remembering that this method of scoring does not differentiate between 'near misses' and total failures.

There is the same limitation in the case of spelling. In general, a 'reading age' and a 'spelling age' can normally be regarded as a reasonably accurate indicator of your performance on a given occasion, but you should of course always remember that numerical scores do not tell us everything!

INTELLIGENCE

This is also true if you are given an 'intelligence test'. There is evidence which suggests that those who are successful in some or all of these tests are also likely to be successful in the skills which are needed in studying for a degree.

However, for various reasons, scores on intelligence tests are somewhat controversial (**see note 2.3**), particularly in the case of dyslexics; and we therefore offer some words of caution. Whatever else, if your tester uses the traditional concept of 'IQ' (intelligence quotient) do not regard the resultant figure as something cast in tablets of stone. Several decades ago it was widely believed that every individual possessed an 'IQ' which was then assumed to be something which cannot change and which imposed a 'ceiling' on what the person could achieve. As a result, people came to regard the IQ figure as being of crucial importance, and this attitude has still not entirely disappeared. In fact, it is known from many sources that all kinds of skills can be developed by suitable training (**see note 2.4**); and we have found this to be particularly so in the case of dyslexics. You would certainly be right to feel encouraged if you find that you have come out with a high score on an intelligence test – it is all too easy for dyslexics to underestimate their abilities; but in our experience we have often found that low scores give a misleading picture (**see note 2.5**). Our advice, therefore, is that if you are keen to take an academic course and if you are willing to put in the required effort a relatively low score should not discourage you. If a course genuinely turns out to be too difficult for you this will almost certainly become apparent in a matter of weeks; and for many people it is better to try something and fail (at relatively small cost in terms of time and resources) than not to attempt it (**see note 2.6**).

As always, we suggest you use common sense. Although our intention is to encourage dyslexics to 'think positive', it is worth remembering that there may be situations where you think you are keen to take a particular course but where, on reflection, you will agree that it is safer to wait for, say, a year or more, so that during this time you can reflect on whether this is really what you want.

Intelligence tests assess a variety of skills, and it is possible that your performance may be uneven. The exact spread of your scores is something that you can usefully talk to your tester about. In fact, there are some items in traditional intelligence tests, for example, items in which you have to recall strings of digits, which, so far from being measures of intelligence, are actually tapping typical dyslexic weaknesses (**see note 2.7**). This is yet another reason why giving your 'total' performance in terms of an IQ figure can be misleading.

One can say in general that if you are dyslexic it is likely that there will be a marked contrast between your intelligence test scores and your ability to spell and write essays. An accurate knowledge both of your strengths and weaknesses cannot but be helpful.

OTHER TESTS

This is also true if you are given tests other than those of reading, spelling, and intelligence, for example the Bangor Dyslexia Test (**note 2.8**). This particular test can often help you to understand more about the kinds of thing which you have found difficult and about why it has been necessary for you to think out particular compensatory strategies. Some dyslexics have found, after being given this test, that various earlier events in their lives 'fit together' as part of their dyslexia. For example, if on the basis of what they do on the Bangor Dyslexia Test one discusses with them their difficulty in remembering verbal instructions or telephone numbers they may call to mind an episode when at a much younger age they were reprimanded for failing to convey a message accurately from the school to their parents; and it is only now that they realize that their failure was a direct consequence of dyslexia. One of us (TRM) has met a famous dyslexic actor who reported both that he tended to be late for appointments and that he could not remember people's names. People had regarded this simply as arrogance; but he said that when he realized he was dyslexic he felt 'forgiven'. In general you may well find as a result of your assessment that you have gained a much better understanding of the part dyslexia has played in your life.

A FINAL WORD

If, as still occasionally happens, you are assessed by a psychologist who in your view does not fully understand about dyslexia, do not be too worried: such people, though they are a dwindling number, are still to be found! In some cases, perhaps through lack of experience, misunderstanding, or simply excessive caution, they may express reservations about the term 'dyslexia'. If you meet such a person the sensible response, in our view, is to make use of information she gives you – reading scores, spelling scores, intelligence scores, and the like – without necessarily accepting the inferences which she draws. This general principle applies, of course, to any counselling situation. Counsellors are only human – and even with the best of intentions they do not always get things right (**see note 2.9**).

Chapter 3

The move to Higher Education

THE STUDENT'S WISHES

When the question of career choice comes up, the central consideration must, of course, be the student's own wishes. Considerable sensitivity is needed, however, on the part of parents and counsellors if they are to strike the right balance between positively encouraging her on the one hand, which is often very welcome, and putting her under undue pressure which is not.

The first suggestion which we should like to make to anyone who is thinking of going to college is: **do not be afraid of taking risks**. In our experience, the ability of a dyslexic person is often underestimated – and this not merely by her teachers but often also by herself. We have frequently met parents who secretly felt that their son or daughter was very bright and well capable of taking academic courses but were reluctant to say this in public, particularly if unsympathetic teachers and educational psychologists – claiming to be 'realistic' – had told them in the past that they were over-ambitious. There may indeed be a completely sincere wish to save the student from disappointment (**see note 3.1**). Yet is it not sometimes kinder to encourage a person to attempt something, even if there is risk of failure, than to allow her to go through the rest of her life wondering if she should have made the attempt? Indeed, we have met many dyslexics who derived considerable encouragement from the knowledge that there were those who were prepared to back them 'against the odds' and in spite of their weak examination results. This has been particularly relevant in the case of mature students on ACCESS courses; such people have often come back into education with few traditional qualifications and therefore might be expected to find academic work difficult.

We do not dispute that there are risks for dyslexics if they attempt college courses. However, such risks seem fully justified provided the prospective student is aware of them, is willing to work hard, and is prepared for possible disappointments. We believe that it can often be a greater error for a dyslexic to set her sights too low than to set them too high (**see note 3.2**). If her interests are academic there is every reason for her to try for a place at college.

ROUTES TO HIGHER EDUCATION

We suggest that parents and prospective students should make themselves aware of the various routes by which entry to higher education can be achieved. During the last few years (we write in 1995) changes have occurred in Britain which are likely to lead to better opportunities for the dyslexic student to display her abilities; and those living in other parts of the world may well be able to explore similar possibilities. A dyslexic with only a small number of passes at GCSE (General Certificate of Secondary Education) may like to consider courses in a College of Further Education (**see note 3.3**). Sixth Form Colleges are also broadening their range of courses. There are step-by-step courses, such as Foundation courses, which can lead on to BTEC or GNVQ courses of varying levels. These can lead on to HND courses ('HND' stands for 'Higher National Diploma'), to higher level NVQ courses, or to courses which lead to a degree (**see note 3.4**).

Older dyslexics who may not have been successful at school may find that an ACCESS course leading to Higher Education is their best option. These courses are specially designed for mature students who wish to return to learning. They contain core skills, such as information technology (IT), study skills, and mathematics, all of which develop the basic abilities needed for Higher Education. In some colleges there are also other short intensive courses, such as Fast Track (**see note 3.5**). Other prospective students may wish to consider reading for a degree at the Open University (**see note 3.6**).

It is also worth noting that the degree courses at some of the new universities often follow the same principles as BTEC and GNVQ courses: they tend to be more practical and less theoretical and academic than traditional university courses. Many of them are tested by continuous assessment, and the students who take them are encouraged to use many different methods of collecting, collating and presenting information. Some of them are structured on a sandwich basis, with their students spending a proportion of their time working in industry. This can give them work experience and provide them with the necessary practical training. Moreover, as in the case of the BTEC or GNVQ, assessment techniques are likely to contain a relatively large oral element, along with evaluation of their work experience and their ability to respond to real life situations. There is less emphasis on the formal written word and the final grading does not place undue reliance on examinations of the traditional type.

CHOOSING BETWEEN COURSES

Many dyslexics have skills and sensitivity in the field of human relationships, and for such people some forms of nursing or teaching, social work, probation work and the like may often be a good choice. Many, too, may wish to make use of their gifts in the area of art or design.

When you start to make enquiries you should look in particular at the content of courses, at the way in which different ones are organized, at the methods of assessment used, and at the spacing between the examinations. You will usually find Course Tutors and Admissions Tutors very willing to offer help and advice, and, if it is at all possible, you should look round the departments and consult with students who are already on the course. Many colleges now have support services for dyslexic students and produce their own publicity leaflets, and there may also be information available in the university prospectus. However, there is considerable variety between one institution and another (see note 3.7); and it should be remembered that there are likely to be many different attitudes to dyslexia not merely within the same institution but even within the same department.

Occasionally one hears of colleges who are reluctant to take dyslexic students because of the cost involved in providing the necessary services. In such places you can scarcely expect much understanding, and – unless you are a campaigner! – we would advise you to look for an institution which is more dyslexia-friendly.

All students, whether dyslexic or not, need to make sure that they choose a course which fits their abilities. At degree level it is essential that you should feel genuinely committed to the subject. At the same time, you need to be realistic about your difficulties. Thus if you find writing essays very difficult you will need to check carefully on the amount of written work which the course involves. Most courses now are organized on a modular basis, which gives students some flexibility in their choices; but we strongly advise that you check what you are committing yourself to before undertaking a particular module.

A few subjects, such as physics, require mathematics at a high level (for instance a knowledge of calculus), while there are some which need a knowledge of basic mathematics because of the use which they make of statistics. These include, among others, psychology, economics, education, agriculture, sociology, and business studies. Do not rule out the idea of taking such courses because you feel that you have problems with mathematics. There may be parts of mathematics which you have 'missed out on' at school, but they can be learned; and it is in fact quite possible for dyslexics to turn themselves into successful mathematicians. Indeed, there is no reason why those who are so inclined should not do an actual degree in mathematics (**see note** 3.8). There are, admittedly, difficulties in the early stages, but they can be overcome, in which case the way is open for challenging and enjoyable academic work. Those who have found mathematics a struggle may like to bear in mind some of the things which are said in Chapter 13.

It has also been shown on numerous occasions that dyslexic students can qualify as doctors or dentists; and it seems likely that a good understanding of anatomical and physiological processes can compensate for relative inefficiency at learning by rote the necessary medical terms. We know of a dyslexic surgeon who claims that his high visuo-spatial abilities actually put him at an advantage in certain forms of surgery in comparison with his colleagues (**see note 3.9**). Engineering calls for less by way of language skills than some subjects, and although written examinations have to be passed and clear thinking is essential, it is possible for a dyslexic student to show in an examination script that he understands a particular issue even if he cannot spell correctly or express himself elegantly. Chemistry, physics, mathematics and computer science have certain difficulties because of the amount of symbolism involved; but once the symbols are learned – which will probably take extra time – a dyslexic student may well be extremely successful. We know also of many dyslexics who have obtained honours degrees in biological subjects and we have first-hand evidence of over thirty who have achieved honours degrees in psychology. With arts subjects there is inevitably more to do by way of reading the relevant literature and writing essays, and it is unavoidable that students will have to spend very much more time over written assignments than do non-dyslexics. Degrees in English, history, sociology, economics and the like are by no means ruled out, however, and we have met a number of dyslexics who have been successful in business studies.

Philosophy has sometimes been a struggle, and although we know of a small number of dyslexic barristers or trainees, some dyslexics could find law difficult because of the amount of rote learning involved. Foreign languages are also likely to be hard going because of the effort needed in mastering the spelling systems of languages additional to English. In no case, however, should a particular course be ruled out without careful consideration of the student's individual wishes and aptitudes.

It is not impossible for dyslexic students to train as teachers. We have, in fact, had reports of dyslexic teachers having problems in dealing with the National Curriculum and with the marking of Standard Achievement Tests ('SATs'); and it is sometimes supposed that there is risk of embarrassment for them if they write a word on the blackboard which the class can see is misspelled. However, it could also be argued that a conscientious teacher will usually be able to forestall possible difficulties by suitable preparation. For example, if he is writing a report on a child he can check his spellings with a dictionary, and if he writes a misspelt word in the board in front of the class – well, it does not seem to us a major disaster if he has to admit that his spelling is poor. After all, it is widely agreed that to retain the pupils' respect one need not present oneself as being infallible (**see note 3.10**).

Some dyslexic students have expressed a wish to specialize in the teaching of dyslexic children. However, most training courses, not unreasonably, require that those whom they accept should have had some ordinary classroom experience first.

There are various additional factors which need to be considered, quite apart from the content of the course. There may well be advantages in being at a small college or in a small department where students are personally known to the tutors. Lectures to a vast audience, particularly if they involve a large amount of overhead projector work, can be quite daunting for dyslexic students. It is also wise to find out what the methods of teaching are: some, though not all, dyslexic students enjoy taking part in oral discussions, and those who do so may like to choose departments where there are regular group meetings and tutorials.

Also, since dyslexic students are likely to do themselves better justice if they are assessed in untimed conditions, it is sensible to apply to a department which does not rely solely on timed written examinations. Many departments nowadays award marks on the basis of continuous assessment and take into account performance on projects, dissertations, and the like. It is worthwhile to check how often examinations are held; in modular courses this is usually twice a year, which allows for a staggered revision load. It is also important to find out whether there is any special examination provision for dyslexics. We have found that such provision is much more common than it used to be, but it still varies considerably from one institution to another. Some colleges have a written policy; others deal with each request individually but indicate the kinds of thing that are on offer.

Another consideration is environment. You need to consider whether you prefer a country setting or a town one. Often a smaller place or a campus university is easier to get around and involves less travelling stress. In view of the extra amount of work required from dyslexic students it is wise not to live too far away from the institution since travelling to and from lectures can take up valuable time. Those who feel the need for continuing parental support should, of course, choose a college which is reasonably near home.

FILLING IN THE UCAS FORM

A problem which is likely to cause considerable heart searching is that of how to fill in the application form. (This is commonly called the '*UCAS form*' – where 'UCAS' stands for '*Universities and Colleges Admissions System*'). The form is complicated and we suggest that you photocopy it so as to have a rough copy on which you can make alterations. You should certainly ask for help in filling it in. A large amount has in fact been written about this, and a video is available from UCAS or the local Career Service (**see note 3.11**).

Some of the entries are relatively straightforward, for example, address of parent or guardian (though who can say that anything is straightforward to a dyslexic if it contains a complicated mass of symbols?). On it you have to indicate your qualifications and your choice of different universities or colleges. You are also asked to write a personal statement, in which you set out your reasons for applying for your chosen subject and outline your personal experiences and interests. If you refer to your dyslexia in this section (see below) we advise you to do so as positively as you can and to mention your strengths as well as your weaknesses. It is useful, in particular, if you can indicate both how you are at present coping with your dyslexia and how you plan to cope with it when you get to college. The same point is important if you are being interviewed. In a recent book (**see note 3.12**) David McLoughlin and his colleagues have said that what makes dyslexic adults do well are: (1) a desire to succeed, (2) being sure of their goal, and (3) being willing to take action to overcome their difficulties. This last point could be particularly important if you are to convince the admissions officer

that you are a well rounded person and that you have the ability
and determination to complete the course.

At the end of the UCAS form a referee (usually your headteacher,
or someone of comparable status) has to write a confidential report
on your suitability to take a college course. In this report it is normal
practice nowadays for the referee to refer to the candidate's
dyslexia. This brings us to a crucial question – should you yourself
mention on the UCAS form that you are dyslexic?

If you are likely to need any kind of help or support, the answer
in our view should undoubtedly be 'yes'. There is now ample
evidence that dyslexic students are perfectly capable of obtaining
high class degrees, and it is hard to believe that any appreciable
number of selectors are so ill informed that they would regard
dyslexia as such to be a barrier to admission. Indeed the opposite
may well be the case, since a dyslexic student with relatively low
grades in his examinations – where inevitably the odds are stacked
against him for reasons given in Chapter 1 – is likely to be a better
prospect, particularly in terms of creative ability and seriousness of
purpose, than a non-dyslexic student whose grades are somewhat
higher. This is a factor which we hope selectors will increasingly
come to appreciate.

A further point is this. There is now a section at the beginning of
the form where you can indicate that you have a disability or special
need. In a later section you are asked to follow this up by indicating
what special arrangements you are likely to require. You also have
to sign a statement saying that what you have put on the form is
true. Clearly, therefore, if you do not declare your dyslexia you
cannot in that case expect your college to make any special
provision.

TAKING MORE TIME?

Some dyslexic students like to consider a 'gap year' before going on
to university. This gives them chance to 'recharge their batteries'
after an intensive A-Level course and perhaps to gain some valuable

experience in voluntary work – or, indeed, paid work (**see note 3.13**). Admissions tutors welcome the idea of a 'year off' but like to see it used positively. Students may also like to bear in mind that if they are over 21 they are classed as 'mature-age' students and qualify for an extra grant. We should also like to call attention to a recommendation in the report of the Kershaw Committee (**see note 3.14**) that

> where . . . a university student is dyslexic he should be permitted to stay at the university for an extra year beyond the ordinary duration of his course. The alternative might well be a final examination level which would not reflect his true capacity.

In view of this recommendation, dyslexic students should not hesitate to discuss with their tutors the question of taking extra time over their courses. The issue is one which needs to be worked out separately for each individual. It is not necessary in the case of every dyslexic student, but our experience suggests that in suitable cases it is extremely beneficial, particularly for those students who feel themselves overwhelmed by the amount of material to be covered or who tire easily. In a three-year course the break is likely to be most useful between year 2 and year 3. During this time the student can consolidate what he has learned in the first two years and perhaps also take an advance look at some of the topics to be covered in the final year. Above all, however, he can have a change of scene and a rest so that he does not feel under too much pressure. It will almost certainly be difficult, however, to secure a grant for anything more than the usual three years.

INTERVIEWS

If the application form indicates that a candidate is dyslexic we recommend to selectors that they invite him for interview. This gives an opportunity for a joint exploration of what the course involves, whether it covers the areas in which the candidate is genuinely interested, and whether he is likely to be able to complete it successfully.

Moreover, we strongly urge selectors, when they interview dyslexic applicants, to make an extra effort to put them at their ease. A skilled interviewer can help the applicant to say what he wishes to say, while an unskilled one may cause him to 'retreat into his shell'. Indeed there is risk that questions which are asked in all innocence (e.g., 'I see your referee says that you are dyslexic – what exactly does this mean?') may be perceived as threatening or as casting doubt on the genuineness of the dyslexia. There is a risk that sometimes they will reopen old wounds, since unsympathetic teachers may have expressed such doubts in the past.

The applicant, for his part, should remember that the purpose of the interview is not to catch him out but to determine whether a particular course is suitable, and he should therefore be careful not to read more into a question than the questioner intended, particularly if this 'more' is perceived as threatening.

For dyslexic applicants' 'mock' interviews are likely to be of special help. What is involved here is that a careers adviser or teacher takes on the role of interviewer and asks searching questions similar to those which the applicant is likely be asked at the interview proper. Indeed it is useful if the 'interviewer' asks extra-difficult questions; then, if such questions occur in the real interview, the applicant will not be taken unawares. One function of the mock interview is to give the student practice at formulating his ideas, and if he is used to the procedure he will find the real interview less of a strain. Many of us fail to find the right words if we are under pressure, and in the case of the dyslexic there is the added risk of mispronunciation, stumbling, or 'going blank'.

If the student is asked about his dyslexia it is probably wise if he talks about it as objectively as possible, neither playing it down nor making too much of it. There is no reason why he should not indicate that there are certain tasks which he still finds difficult, but he should also call attention to the compensatory strategies which he has found to be useful. If his interests are academic he should make this clear, and in areas where he is enthusiastic it is an excellent thing if some of this enthusiasm can be conveyed to the interviewer.

SOME GOOD NEWS

What is good news is that the whole scene for dyslexic students has altered beyond recognition over the last twenty years. There were about 100 dyslexic students identified in British universities in 1981; in 1995 there are probably about 5000 (**see note 3.15**). In response to this rise in numbers there has been a corresponding rise in awareness and support units in higher education institutions. The Disabled Students' Allowance has meant that students can obtain help to enable them to progress through a university course more easily. SKILL, the National Bureau for Students with Disabilities, has been of particular support to dyslexic students and is always ready to offer advice both to them and to their tutors; there is also ADO, the Adult Dyslexia Organisation, which works for dyslexic students as well as adults in the workplace (**see note 3.16**). To some extent, the growth of these support services has been the result of the successes of small numbers of dyslexics who from the 1970s onwards 'beat the system' and worked their way to college despite all kinds of initial disadvantages.

Chapter 4

Preparations for college

A LOOK AHEAD TO POSSIBLE DIFFICULTIES

Many of those aged 18 and 19, when they go to college, will be leaving home for the first time. This is something which can be exciting and challenging, but inevitably the start of a new life has its complexities. Similarly, mature students, maybe newly assessed as dyslexic, will now be undertaking a much more complicated lifestyle; for instance they may be commuting into college on top of running a home and family. There may even be some doubts and misunderstandings to cope with from family and friends. In our experience if it is possible for students to develop some habits of **planning** and **organization** (don't groan!) the early months at college can be much easier. It is, of course, a bonus if you can start on this before you go to college; but it is never too late to learn even if you are part way through your course.

We begin with a comment about attitude: **Think positive**. We have given to some of our students a poster showing the following words: **No negative thoughts – I can do it**. It is very easy if you are dyslexic to feel bad about yourself and to develop a low self-image. If things start going wrong, you tend to blame yourself – and perhaps your dyslexia as well. If you forget something and blame yourself for always being forgetful, you are more than likely to forget something again – and so it goes on. Watch out, therefore, for the negative thoughts; look at what you have already achieved in getting to college; realize that most new students – and those well on in their courses – forget things, muddle dates, go through patches of disorganization. It is not all down to your dyslexia!

Next, a word of caution. If one tells a dyslexic that he needs to be 'tidy' and 'structured' this can sometimes be perceived as threatening. Many people get through their work quite successfully with a considerable amount of 'chaos' in their lives; and such people may find that too much order imposes too rigid a discipline and hence is too stressful to deal with (see note 4.1). On the other hand, we have seen dyslexic students unable to cope with their work and almost come to a standstill because they cannot sort out their muddle. What we have to say on organization, therefore, will not necessarily be applicable to everyone; but we suggest that you consider whether it is relevant to your particular circumstances.

Large numbers of students, whether dyslexic or not, find their first few weeks in college somewhat bewildering. Even those who have been away from home before may not be used to the responsibility of organizing their lives with only minimal guidance from others. 'Life', said one student, 'was so easy when you were 14 – everything was planned or done for you; all you had to do was toe the line!' This was said as he clutched a bag of dirty washing, a file of notes for an overdue essay, and a demand from his mother for some communication. To make matters worse he had just broken his spectacles!

For the dyslexic student there are extra difficulties. You are likely to be confronted with forms to fill in, with seemingly complicated messages on notice boards telling you where to be at a given time, with unfamiliar acronyms such as 'NUS' ('*National Union of Students*') and 'JCR' ('*Junior Common Room*'), and with a bewildering amount of invitations to join political and religious groups, sports clubs, aerobics classes, and the like. You may also be having to deal for the first time with an unfamiliar bus service – perhaps one which has a very complicated timetable.

Even for such apparently simple tasks as reading a message or filling in a form it is well established that a dyslexic needs more time than a non-dyslexic (see Chapter 1, note 1.3); and the problem is likely to be aggravated if you are under pressure of time or if there is jostling round a notice board. You may even feel nagging doubts as to whether you should have come to college at all, particularly if you had to make your choice in the face of discouragement from teachers, friends or relatives. Occasionally, we have met students who went for several weeks without getting in touch with their homes – in part, it seems, because they felt that they could not cope with letter writing or even, trivial as it may seem to the rest of us, because they could not get around to using the telephone. Many of our students put off doing the paperwork for the Disabled Students' Allowance – it seems to be just too much hassle. If you can make plans in advance to forestall some of these difficulties then life when you reach college is likely to be much easier for you.

LEARNING TO BE INDEPENDENT

From our discussions with dyslexic students we have noticed that many of them have had at least one person as a 'prop' during their school career. This 'prop' is often a parent or other relative, or sometimes a teacher, a tutor, or a member of a local Dyslexia Association. Such a person will have guided them in a variety of ways, for instance, by showing them how to fill in forms, by reminding them of appointments, by supplying them with addresses and telephone numbers, and by making suggestions as to how they might plan their studies and revision.

We suggest, therefore, that while you are still at school – or as soon as possible thereafter – you make yourself aware of the help which is being given by your mentors with a view to making yourself gradually more independent. This need not be too hurried a process, and so long as you are at home you will always know that there is someone to turn to for help if necessary. It is likely, in fact, that when you reach college you will find fellow students who are willing to assist you; but this may take time, particularly if you are hesitant at first to tell people that you are dyslexic.

If, however, you have become used to *filling in forms*, to *writing letters*, to organizing your own *bank account*, etc. *before going to college* there will be less need for you to be dependent on others. In the next few sections we shall offer some suggestions as to ways in which prospective students can prepare themselves for greater independence.

ORGANIZING A FILING SYSTEM AND OTHER AIDS

Filing

One of the things which you can usefully do is to spend five to ten minutes each day training yourself to tidy and sort out papers. Few students ever file things perfectly, but it should be possible to have drawers, files or boxes, preferably labelled in colour, for different kinds of paperwork. It is all too easy to let muddle accumulate; and if this muddle continues during your college days there is a risk that your desk will contain a disordered mess of undated lecture notes, uncompleted essays, unanswered letters, out-of-date invitations to meetings or social events, bills, paper clips, rubber bands, unwashed handkerchiefs and . . . you name it! If the chaos has gone beyond a certain point it is a very daunting task, particularly if you are dyslexic, to set to work and sort it out – the more so as you may well not know where to begin! In this connection some readers may remember a delightful poem by A.A. Milne (**see note 4.2**) about an old sailor who was shipwrecked. His plight was that he 'had so many things that he wanted to do' yet *'never* could think which he ought to do first'! He in fact ended up by doing none of them and got away with it. Regrettably, however, we cannot advise dyslexics at college to follow his example!

During the years before you go to college we recommend that you acquire the habit of keeping your desk tidy so that you know where to find things. You will then be better prepared to deal with the larger number of documents which are likely to confront you when you start your college course. As the authors know to their cost this is the kind of advice which it is easier to preach than to practise. One of us (TRM) had a grandmother who used to admonish us by saying, 'A place for everything and everything in its place' – but few of the family have had much success in bringing this state of affairs about!

Memory joggers

Many dyslexic students grumble about their poor short-term
memories. Unfortunately, they have to use them constantly at
college. If you cannot remember things, we suggest that you work
out ways of 'jogging' your memory. A *notebook* or *voice organizer* (see
next section) is likely to be very useful. Also you could try leaving
yourself notes where you will see them: small yellow sticky labels
are excellent for this purpose. One student writes on the mirror
every night (with a whiteboard pen); another props a list up by the
kettle. If you do have a poor short-term memory, it may help you to
try to develop the habit of writing down anything that crops up
during the day. Even if you do not consult your memory joggers,
the very fact that they are there relieves you from the worry of
wondering what you have to remember.

Other aids

We recommend that, well ahead of going to college, you train
yourself to use

1 a notice board;
2 a planner calendar;
3 an in-tray or a set of stacking trays;
4 a personal filing system;
5 a diary, notebook or filofax;
6 an address book;
7 a dictaphone or cassette recorder;
8 an electronic organizer or a voice organizer (possibly);
9 a kitchen pinger.

These and other aids can mostly be obtained from stationers,
computer shops or office suppliers, and if you are at a College of
Further Education or at a large school with a business studies
department, you may find that the staff can offer useful suggestions.
If these aids are used intelligently, certain routines – for example the
filing of personal correspondence as soon as it is received – will

become a habit and therefore take less effort. The following are suggestions as to ways in which the different aids might be used:

1 *The notice board*

What we have in mind is a small portable board made of cork or wood which can be placed on a desk or hung on the wall. On to it can be pinned slips of paper noting urgent messages, reminders, and the like – for example, telephone numbers, important spellings, lists of equipment needed for laboratory classes, details of the opening hours of the library or the sick-bay, and things which one might otherwise forget, such as 'Mum's birthday – *Friday* – post parcel Tuesday'. You can use highlighters, coloured stars or stickers to make things stand out. Posters can also be attractive on the eye, and they offer a change from the none-too-legible entries in diaries or notebooks. (For further suggestions as to their use in learning see also Colin Wilsher's suggestions in Appendix I.)

2 *The planner calendar*

This enables you to enter events for a year ahead (or for 6 months if you buy a 'half year' calendar) and remind yourself of them in plenty of time. Some planners are designed specifically for the academic year. We suggest that you buy one with large clear spaces. It is also possible to buy plastic-covered charts and use magnetic shapes and wipe-off pens. Different colours can be used for referring to different types of activity; and some events – for example, family birthdays and dates of holidays – can be entered up before you leave home. A major advantage of a planner calendar is that you can see your term's work as a pattern; and where there is a cluster of submission dates, you can try to stagger your work.

3 *The in-tray or set of stacking trays*

These can be bought from a stationer's and may be made of wire mesh or plastic. Some students, however, may prefer to construct their own trays, for example, by making suitable adaptations to cardboard boxes. (One of our students uses empty cereal packets.) The advantage of such trays is that all unanswered correspondence can be placed in them. Thus if, as may sometimes happen, a complicated letter arrives and you have no time to read it then and there, you will know that it is in a place where you can easily find it, and you will be able to reply to it when more time is available. Labelled stacked trays can hold notepaper, envelopes, college correspondence – all within view and yet sorted.

4 The personal file

A suitable file, which might perhaps unfold like a concertina, can be bought from any office supplier or stationer. (They make useful birthday presents.) It is likely to be of most help if it is divided into sections. For example, there might be separate sections for your birth certificate, passport, bills, receipts, bank and credit card, correspondence over your student grant, membership cards for clubs and societies, and so on. Plastic clip-on or slide-on headings can be bought to name each section of the file.

5 The diary, notebook or filofax

This is essential at sixth form level and, indeed, earlier. It is helpful if you develop the habit of writing down every date, book, suggestion, reference, etc. which you meet during your working day, and it can contain a list of tasks which need to be completed. A shorthand pad is often advantageous because used pages can easily be torn out and discarded. You may also find it useful to insert at the front of the notebook the letters of the alphabet set out in order; this will help you when dealing with telephone directories, index references, library catalogues, etc.

It is, however, better not to acquire too many notebooks since this may be confusing. When you reach college, your 'master plan' will probably be the planner calendar in your room. When you are away from your room you will need to make entries in a diary. If this can serve the dual purpose of notebook and reference book there is less risk of having 'things to remember' scattered in too many different places.

A filofax can be very useful as it is already quite well organized and replacement sections can be bought each year. Many sections will be ongoing from year to year, and this saves tedious copying out.

6 The address book

This is an essential aid to memory. Before leaving home you should check that all the addresses and telephone numbers which you are likely to need for the next few months are written in it. If you have a problem in remembering the initial letter of any awkward names you should write them down at the front of the address book. In the case of STD codes and telephone numbers which you are likely to use regularly, mnemonics can be devised. Adhesive labels with the addresses of relatives and friends printed on them are also useful – particularly if your handwriting is not very legible! Addresses can be added on to a 'label' template on your computer. Under stress, some dyslexic students may find even the seemingly simple task of writing an envelope very demanding, and any device which saves time and energy is to be welcomed. If your parents are in a benevolent mood they may even be induced to provide stamped addressed envelopes!

7 The dictaphone or cassette recorder

This is a further example of a labour-saving device. There are a number of dyslexic students who find it a real effort to write letters home but who have little difficulty in giving their news by speaking into a tape recorder. The Post Office now supplies special padded envelopes which enable cassettes to be sent by post, and for those who cannot easily write letters this seems an excellent way of staying in touch with their families. Also, if any other member of the family is dyslexic he is likely to welcome a method of communication which involves listening rather than reading. Dictaphones as study aids will also be discussed in Chapter 9.

8 The electronic organizer or voice organizer

These are like small dictaphones into which you can speak; they can be made to ring at pre-programmed times so as to remind you of your appointments.

9 The kitchen pinger

Some of our students seem to lose track of time; they get absorbed in their work or on even possibly drop off to sleep for a while. They find a kitchen pinger can act as an alarm clock: it can remind them when they have only 10 minutes to go before going out and it can be used for timing study sessions.

FINANCE

This is another area in which you can usefully be given training before you leave home. You should make sure that you know how a *bank account* operates and how to use a cash point. You should also get to know your bank's opening hours. You should develop a *consistent signature* and practise it regularly. (For some dyslexics this may not be as easy as it seems, particularly if they find themselves being watched by a bank clerk or shop assistant.) A number of our students have reported embarrassing moments when, because of untidy writing, the signatures on their cheques have seemed not to tally with those on their cheque cards. There may also be certain *numbers* which remain difficult to spell – for example, 'eleven',' eight' and 'forty'; and some students may find it useful to write these words down in a diary or in their cheque book.

You may also need to know your *cash point number*. Here a mnemonic seems desirable, since there is appreciable risk in having the number in writing anywhere near the cash card. If a cheque has to be made out in the presence of a shop assistant it is perfectly acceptable to ask for help in spelling the shop's name, or, indeed, it is possible to note the spelling of the shop's name before entering.

If you qualify for the *Disabled Students' Allowance* it is a good idea to set in motion the procedure as soon as you have been firmly accepted by a college; this will save you having yet another job to do when you actually arrive. For more information about the allowance see Chapter 2.

TRAVEL

Many students go abroad during their years in college; and you should remember that the paperwork involved in filling in an *application form for a passport* may be extremely laborious and time consuming for a dyslexic student, particularly if you have to make your application during the pre-vacation examination period. Considerable worry can be avoided if you are equipped with a passport before you leave home. You may also wish to consult some of the books which are now available on the filling in of forms (**see note 4.3**). *Train and bus timetables* can also be somewhat daunting: make sure in particular that you fully understands the *24-hour notation*, e.g. that '1600' is the same as '4 p.m.'. (Some dyslexics, when they are younger, fail to grasp this.) Also a cardboard marker will serve as a safeguard against losing the place – and can be used if you need to consult mathematical tables.

It is wise too to have a supply of passport-size photographs to take to college; and it is a good idea to have one or two already filled-in forms, giving your date of birth, nationality, etc., so as to save an extra job when you are under pressure later.

SPOKEN LANGUAGE

You will almost certainly find that the ability to speak fluently is an extremely useful skill during your time at college. After all, it is through our spoken communication that most people get to know us.

Here is an example. One of our students was outstanding in her spoken answers to questions about her laboratory work. She then wrote an essay for which she got a poor mark. When she went to see her tutor he instantly realized the difference between her oral and written ability, looked more deeply into her essay and then upgraded it. She had proved herself orally. In general oral communication is becoming more important in assessment. It is common practice to examine candidates orally, and, as will be seen in Chapter 15, some students in examinations are now allowed to speak their answers to an amanuensis (a person who writes down their response) or record their answers on to tape.

There are also courses on which students take the lead at seminars and present papers to quite large groups. This can give them the chance to do well without relying on the written word. Practice at oral communication will also give them confidence if they wish to speak in a debate or chair a committee. Most of our communication is through the spoken word, and in the case of dyslexics the use of spoken language provides the opportunity of demonstrating their knowledge and understanding.

Slight mispronunciations and other errors sometimes occur in the speech of dyslexics (compare p. 4), and we suggest that you listen to words carefully, as this will enable you to say them accurately. This may also help your spelling; and, conversely, if you know the spelling of a word you will be better able to say it accurately (**see note 4.4**).

Reading aloud can be a real ordeal for dyslexic students; and at college you may sometimes have to read work in a tutorial group. As a preparation it is a good idea before you go to college to give yourself plenty of regular practice at reading aloud. A member of your family or a friend may sometimes be available to listen and to comment, or, if no one is around, it is always possible for you to read into a tape recorder and afterwards monitor your performance by comparing it with the printed text. This will require self-discipline and is not easy to do, but it is worth it!

WRITTEN LANGUAGE

In many first year college courses the student has to take several different subjects, often now organized into modules. If you have taken a practical or science-based course before going to college you may find the written work difficult to cope with. Prospective students should be aware of this and make every effort to keep up their *written English* (or other language) during the pre-university period. It might be worth going to an evening class in writing skills at a local college, or doing a short correspondence course (**see note 4.5**).

In our experience, it is quite possible for dyslexics to learn to write grammatically and to punctuate. If they are weak in these areas it may not be because the required skills are beyond them; it may rather be that because they had so much else to cope with in their early teens they did not pick up things which their non-dyslexic colleagues learned as they went along.

Students who have taken a year off should also try to get back into the writing habit before they return to academic work. Mature students should consider a pre-university course – ideally an ACCESS course. These courses often provide the chance for practice in note taking and essay writing. The Open University also has various courses in essay writing and study skills.

Prospective students need to concentrate in particular on *precis writing*, *paraphrasing*, and *note taking*.

Precis writing forces one to think out carefully what are the key ideas in a particular passage and to express them clearly and concisely. *Paraphrasing* involves similar demands but makes one consider the style of the original and to be critical of one's own attempts to represent what has been said. A good newspaper or journal can be used as practice material. *Note taking* will be very important at college; it makes similar demands with regard to the grasping of key ideas and the selection of concise phrases, and in addition it is something which has to be done at speed. A possible exercise is to listen to talks on radio or television and to write down the important points.

In the years before college we strongly advise you not to let your skills in written language deteriorate from lack of practice.

THE WRITING OF BUSINESS LETTERS

Many students need to put together formal business letters during their time in college. Rightly or wrongly many recipients set considerable store by the layout and appearance of such letters, and these are things which some dyslexic students cannot achieve without considerable practice. Many reference books are available on this topic (**see note 4.6**), and in addition it is well worth while for the prospective student to obtain guidance from teachers or parents.

A helpful suggestion, in our view, is that you should try to *put yourself in the position of the recipient*. It can usefully be assumed that the recipient is a busy person who does not have time for non-essential details, and it is therefore important to say what one has to say in as clear and concise a form as possible. As a check, see if you have stated the *purpose* of the letter clearly at the start and then given all *necessary details*. You should also check that the letter reads courteously. Sensitivity to shades of meaning is important here. We were recently told of an executive who instructed his secretary to check why a colleague had not replied to a letter. Her draft began:

Dear Mr Smith

Why haven't you replied to my letter?

It is true, in a sense, that this was what she had been told to ask, but the wording is sharp and aggressive. A dyslexic person may not readily pick up nuances of this kind, but he can certainly be trained to do so. In this case the letter could perhaps have started:

Dear Mr Smith

I am somewhat concerned about my last letter and I think it possible that you may not have received it.

It may also be useful if you include in your spelling notebook a list of words likely to be needed in letters. Some of the important ones are: *grateful, reference, acknowledgement, enquiry, advertisement, faithfully* and *sincerely.* These words should be available to you in advance; otherwise the 'flow' of the letter may become interrupted while you stop to think about their spellings. You can create your own letter heading and store a sample letter with useful phrases in it on your computer. In the case of important letters you should use clean, unlined notepaper of consistent size. We have met students, both dyslexic and non-dyslexic, who clearly had no idea of the extent to which recipients can be put off by a scruffy-looking letter.

FURTHER PREPARATIONS

Before you leave home you should study carefully the literature which the college has sent you. This may tell you when and where to register for courses, how to join the Students' Union, and much else. You may find it helpful to mark the important points with a felt pen or fluorescent marker; and all relevant times and dates should be entered as soon as possible into your diary.

It is also useful if you acquire *a map of the college* and its precincts and mark on it your lodgings or hall of residence, the relevant lecture rooms or laboratories, the Students' Union building, the library, and so on.

If it is at all possible you should make a short visit to the college before your course starts so that you can become familiar with the layout of the campus. During your first days in college continually having to ask to be directed to places may be an extra worry; and if you then receive complicated verbal instructions ('First left; then second right, and then it's the third door on your left when you've been through the arch'), this will certainly add to your bewilderment at the very time when you have all sorts of other things to think about. In this matter, as in so many others, careful preparation at an early stage can save worry and embarrassment later on.

Chapter 5

Social and academic relationships

ESTABLISHING A ROUTINE

During your first few days in college you are likely to meet many
new people. To prepare for this, we suggest that you think about
yourself carefully. Do you have difficulty, for example, in
remembering the things that you are told? You may well find
yourself being given far more information than you can possibly
remember – people's names, addresses, room numbers, telephone
numbers, and much else. In the case of names you can try to 'fix'
them by repeating a particular name when it is said to you and by
using it when you speak to the person concerned. It may also be
possible for you to call to mind an obvious feature of that person or
to think of other people with that name.

As for addresses, telephone numbers etc., you will probably find
it helpful to write all relevant material in your diary or notebook. It
is also useful to carry a map of the college around with you and, if
you need to remember where someone lives, to make a suitable
mark on it. You should make sure that you locate the important
university buildings: several dyslexic students have missed their
first lecture by going to the wrong place!

If you find a diary hard to use, we suggest that you carry with
you a simple day-to-day calendar and write all appointments down,
highlighting the times. It will probably help if you adopt a set
routine: this could include checking your notebook, diary or
calendar each day before going out and emptying your in-tray at
least twice a week. You may well find that such a routine helps you

socially as well as academically, since it will be a safeguard against missed appointments and the like, which can be very irritating to the person on the receiving end. Dyslexia should certainly not be seen as an excuse for being unpunctual! Over the years we have had many telephone calls from tutors, administration officers, the computing laboratory, and so on, asking irritably where a student is.

We suggest that you try to communicate with your family at a regular time each week since (as most of us know to our cost!) if things are not done at fixed times there is a risk that they will not be done at all.

DO I TELL OTHER STUDENTS THAT I AM DYSLEXIC?

We have met students who have worried considerably over this point. Some of them have wondered whether such an admission would make them 'different' from other students in some uncomfortable sense or give the impression that they were looking for preferential treatment. If they were the victims of such accusations when they were at school then it is understandable if they do not wish to run the risk of anything similar happening at college. From time to time, we have met students who, not surprisingly, wish to make a fresh start and leave their dyslexia behind. To quote one student, 'So much was made of my dyslexia when I was at school that I was determined, when I came to college, to forget it.'

Some students – perhaps as a result of some misapprehension as to what dyslexia is – feel ashamed of being dyslexic and for this or some other reason do not wish any mention of dyslexia to go into their records. These are all points which you may wish to talk about with a counsellor or with another dyslexic student.

We, ourselves, strongly believe that telling is the wisest policy. Not only may keeping your dyslexia secret involve you in all kinds of stress; more importantly, it is our experience that almost all students, when they learn that someone is dyslexic, have been extremely supportive and sympathetic. Many take pride in the fact that they have a dyslexic friend and wish to learn more about dyslexia; they are genuinely glad if they can help, and they can share the pleasure when he succeeds. It is a different environment from that of a school, and we have seldom encountered anything other than an interested, positive, and sympathetic attitude to dyslexia among the student community.

You may sometimes be asked what dyslexia is, and it is worth giving thought as to how best to explain. You could say, for instance, that dyslexics can be gifted in all kinds of ways but that they have difficulty in processing symbols and language. If necessary, you could add that the condition has a physical basis and quite often runs in families.

As was pointed out in the Foreword, there are now large numbers of dyslexic students in British universities (for figures see Chapter 3, note 3.13). This is greatly to the credit of the students, their schools, and their families. Very occasionally, however, we have heard seemingly unsympathetic comments; for example one student said in a loud voice, 'There are an awful lot of dyslexics around here.' (Remember, of course, that even this remark may simply have been made 'off the top' with no hostile intention). If by any chance you meet with hostility – which *can* occur, though we do not believe it to be very frequent – perhaps your answer could be that there is no reason why there *shouldn't* be dyslexics at college, and you could explain that there were not so many in the past simply because they did not get the chance to use their ability.

If someone makes a snide comment about your computer allowance you could well find this upsetting. However you may like to point out that a student has to be very carefully assessed in order to get the allowance, and you may even like to quote the words of the dyslexic student who said, 'I'd rather *not* be dyslexic, and do *without* the computer.'

If comments are made in a semi-joking way, take them lightly; some dyslexic students can be very sensitive and perhaps over-react to what seem cruel jokes. It is better not to turn nasty, but to make up your mind that at some convenient stage in the future you will have a chat to the person who has made the comment. You might also offer to share your computer with other students – we have known several students who have done this with very positive results.

It is also very important that you should not give the impression of being self-centred about your dyslexia or of being unwilling to take an interest in the needs of others. Some students with a problem (not just dyslexia) relate everything back to their difficulty and blame it for every disaster that happens to them. Although this is to some extent understandable it can be most off-putting for others! Almost everyone has difficulties of some kind – and it is therefore up to you to take an interest and try to be helpful.

COPING WITH STRESS

Your social relations can also be affected if you allow yourself to harbour resentful attitudes. Some of our dyslexic students have, not unreasonably, felt very bitter towards their schools, where they were perhaps discouraged or put into the wrong stream. There may be all kinds of scars from the past (**see note 5.1**), and sometimes their very success at college opens these up – for instance a grudge towards those of their teachers who had not recognized their ability. In the case of mature students who have been recently assessed there may be feelings of deep regret over their 'wasted years'. Bitterness is a negative feeling, however. If you can – and we know it is not easy – it is better to forget, forgive, and determine to do your best in *this* stage of your career rather than harp on the past. We have in fact found that many of our students, after graduation, have taken a genuine pride in telling their schools about their degrees – and this can be good for future generations of dyslexics from the school.

Stresses also occur when a combination of academic and personal demands accumulate and students feel both tired and pressurized – there is just too much to cope with! Dyslexic students are particularly prone to this kind of stress and what distinguishes them from the non-dyslexic student is that they seem extra vulnerable – and the stress, in its turn, seems to make the dyslexia worse (**see note 5.2**).

It is important that you should realize this and watch out for signs of feeling under too much pressure. Some students become very tired – things 'fuzz' or 'blur'; others can be very tense, while with others things can get out of proportion and the smallest event can seem a catastrophe. Some students can almost come to a standstill when acutely stressed and their work will then deteriorate. Others show their tension by being overactive – in which case the mind may become confused and make irrational jumps: it is hard for the student to unscramble his thoughts, and his work, in general, becomes disjointed.

Many students have found that learning about *stress management* has been very useful. Dyslexics under stress may find it difficult to organize or structure things. It is important in that case to decide which are the priorities (or, in the fashionable jargon, to 'prioritize'). This involves creating a list of the essential tasks to be done so that one can work through it steadily and systematically taking one thing at a time (**see note 5.3**).

Communicating with other dyslexic students in a student group can also be very helpful. Many colleges run yoga or relaxation/ meditation sessions. Music can be very soothing, and there are also relaxation tapes (**see note 5.4**). Some of our students practise reflexology or aromatherapy. If the stress symptoms become too strong it is wise to seek help from a counsellor.

Finally, as part of 'dealing with stress' may we throw in some grandmotherly advice? Make sure that you eat properly and that you take regular exercise, or at the very least allow yourself relaxation of some kind. We have in fact found find that dyslexic students can be prone to ongoing illnesses – sore throats, asthma, colds, and, more extremely, glandular fever or even ME (myalgic encephalomyelitis). Dyslexia can be fatiguing to live with, and perhaps the extra strain it places upon the whole coping mechanisms can lead to a student becoming physically run down. Then, as a result, it is harder to keep up with the work. If possible we suggest that you try to prevent this by **building up your strength with healthy eating**. This does not necessarily involve cooking: there are all kinds of foods where cooking is not needed: for instance, cheese, salads, wholemeal bread, bananas, raw vegetables, or yoghurt. Several of our students go swimming once or twice a week – and we highly recommend it! If you think it would help you could read some of the many leaflets and books written for students on the subject of health. Our overall advice is that you will function much better if you take care of yourself!

COLLABORATION BETWEEN STUDENT AND TUTOR

At an early stage of his course a dyslexic student should make a special effort to get to know his tutors and to establish friendly terms with them. If things go well there is every chance of effective collaboration.

There are, of course, different kinds of tutor. The terminology at different colleges may vary, but the three main types are as follows.

1 First, there is your *academic tutor*. It is his job, primarily, to help you with your academic studies. This is not to say that he will not try to help you in other ways should the occasion arise, but primarily he is there to help you over your choice of reading, over your written work, and the like. You may, of course, have different academic tutors at different times.

2 Secondly, there is your *personal* tutor. (Some colleges used, in the past, to speak of 'moral' tutors, but this somewhat quaint description is now largely obsolete.) He is the person to approach on personal matters, for instance, changes of course, difficulty over finding accommodation, or inability to get down to work. He will usually be a member of your department and may therefore also be advising you on your academic work, but his prime role is to help you in the event of difficulties other than those which arise from your academic studies.

3 Thirdly, both here and in Chapters 6 and 7, we shall be referring to the *Support Tutor*. This is the role that one of us (DEG) has played in relation to the dyslexic students at Bangor. There are

many forms of 'support' available for students, and there may be Support Tutors e.g. for blind or physically handicapped students.

Quite a number of colleges now have Support Tutors for dyslexic students, and their job is principally to provide a service which these students can use. This is a point to which we shall return in the next chapter. Help is also available from *doctors*, from *chaplains*, from *student counsellors*, and from *student welfare services*.

In all cases, if harmonious relations are to be established there needs to be effort on both sides – both by the student and by the tutors and counsellors.

You will probably find that there are some lecturers and academic tutors who do not have a clear idea as to what dyslexia is; and if there is occasion to discuss your dyslexia with them it is wise to think out clearly in advance what needs to be said. In particular, you will need to explain your difficulties and be prepared to make suggestions as to how the tutor can be of most help. It could well be useful if you take along a copy of your dyslexia assessment so that the tutor can read it.

If there are any feelings of strain it should be remembered by both parties that it is the other who may be feeling uncertain or shy! For example, a student may be in the position where he has to come forward and ask for help yet may find it difficult to admit, even to himself, that any help is needed. In these circumstances what seems like an abrupt or aggressive manner may be a cover for feelings of insecurity. Similarly, the tutor may naturally be a shy person or may act aggressively because he is inwardly unsure as to what help he should be trying to give.

There are further complications. The student may well have had 'brushes' with his teachers at an earlier age: they may have accused him of being 'lazy' or 'careless' or even have implied that he was using his dyslexia as an excuse for doing no work. If this has happened it is hardly surprising if he assumes – perhaps without any serious reflection – that his college tutors are going to treat him in the same way. It follows that remarks which they make in all innocence may be misinterpreted. To tell a dyslexic student that his spelling is poor, for example, may be no more than the truth; but if it is adequate for his needs the comment is unnecessary, and if it is not, then something more constructive is called for.

Similarly, if you – and for the next few paragraphs 'you' means the tutor – are unfamiliar with dyslexia it is very easy to assume, wrongly, that if the student hands in a meagre, untidy, and poorly spelt piece of work it is because he has not taken enough trouble. It is far more likely, if his work gives this impression, that he has in fact put in considerable effort and that he has reverted to his earlier weakness of failing to express his ideas adequately in writing. It is good if you can bear in mind what it is like to have language difficulties in a language-based environment. It may also be helpful if you ask the student how long he took over a particular piece of work. Regular checks on the student's progress are particularly important, since if things are not going well the cost of delay may be very heavy.

If you have heard the word 'dyslexia' but have not had it explained to you, you may be under the mistaken impression that a dyslexic student is a weak student. This impression may be reinforced by the regrettable tendency to speak of 'concessions' to dyslexic candidates when they take examinations. As will be seen in Chapter 18, what is needed is not any kind of concession but machinery by which students are not marked down for lack of skills which from the Examining Board's point of view are irrelevant. (The word 'provision' has now largely replaced the word 'concession', and this is a great improvement.)

You may also be misled, as a result of the student's obvious competence in some areas, into assuming that his alleged difficulties are a fiction. In this connection we should like to emphasize the harm which can be done if you give the impression that you are questioning the genuineness of the handicap; a sensitive person can find this very demoralizing. It is possible, too, that things which a tutor says lightheartedly may nevertheless be misunderstood. This happened recently when a tutor told a student that he ought to have been in the secret service since so much of what he wrote was in code! Although no malice was intended, this particular student found the remark very wounding; and it is important that you should remember that dyslexic students may be extra sensitive to criticism because of their earlier failures. It is also possible for a tutor unfamiliar with dyslexia to write off a dyslexic student as 'stupid' through being unaware of the kinds of thing which can happen on a 'bad day' (**see note 5.5**).

There are many ways in which an academic tutor can give practical help. For example, if the student has had difficulty with note taking, you could supply him with copies of your lecture notes or of the sheets which you have used on the overhead projector. Several of our tutors have put dyslexic students in touch with second year students or with good note takers in their own year. Students who are entitled to the Disabled Students' Allowance may sometimes wish to consult their academic tutor on the type of computer that they should order.

Occasionally we have met academic tutors who did not appreciate that their relationship to a dyslexic student needs to be a professional one. In such a relationship the student is no less entitled to confidentiality than when he confers with his doctor, solicitor, or student counsellor. It is therefore quite improper, for example, for a tutor to proclaim in a lecture room, 'I knew you might not follow this because you are dyslexic' or 'Which of you are dyslexic? Come and sit at the front.' Not all students object to it being publicly known that they are dyslexic, but the choice is theirs, not the tutor's.

As we indicated at the start of this chapter, there are some students who decide not to let it be generally known that they are dyslexic. Even, however, if this is your decision – we are now back to addressing the student – it may still be wise to take your personal tutor into your confidence. If it is your wish, he will probably say little to you about your dyslexia, but it will help neither him nor you to deny its existence. At the opposite extreme, as we have said, are those who attribute every minor incident of forgetfulness to their dyslexia – not realizing that we all forget things – and these are sometimes the students who write, '*I am dyslexic*' at the top of every examination script – a practice which we do not encourage

(**see note 5.6**). Perhaps the most important task for tutors and
counsellors is to help students to view their dyslexia realistically,
neither making too much of it nor too little.

Finally, there is the question of the relationship of a dyslexic
student not with her personal tutor but with those who lecture to
her. Some students have indicated to us that they would have been
helped if the lecturer could have repeated or clarified something
that she had said but were hesitant to approach her. In our view,
such reluctance is misplaced. As in any social situation one cannot
go far wrong if one shows normal courtesy and consideration. Thus
if the tutor is looking busy or harassed it may be best to ask for an
appointment later. If you feel unsure of yourself you can always ask,
'Do you mind if . . . ?' 'Would it be a trouble to you if . . . ?', etc. We
believe that there are few lecturers who are so busy or so unsociable
that they would be unwilling to respond to requests of this kind,
and many of us who are ourselves lecturers positively welcome it if
members of the audience approach us afterwards.

If a later appointment is fixed it is important to be punctual –
some dyslexics do not have a very secure sense of time! It is also
important not to overstay your welcome – some dyslexics do not
pick up what may be called the 'being-busy vibes'. Occasionally we
have met students who, perhaps because they were over-anxious,
have gone into a tutor's room and been quite aggressive or pushy.
This can easily put the tutor's back up, and will not do the cause of
dyslexic students any good. We have also had students who have
telephoned their academic tutors late at night or at weekends.
Although your anxiety is understandable, this is not the right thing
to do!

Chapter 6

Organizing a support service

INTRODUCTION

There is a growing need for support services for dyslexic students in Higher Education – a need which has evolved as the number and range of students has increased (**see note 6.1**). Many of these students will have had support and provision at school and will therefore look to their college to provide a similar service. For example the administration of the Disabled Students' Allowance is complicated and most students need some help over claiming it.

In this chapter we should like to share with Support Tutors and counsellors some of our experiences in setting up such a service. (In what follows, 'you' should be understood to mean the Support Tutor.)

The support service for dyslexic students should, of course, operate within the framework of other services: the counselling service, student welfare, the disabled students' advisory service, and the like; but the dyslexic student is likely to have certain distinctive needs.

We cannot, in fact, offer any one model as the only appropriate example. Support services vary according to the type of student, the size of the institution, the staff available – and, of course, the budget. Within a support service, too, the help offered to a student needs to be flexible: there are, for example, students who require to be taught academic skills by means of a structured programme; there are those who have worked out their own strategies and who wish to consolidate them, and there are also those who for all kinds of good reasons simply need to drop in for an informal chat. We have found that many younger students, products of the 1981 Education Act, have already been taught a considerable amount about study skills and need little assistance, whereas mature students, especially those recently assessed, are often very anxious to receive as much help and guidance as they can get.

In some cases, what starts by ostensibly being a tutorial in essay writing or on study techniques may quite well turn into a counselling session. It is important, therefore, that you, as tutor or counsellor, should be sensitive to the student's needs at a given time.

Students will probably need to call on a wider network around the immediate study/counselling service. This is particularly the case if they are applying for the Disabled Students' Allowance. They will almost certainly need help with the paperwork; and, as part of this allowance involves purchasing a computer, they may also need advice and details of costing from a computer specialist – preferably one who also knows what is likely to be appropriate for dyslexic students (**see note 6.2**). If they want special examination provision, they will need to discuss their requirements with the examinations officer (see Chapter 15 for more details), and, ideally, there should be sympathetic contacts in the college library and in the Careers Service. Sometimes you, as Support Tutor, may take on some of these roles, or if you do not do so yourself you will probably have to act as a link between the student and the appropriate members of the college staff. From time to time you may also like to undertake awareness-raising among your colleagues.

The needs of dyslexic students are likely to be fairly complex, since they may well need counselling as well as academic support. You may well have to help them, for example, over their study habits or over the management of their time. It is important that when support is provided this should be on a regular, organized basis. It should not only cater for their academic needs (such as being able to complete an assignment on time); it should also deal, for instance, with the feelings of doubt and anxiety which many of them experience when they reach college and with the last minute panics which sometimes arise as they approach examinations.

PUBLICITY

In any large university, polytechnic, or College of Higher Education communicating with students can be a problem. If you are the organizer of a support service for dyslexic students you should therefore explore every possible means of publicizing what is available. In particular, the need is for clear and simple information which reaches as many students as possible and tells them about the help available.

It may be possible to contact new students directly if they indicate that they are dyslexic on the UCAS form. However, this is not possible in all institutions, since it is sometimes argued that revealing information which appears on the UCAS form is a breach of confidentiality. If this is the college's policy (and it is a reasonable one) it is still possible for you to send information to the academic office which administers the UCAS applications.

The existence of a dyslexia support service should be mentioned in the college prospectus. In addition, a comprehensive system of publicity should be established within the college. Both hand-outs and posters with an effective logo should be designed, and the wording should be friendly and informal – for example, 'Drop in for a talk.' An indication of the form of the service which is being provided should be shown on the poster. Dyslexic students are often extremely sensitive and will hesitate to enter a group situation until they have first established a firm contact with the tutor. They will also need to be assured that the service is entirely confidential and that they can approach the tutor without necessarily being identified as dyslexic. A notice such as 'Dyslexic Students' Meeting' should never be displayed (**see note 6.3**).

The publicity should be distributed to all areas of the college, including individual departments, the library, the Students' Union, the rooms where students register for courses, the administration offices, Student Health, Student Services, Counselling, Nightline, the chaplains, the students' shop, the canteen, etc. Reference to the service should be made in the relevant student diary, calendar, newspaper or handbook. Explanatory letters should be sent to all heads of departments, personal and academic tutors, chaplains, and others concerned with student welfare. Even if a dyslexic student makes only infrequent use of this service it is important that he should know of its existence.

As a minimum, some kind of room should be set aside for the use of the Support Tutor at a regular time each week. You should also retain an emergency meeting place if your room is not always available. A kettle and a box of tissues are often useful! A discreet waiting room is also important.

Ideally, part of the student service should comprise a resource base, and even a study area. The resource base would contain study materials, information on dyslexia, books of all kinds, and spelling dictionaries. There could be equipment for the student to test out, including computer and software, spellmaster, and dictaphone. There could also be materials with which the student could experiment – coloured paper, plastic overlays, and postcards and posters for revision. This is the ideal: practicalities – such as cost, staffing, administering a loan service (dyslexic students are not very good at returning books!), security, and insurance – could make this prohibitive in terms of money.

Because concentration is not always easy for dyslexic students many of them welcome somewhere quiet to work. Some in fact prefer total silence; others like to have music in the background. It may also be useful if a room is provided in which they can revise together and learn study techniques from each other.

TYPES OF SUPPORT

The ever-increasing numbers of dyslexic students place heavy demands upon one Support Tutor, and in many institutions services are 'bought in', which use expertise within the college. (Some of these services can be usually be paid for out of the Disabled Students' Allowance.) Students have also set up their own self-help groups – these will be discussed later on in this section. We suggest however that the followings patterns act as a basis for support.

One-to-one meetings

The simplest way in which you can operate as Support Tutor is for you to make yourself available to see students on a one-to-one basis at a fixed time during the week. If this method is used, every effort should be made to ensure constancy and regularity since it is an extra difficulty for dyslexic students if the time and venue of the meeting are continually being changed. Their first visit may be difficult for them and you should be aware that for many students it takes a great deal of courage to come forward asking for help.

In the first two or three meetings you and the student might decide to look at her assessment and discuss how she approaches her work. Once the contact has been established it is up to the student to choose what type of support she wishes to have. This could be some particular aspect of study skills, an essay which needs to be checked, spelling difficulties, problems in organizing her personal life, requests for help with form filling, and so on. If she comes with a personal problem which needs more detailed discussion then a further meeting can be arranged. We have found that many students have benefited from one-to-one guidance on ways of studying their own subject, and there have been others for whom the possibility of such guidance has been a reassurance. In the words of one of them, 'I may not come very often but I always know you are there.' At times the Support Tutor may need to liaise with the teaching staff in the student's department; and, provided the student agrees, it is good practice to inform the department of the work that is being done.

Some colleges provide 'mentors' – people with training in general study skills – who can also give one-to-one support (**see note 6.4**). In some cases it is possible for a post-graduate student to provide help with such things as spelling, statistics or essay writing. It is also possible that a 'buddy' service may be in operation: in that case another student 'chums' a dyslexic student, perhaps taking notes for him or helping him with reading. This can either be 'for free' or, where appropriate, for a small payment.

Group meetings

Another way of working is to have group meetings, perhaps two or three times a term or more, according to demand. These can operate as small, formal classes, or as study groups with a set subject to be taught and discussed. For first year students a discussion of dyslexia could be a useful starting point and could be followed, for instance, by an introduction to study skills. There could then be discussions of note taking, essay writing, reading up material for assignments, or of improving one's spelling. As examinations approach, we have found that time spent on revision and examination techniques is particularly valued. Outside speakers, including other dyslexic students or ex-students, can be brought in both to address the group and to participate in discussion.

However, besides formal teaching (of which most of them have plenty every academic day) something more informal may also be of help. For example, as Support Tutor, you could give a brief lecture on an everyday topic (pollution, the monarchy, the local area, sport, etc.), while the students would be encouraged to take notes, to compare what they have written with what has been written by others, to discuss what is good or bad in each, and, individually or jointly, to produce a set of notes which, with the tutor's guidance, is better than any of them could have produced individually. In these circumstances a really interesting learning situation can develop: each student will have his own approach and the various different techniques can be 'pooled' and discussed.

Perhaps the most positive aspect of a meeting of dyslexic students, however, is the remarkable group atmosphere which emerges. In the experience of one of us (DEG) every group, without exception, has developed its own distinctive feelings of 'togetherness'. For many dyslexic students it will be their first meeting with others who are dyslexic. They can offer each other quite striking personal support. We have also found that the second and third year students have fostered and guided the first year students, offering them help with their studies, their examinations and their approach to the academic staff. The group can be particularly supportive to any one of its members who may have a problem. A student may storm in, smarting from the latest 'insult', and find complete understanding, immediate sympathy and many practical suggestions as to how to cope with it. Students are always pleased to find that some of their difficulties are not just theirs but are shared by the others.

We have also found that as a group the students worry about any of their members who may not have attended for a while. They are all willing to offer each other their 'tricks' and devices for coping with dyslexia in day-to-day life. Basically, they all understand each other; and this is clearly a vital factor in the successful working of the group.

We have found that it is of particular benefit to the less experienced students to know that others have gone before and not only coped and survived but actually succeeded. Some of our previous students have written back to the group with encouraging stories of their successes (**see note 6.5**). We have also found that a discussion of someone else's problems can help a student to get his own problems into perspective. In general, a study group can act as an important lifeline for students who wish to open up and discuss their problems with each other.

From your point of view, too, as Support Tutor, the experience may be a rewarding one. Although (if you are not yourself dyslexic) you are in a sense an outsider, your understanding of the problems can be very much enhanced simply by careful and sympathetic observation of the ways in which the students interact with each other. There is the possible difficulty that you may sometimes have to listen to harsh criticism of your academic colleagues, if the student believes them to have been unsympathetic, or even embarrassing praise. In these circumstances it is probably wise, if the necessity arises, for you to make clear that for professional reasons you may not discuss the merits or otherwise of individuals; but this need not prevent you from discussing how the student feels about people who have come into his life. It is, of course, widely agreed among counsellors that they should not take sides with a client in finding fault with a particular person, even though they may make clear that they understand the client's feelings about that person.

It may sometimes be possible for you to use your 'outsider' role in guiding the group. We have found that now and then there is a tendency among certain students to 'have a good moan'. This may at times be necessary, but it can become very negative and be off-putting to other students. At some point you may like to announce humorously that there is a ban on negative comments and that only positive thinking is permitted.

Our students have set up their own 'self-help' groups outside the main group, working with computers, sorting out notes, revising, and so on. There is a strong informal network among them. We have discussed whether they would like to run their student study group as a total 'self-help' group. This raises the question of the type of support which they need; at present the consensus is that they feel that a tutor is essential who will present ideas and patterns 'from the outside' and who will prepare materials, obtain books, help with work, and liaise with their academic tutors and others. We feel that it would place heavy demands on dyslexic students to be totally 'student-centred', although there is certainly a place for student-led groups alongside tutor-led groups.

There have been occasional students who for various reasons have not wished to participate in group work. It may have been the 'flavour' of such meetings which they disliked; indeed one student said that the meetings 'smacked of Alcoholics Anonymous'. In our experience it is wise that all students known to be dyslexic should be informed if a group meeting is to take place; but it should be clearly understood that there is no pressure on anyone to attend it.

Instant help

Another way in which you can help your students is to let them have your telephone number or address. This will enable them to get in touch with you at any time if they feel depressed, frustrated, muddled, or unable to cope. (Obviously this is more feasible in a smaller college.) Dyslexics find it difficult at times to deal with pressure, and stresses may accumulate until their thinking becomes befuddled and the various problems begin to seem insurmountable. At this stage they may call for help, and if you are readily available you will be in a position to go immediately and listen. In this situation it is perhaps better to meet in a less formal setting, in your house, for instance, in the student's room, or even in a pub or coffee-bar.

It has been our experience that stress is more common at certain times of the year than at others. The third or fourth week of the first term is a bad point for first-year students, and in addition pressures often seem to mount in February or March: it is the mid-year low point – one set of modular exams have just been completed and the next modules have started with an new workload; at this time also students are often run down after the winter. Any examination times are of course almost always stressful. Some dyslexic students withdraw into a shell at bad times and cannot cry for help. It is important that you should know where to find your students and, if you have not seen a student for some time, you could perhaps drop in casually to check that all is well. It is always possible that problems may have accumulated. On various such occasions, DEG has found herself doing the washing up, refiling notes, helping with application forms, writing a letter, and taking home a load of washing!

There is no reason why all these forms of support should not be available concurrently; and it is important to recognize that dyslexic students may need different kinds of help at different stages of their course.

THE TUTOR AS COUNSELLOR

Although a support service may be seen principally in terms of academic support, it will have become obvious that there is also a strong need for a service which can provide for personal counselling. Problems with study trigger off anxiety; a student becomes tense and many underlying insecurities might well up from the past. Hence a session with a student might involve study skills to cope with the immediate problem but also some discussion of past difficulties: into that might come problems with personal life, which could easily have got out of proportion because of the general stress under which the student is labouring. In such a state it seems that the holistic, lateral way of thinking of a dyslexic (compare Chapter 1, p. 6) can lead him to jump from one thing to another – all his problems crowd in together and he cannot structure either his thoughts or his work. This can easily happen if he is under pressure or has too much work to do.

A distinction can usefully be drawn in this connection between 'generalist' and 'specialist' counselling. A counsellor with 'generalist' skills is a trained listener who helps the client to talk through possible courses of action but does not have the specialist skills of, say, a doctor, solicitor, or college lecturer. These have expert skills in their own particular areas and can advise accordingly. In contrast, a generalist counsellor is not that kind of 'expert'.

Now it seems to us that if you are to act as tutor to dyslexic students you need to be *both* a generalist *and* a specialist counsellor – generalist in that you need to be a good listener but specialist in that you need to have a knowledge of dyslexia (**see note 6.6**). Your job is both to deal with the anxieties which the students bring up and to know what aspects of their academic work they are likely to find easy and difficult.

Finally, dyslexic students are often highly sensitive and can easily become upset by negative criticism; for example, it has recently taken one student two months to come to terms with some severe comments on his use of grammar. Occasionally, too, you may come across a student who has not wanted to admit to his dyslexia but who finds that he cannot cope on his own and therefore has to come forward to seek help. This can often cause loss of face. Such a student can sometimes be quite aggressive until he has settled down, and it is important for you, as tutor, to understand the reasons for this.

Chapter 7

Study skills and the Support Tutor

ON BEING BOTH COUNSELLOR AND ACADEMIC TUTOR

In the last chapter we discussed the role of the Support Tutor as a counsellor. We are now going to discuss how the Support Tutor can help the student with her studies. (In what follows 'you' again means the Support Tutor.)

We believe that the roles of counsellor and adviser on study skills are inextricably intertwined. In the words of Dr Gerald Hales:

> We cannot – must not – separate an individual's dyslexia from other aspects of existence [in this case – study] and some assessment of the effects on personal structures is, and should be, a part of our service to the individual dyslexic person.
>
> **(see note 7.1)**

Thus your aim should be to support the student as a person: this means encouraging her motivation by developing her self-confidence and feelings of self-worth, while at the same time supporting her ongoing academic work – coursework, dissertations, and essay writing. Alongside this, it is important to help the student to develop her own strategies, so that she will acquire sufficient self-awareness to monitor and control her own learning (**see note 7.2**).

You should also encourage the student to think positively about herself, about the way she studies, and about what she is expecting as a result. It is important that she should go into a period of work actively, thinking about her aims, rather than just reading and writing passively or mindlessly (**see note 7.3**).

In the dyslexic student's eyes you may well be the most stable and caring person whom she will encounter in what could be stressful weeks in a college term. In your whole approach to the student, therefore, you yourself need to be calm and unrushed (and punctual!). If you can, you should develop a relationship with the student which will help you to understand her needs and abilities. It is therefore important to know your student – in order to find out what strengths to build on, what difficulties to work on, and what causes of stress are likely to affect her academic performance. Some students come in to us only if they have a personal problem which may be interfering with their work; and, once one knows the student, the first question could be, 'How are you?' or 'Is everything all right?' Although it is a mistake to probe uninvited into personal relationships or family background, in practice what often happens is that we are given accounts of difficulty with living arrangements, of flat-mates 'not understanding', or of problems with money. It is plain in such cases that the student needs a listener who appreciates that these things are worse because she is dyslexic and who can see that they interfere with her study. It may be necessary for you to discuss the student's relationship with other students. As we have seen, some dyslexics are very open about being dyslexic, while some go to great lengths to conceal it. It is useful if you and the student jointly discuss ways of telling the 'world outside' what it is like to be dyslexic.

As a Support Tutor you should never forget the extent to which many dyslexics have low self-esteem (**see note 7.4**). It is therefore important that you do your best to encourage your students and give them confidence. There is plenty of research which suggests that people who think badly of themselves make poor learners (**see note 7.5**). It follows that you should look at your students' strengths and *make them aware of these*. Dyslexics desperately need self-respect.

It can also be useful if both of you discuss the psychologist's report. In some cases the student may not have had it explained to her and may still be unclear as to what dyslexia is. It is possible to work through the report so as to help her both to develop strategies for learning and to increase her self-understanding. Ginny Stacey has spoken of dyslexics 'being wired differently' (**see note 7.6**); and this can mean a different pattern of skills and hence a different approach to work. It can sometimes be useful to talk about left-brain and right-brain activity (see Chapter 1, p. 6). This may help the student to get to know herself, to become aware of her own thinking and learning processes, and of the way in which her memory works. You should discuss how to study, how to relax, and how to plan a work session. Remember that many dyslexics have 'good days' and 'bad days'; the 'bad days' need to be talked through and some kind of coping strategy worked out. Above all it is important to convince your student that she is not 'thick' but rather has a different and distinctive approach to learning.

Many students will tell the Support Tutor of difficulties which they have had with their mainstream staff. They sometimes get these difficulties out of proportion, and it may therefore be important to give them the confidence to go and seek help. A possible procedure is to talk to her about how to approach other tutors.

It is particularly useful if you can help to make her aware of the pressures which there are nowadays on most mainstream staff – though not in such a way that she is deterred from approaching them! For whatever reason there are some dyslexics whose interpersonal perceptions are not very acute. To such people their own problems are paramount; and if, in addition, they have poor language skills the result may be an abrupt or seemingly aggressive manner of confronting their tutors. You will often find that you need to act as a link between the student and your fellow staff. A procedure which we ourselves often use is to obtain the student's permission to approach your colleagues and then do so on the understanding that all correspondence between you and her other tutors is open for her to see. Finally, she will probably experience certain struggles within a structured college environment and within that environment you can act as the buffer and stabilizing influence.

HOW FAR SHOULD THE SUPPORT TUTOR TAKE OVER?

We should like to consider this question by citing a particular example. One of us (DEG) has recently worked with a final year student who came in looking pale and thin and very stressed. It was late January. He had six essays to hand in, a dissertation of 9000 words to complete, and application forms for jobs to fill in. There were finals coming up and he had not been eating. He said that he was 'working all the time but not getting anywhere' and that his mind had 'gone all blurry'. In fact, the essays and the dissertation did not have to be in until the second week in May, and the application forms were to be completed by the end of March. Because there was so much looming, however, it seemed that he was unable to put any structure on to the various tasks.

We therefore discussed each part of what lay ahead and broke his work and his timetable down into manageable chunks. Since as a final year student he only had four lectures a week we decided to split the week into two sections – either all the mornings as one section and all the afternoons as the other, or two blocks of two and a half days each. One of the blocks would be spent on the dissertation, the other on the essays.

We also decided that he would do an essay to a deadline every two weeks and that he would hand them in to DEG. We worked out that he should be able to complete the dissertation by mid-March and that he could then start revision. We photocopied the application forms and he decided that he would take them one at a time.

There were still two days each week free, and we discussed the importance of 'time out' without feeling guilty. We also had a chat about the least stressful way of keeping oneself fed. After all this DEG asked him if he wanted her to write it down for him (it might have seemed patronizing to do so peremptorily). He in fact said that he did; and he actually asked for it to be put on a postcard so that he could keep it in his pocket and look at it when he needed to. This procedure worked!

From this example it can be seen that coping with college life, both academic and personal, makes it virtually essential for the student to have some structure in his weekly routine. Study at college can be much more open-ended than study at school, and students have more responsibility for their own private work. There seems to be more free time to fill in; there is no set homework timetable, and submission dates for essays are often set weeks ahead. This can involve planning and time-management tasks which can be very stressful for dyslexic students. In addition, the organizing of their studies may place many demands upon their short-term memory – and there is usually much diverse information to process during an academic week.

Our dyslexic students have often described themselves as having 'blurred brains' or, to use an expression coined by Ginny Stacey (**see note 7.7**), 'muddle in our minds'. One could perhaps speak of an 'overcrowding' of the brain so that, as in our example above, the student cannot sort out his thoughts into clear structures, particularly when he is under stress. When such a student comes forward for help, you will need to assess how far to impose a structure for him and how capable he is both of organizing his work and of sticking to the plan.

Work with an individual dyslexic student or group of students should be a dialogue: the tutor can present structure, ideas and strategies 'from the outside' but each student may have his own strengths and difficulties. The study skills hand-outs which we provide for our students (of which examples are given below) are very simple: they present general ideas which can be discussed and adapted according to individual needs.

THREE SAMPLE WORK SHEETS

Here are three examples of the work sheets which we use. They are kept simple for two main reasons. In the first place they can function as discussion points, either with individuals or with groups; this means that the students can then add their own ideas and strategies while you, as tutor, go over each point with your comments.

Secondly, dyslexic students have so much complicated material to process during their working week that it is a relief to have something which is both challenging and simple.

I Basic study skills

1 Plan out your work
   Work for short periods of time
   Target your work periods
   Look forward to finishing
   Take a timed break

2 Never work when you are tired (the mistakes will get worse)
   What are your best times for working?

3 Can you keep tidy . . . How?
   Colour coding
   Folders for each subject
   Desk

4 How can I learn?
   Notice board, posters (subconscious learning)
   Tape
   Mind-maps
   Colour
   Shape

II Taking notes

1 Why is the lecturer lecturing?
   • ideas
   • facts
   • for exams
   Ask the lecturer?
   Ask other students?

2 Look at lecturer's programme
   • pick out key words

- read around it
- prepare key spellings/names

3 Prepare shorthand
  - What ideas have you? ('Shks' for 'Shakespeare'); ('envr' for 'environment')

4 Techniques
  - headings
  - sub-headings
  - key words
  - signposts

5 How to get extra help?
  - approaching lecturers? how?
  - what about tapes?
  - friends?
  - photocopying notes?

III Approaching a session of work

1 What is my goal tonight?

2 Avoid those chasing thoughts

3 Can I monitor myself?

4 Am I controlling my work patterns?

5 No negative thoughts

6 Am I getting tired?

7 Relax . . . do something else

Chapter 8

Study skills and the student (I)

TIME MANAGEMENT AND SELF-ORGANIZATION

(This may seem a frightening heading – do not let yourself be put off by it! 'You' in this chapter means the student.)

From the time when you first come to college, you are likely to achieve more if you *plan in detail* how to spend your time rather than leave matters to chance. If you, either alone or with a tutor, can create a structure or framework for your studies, it is likely that you will work better and feel more confident. Your teachers may have done this for you in school and such a framework exists in the case of ACCESS, BTEC, and GNVQ courses. For college courses, however, long-term planning is needed; and there may be no one standing over you to make you get on with your work.

You will probably find it helpful to work out *a timetable*. To start with, there will be a number of hours during the week which are committed in advance – those in which there are lectures, practical classes, tutorials, and the like. Time also needs to be set aside for meals and for regular social activities such as club meetings, aerobics, sport, social events, etc. This still leaves a large number of hours available for private study.

It is most unwise to assume that *private study* can be 'fitted in at odd times'. It needs to be built into your timetable. Once particular slots have been set aside they should be regarded as no less firm a commitment than attendance at lectures. Study hours should be integrated with the lecturing timetable; for example, if there is an hour between classes this may be the right time for carrying out certain tasks in the library or printing out some work which you have done on computer.

The planner calendar can be used to ensure that study plans are made well in advance. Since it is difficult for a dyslexic student to 'dash off' an essay at the last moment the dates for handing in should be marked in as soon as they are known, along with dates of tests, examinations, and the like. Some students use large sheets of card divided into columns, with a column given to each subject: the weeks are then divided horizontally. The students write down the lists of tasks for each subject as they occur so that they can then visualize how the assignments are spread out.

Time is precious and you should try to get straight down to work. You should be aware of the risk of **erosion of study time**. Five minutes here, ten minutes there, an extra break for coffee – these always seem minimal, but together they can result in serious loss of time.

Although it may seem very unfair, it is virtually inescapable – from the way in which he is made (see Chapter 1) – that a dyslexic student will need to spend longer hours than a non-dyslexic student on his work; indeed, written assignments may take twice as long and more. It may also be more difficult for him to catch up in the same way as the non-dyslexic student does, for example, by copying reams of missed lecture notes or by staying up all night to complete an essay.

It is therefore important to aim at **regular controlled working hours** and to avoid shelving work or missing classes. As a rough guide we recommend a total working week of **about forty to fifty hours**. If you spend fewer hours than this on your studies there is a risk – because of the time needed for reading things up, for checking what you have written, etc. – that you will find that you are not keeping up with the workload. We have seen students who have started to drop behind, who then cannot face the accumulated backlog, and who end up not knowing where to turn to sort it all out. On the other hand, if you spend more hours than this you may become over strained, and in any case it is a pity to miss out entirely on social life and college activities. We have come across many dyslexic students who work too hard and become very run down – it is necessary to be like the tortoise in the fable and plod solidly along.

We have found that many dyslexic students (and, indeed, other students) **can work better at certain times of day**. You should identify these and allocate your time accordingly. If you find reading very tiring you should aim at doing the bulk of it when you are at your freshest, and the same of course applies in the case of other things which you may find difficult or laborious, such as completing essays or transcribing formulae.

It is unwise to work for too long at a single stretch. We have found, on the whole, that a dyslexic student can achieve good results if he continues for about an hour but that after that his work deteriorates. In that case it is not worth continuing, since the errors associated with his dyslexia tend to multiply. This is particularly so if you are working on the computer, which can place strain on the eyes, hands, and back, apart from the brain. You should learn to watch out for signs of tiredness – the ideas do not come as quickly, the handwriting gets worse, the keyboard errors multiply. Take a short break and move away from the workplace. If you can work to a rhythm of, say, fifty minutes study and ten minutes break, you will find that you can cover a large amount of ground and yet still remain fresh at the end of it.

Similarly **regular but limited amounts of study** each day are likely to be more beneficial than occasional days of intense effort. The time taken off work is important because it gives you the chance to relax and unwind. We recommend that, in addition to shorter breaks, your time off should include one whole day per week as well as one evening and one afternoon. It is important that these should genuinely be periods of relaxation and that you should look forward to them. Some dyslexic students have found yoga classes very beneficial. If periods of work and periods of relaxation are not clearly distinguished you may find yourself half-working instead of working at full stretch – and then worrying during your spare time because you feel you ought to be working! As a result you may end up achieving very little.

If it is possible (and we appreciate that sometimes it may not be) **avoid working when you are tired, rushed, or under pressure**. If you do you will not produce your best work and there is a risk that the dyslexic errors will multiply. You should try to plan to avoid such pressure. Late night study is liable to be extremely tiring, and if – unavoidably – some 'catching up' time is needed, you should consider whether it might not be better to get some sleep and start early the next day rather than make yourself very tired working through the small hours.

Some students may find themselves unwittingly making use of **avoidance tactics** – that is, excuses for not getting down to work; and it is important that you should recognize when you are doing this. It helps, for example, to keep your desk tidy and organized, with spare pens and pencils so that there will be no time wasted at the start of a period of study in looking for the things that you need.

A fixed time should be set aside each week for the **revision of lecture notes**. You should make sure that you understand them, and you should bear in mind that you will need them to be intelligible for revision purposes at a later stage in the course. You may like to consider transferring them on to a tape recorder. Whether or not you do this, it will certainly save a large amount of time later if you date them and, when they are complete, catalogue them; and you will probably find that colour coding with felt pens will help in later identification. They should also be filed carefully, as it is difficult to sort out a mass of notes long after the lecture.

Nowadays as a result of the Student Charter (**see note 8.1**) you can expect that most lecturers will provide an outline of their lecturing syllabus. It will help you if you can use some of your private study time to **look ahead**, in order to gain maximum benefit from future lectures. You can obtain some knowledge of what is to come by a brief scan of the syllabus, and if possible you should try to **familiarize yourself with any names**, **specialist words or diagrams** which are going to be used; this will save you from having to puzzle over these during the lecture.

All these points are matters of common sense; but it is easy in the stress of the moment to forget them, and we would reiterate the point that tutor and student need to work as a team and to ensure by their joint efforts that common sense is not thrown out of the window.

Finally, you may at some stage in your college career feel overwhelmed if large amounts of written work have not been completed. You may feel that you cannot cope and may even consider giving up your course. If this happens you should talk to someone, whether counsellor, tutor, or even fellow student. The simplest procedure is to make a list of priorities, with help from the tutor if necessary, and to work steadily through them. You may well find it daunting if you try to look at all the tasks together.

If the pressures seem too great it is a good idea to **take a complete break,** such as a weekend away. You can then slowly 'retrain' in your studying: one student re-started with just ten minutes three times a day and built up from there. It is also useful at these times to practise relaxation as this helps one to 'unwind', particularly last thing at night. If you find that you cannot sleep, it is important not to worry: in our experience worries over not sleeping can sometimes be more damaging in their effects than the actual lack of sleep! We suggest that you try to work out ways of combating the problem – by practising relaxation during the day to use at night, by treating yourself to a warm drink, or by listening to music. Above all, we recommend a calm and methodical approach: if you and your tutor deal with your problems one by one they are likely to seem much less formidable.

WHERE TO STUDY

You need to think carefully about the place where you can best study. It should, if possible, be somewhere where there are no distractions. If you use your own room it should be organized so that it contains both a place to work and a place for relaxing. All students, not least dyslexic students, require breaks in their studies, and a cup of coffee over a desk covered in papers or by a keyboard is insufficient. It will give you a much better break to move away to a different environment, if only to sit in an armchair by the window.

If you decide that your own room is not a good place for study –
you may, for example, want to escape from the computer for a while –
you could consider the college library or perhaps somewhere in
your department. Your tutor or some of the other students may
have helpful suggestions. Some of our students meet together about
once a week in groups, checking notes and discussing work, and
this is something which they have found very useful.

READING WITH UNDERSTANDING

Many dyslexic students have reported that they find *'reading up' a
subject* difficult and time consuming. We think it unlikely that, even
with practice, you will be able to 'skim through' a book, abstracting
the essentials, as quickly as a non-dyslexic student.

As a result of this, it is sometimes possible to buy essential texts
under category 1 of the Disabled Students' Allowance. You will
probably need a letter of support from your department and you
will have to keep all the receipts for possible presentation later (**see
note 8.2**). Some college libraries allow dyslexic students to have a
longer loan period, particularly for the restricted loan texts. You
might also check whether your Information Technology Centre has
a reading machine. There are also CD ROMs, which convey
information through text, sound, and visual imagery. All these may
give you easier access to texts but you will still need to extract the
information from them.

There are various approaches and strategies which you can use.
We suggest that you think about the whole process of reading – **why
you are reading and what you want to learn from it**. You may sometimes
be reading for background knowledge – to broaden your general
awareness of the subject and to help you understand lectures; you
may be reading to expand your lecture notes, or you may sometimes
be reading up material for an essay or a tutorial paper. Identify your
reason for reading: do not read vaguely!

Read actively. If you read with a **pen or pencil in your hand** it
may help to focus your attention. It may also help you if you place *a piece*

of card under the line that you are reading. We strongly suggest that
when you read you always **make notes** of some kind; if you do so,
this forces you to think and may help your concentration. If you
have books of your own or photocopied journal articles, try using a
highlighter or *coloured felt pens* to make important passages stand out.
In the case of library books (which, of course, cannot be marked)
particular passages and diagrams can usefully be photocopied and
suitable markings and underlinings made on the photocopy. You
might even adopt an old Victorian habit and put key words or short
summaries in the margin of your text. *Bookmarks* (of cardboard, not
flimsy paper!) can also be of help, while *references* on a particular
topic can usefully be *put on cards* so that you do not have to return to
the index over and over again.

Another aspect to active reading is that, as well as taking written
notes, you should *listen to the sounds and say them to yourself*. In
particular, you may find it useful to pay special attention to all
relevant names and to make sure that you know how to pronounce
them. It may also help if a friend reads them aloud so that they can
be stored on a tape recorder, in which case the correct pronunciation
may help you with the spelling. If you are writing down names and
dates they may be easier to remember if you highlight them or write
them in a different colour.

Sometimes *reading a piece aloud* helps you to get the sense of it and
thus gain more from your reading. There is also a special variant of
this procedure in which you can use what is called the ARROW or
'self-voice' technique. This is a technique by which you *hear your
own voice*; it is brought about by means of a special speech recorder
linked to a headset. Several of our students have reported that they
found it beneficial (**see note 8.3**).

If you find some text, e.g. journal articles, very dense, it is possible
to get the text *enlarged*, for example, by means of a photocopier.

The final strategy which we wish to mention is that you should
monitor your reading: check on whether you understand by asking
yourself what you have learnt from a particular reading task. You
may also like to add a brief summary at the end of your notes
(**see note 8.4**).

Meredeen has given a useful list of questions for checking your understanding (**see note 8.5**):

- How much do I remember?
- How well did I understand?
- How much can I explain in my own words?

As we have seen already (Chapter 1), the dyslexic student is likely to be weak at deciphering and strong at comprehension. If, therefore, you think of reading simply as deciphering – as translating marks on paper into spoken words – then your slowness and weak immediate memory may well be a severe handicap. If, however, you know what you are looking for and try to read with understanding you are making better use of your strengths and, in the process, saving yourself a large amount of time and energy.

USE OF READING SERVICES

In some cases your college may run a *reading service* in which books and articles are recorded on tape. There are also tape/listening libraries (**see note 8.6**). This service was primarily intended for blind students; but there is no reason why a dyslexic student should not make use of it. Alternatively, if no service is available, you may be able to find a friend who is willing to read books and articles aloud so that they can be recorded on tape; and it is sometimes possible to reclaim the expenditure under the Disabled Students' Allowance.

Local libraries have a large stock of novels on tape, as well some non-fiction books; and in some cases you will find tape-recorded guides to particular areas which can be a substitute for maps. You may find that you can use these for pleasure, particularly if you drive into college and can listen to them on your car radio. You could also look at their large print books.

READING LISTS

Most lecturers provide *reading lists*. Sometimes these are long and formidable, and a lecturer seldom intends that every book in the list should be read from cover to cover. An obvious step is for you to approach the lecturer for advice: which books are the important ones and which topics require most time? If you are in your first year then second and third year students can often give useful advice (though their opinions may vary!). Mastering certain key texts as background reading is likely to be more valuable than ploughing dutifully through a list of books one by one.

Let us now appeal to your imagination. It is possible to see reading or note taking as being rather like a *pyramid* or a *triangle*. The point at the top is the theme or main subject of what you are reading, and, as you read, the topic broadens out into the dense mass underneath. Dyslexic students can get lost in this dense mass: the risk is that they may read large amounts of detailed material without knowing how it fits into the more general structure higher up.

In this connection we cannot resist quoting the disastrous instructions (from a dyslexic's point of view!) given to Alice by the King of Hearts in *Alice in Wonderland* '"Begin at the beginning," the King said gravely, "and go on till you come to the end: then stop"' (**see note 8.7**). For a dyslexic student confronted with a book we believe this to be the worst possible advice! We suggest that, instead, you formulate to yourself as early as possible what you hope to obtain from it. You can then approach the text with a clear purpose in mind.

If you still find the text too dense, it may be useful to go to *an easier book* which could help you to see an outline. One of our students 'over-read' for an essay and could not sort her notes out. She was in her final year. We then looked at a GCSE Sociology textbook which explained the whole topic in clear outline; and as a result she could then fit her detailed and very academic notes into this outline. She got an A!

If the books on a particular topic seem extra difficult you may like to consider an encyclopaedia or a CD ROM as a starting point.

Once you have some general idea why you are reading and what you are looking for, you should then look in the text for *more specific information*. You can use certain parts of the text as signposts, namely the preface, the introduction, the table of contents (including the chapter headings and sub-headings) and the index. With practice you will be able to learn to ignore irrelevancies (such as acknowledgements) and spend time on those points which you have already selected as being important.

The start of the book and the concluding chapter are often particularly useful in indicating its general direction, and the beginning and end paragraphs within a chapter can be a useful source of information as to the contents of the chapter as a whole. Some textbooks have brief abstracts (summaries) at the beginning of each chapter. It is important that you concentrate on important points and do not stray off into irrelevancies.

Some of our students have gained considerable benefit from the books by De Leeuw and De Leeuw or Tony Buzan on *'rapid reading'* (**see note 8.8**). The main principles are that one should focus on and absorb the topic sentence and concluding sentence of a paragraph, and that one should not read every word (still less every letter) but only groups of words or thought units. The reader has to develop a 'recognition span' in which he isolates and absorbs a phrase by its key words. Other students have found this too difficult to cope with.

Some students report that they find it difficult to tackle the text directly, even when they know what they are looking for. We would like to repeat what we have said about study in general: *read when your mind is fresh; do not try to read complicated material when you are tired or stressed; it is very hard to concentrate. It is also important to take breaks from reading as soon as your mind starts to wander.*

We have already suggested that you should read with a pencil in your hand. If you then run it along the line it will help to focus your eyes. Tony Buzan (**see note 8.9**) illustrates in a diagram how you can use the third, fourth, and little fingers in a wedge to act as a guide for the eyes.

COLOURED FILTERS AND COLOURED LENSES

You may also like to consider the use of coloured filters or coloured lenses. Some dyslexics report that, when they read, they experience visual distortion: the letters on the page seem to blur, or wobble, or jump up and down. It is possible that they are being affected by the contrast between the white spaces on the page and the black letters. Some psychologists test for this, and there are sometimes references to it in a dyslexia assessment (**see note 8.10**).

The important point is that this distortion can sometimes be reduced or even eliminated if you use coloured overlays (sheets of transparent plastic) which are placed on the page. The colour varies from person to person and it is worth a support tutor or unit investing in a screening pack for the students to experiment with (**see note 8.11**). Quite a number of our students have reported that the use of coloured overlays has made their reading much easier: the overlays give an improvement in reading fluency and seem to reduce eye strain so that they can read for longer stretches of time. Not all dyslexics benefit, and there is considerable controversy in the whole area (**see note 8.12**); but if you find reading tiring the matter is certainly worth your consideration.

If the overlays are used for about six weeks and appear to be successful, you may like to consider being tested for coloured lenses; then, if they turn out to be beneficial, you can have glasses made up in your particular colour. Some students have tried using photochromatic sun glasses or, if they already wear glasses, having a tint put on them. We have, in fact, met students who did not know about the research in this area but who had, nevertheless, turned independently to coloured lenses to help with their reading and writing. Even if you do not use coloured overlays or lenses, it is possible that using coloured paper of a similar shade or working under a coloured light bulb may sometimes help to reduce distortion and glare. We also recommend that you experiment with the colour and contrast on the screen of your computer monitor.

Chapter 9

Study skills and the student (II)

SOME THOUGHTS ON NOTE TAKING

Note taking at lectures is a skill which many dyslexic students find difficult when they first come to college. Like reading, however, it is one which can be improved with practice (**see note 9.1**).

In this connection, S.H. Burton has distinguished two extremes – 'the eager first-year student who tries to take everything down and the exasperated second-year student who has given up the unequal struggle and doesn't take notes at all' (**see note 9.2**). We agree that both these extremes are undesirable. No student – least of all a dyslexic student – will be able to write down all the points made in a lecture, but we suggest that you try to sift out the important ones, making sure that they are not forgotten. First of all it is worth considering how you can **prepare yourself in advance**.

PREPARING FOR LECTURES

As in the case of reading it is a good idea to work out **why the lecturer is lecturing**. Is it to present you with ideas to make you think and do further reading – something which is more likely to be the case in arts subjects? Is it to present you with facts and the latest research which you might not easily find for yourself – something which is more common in science subjects? How necessary are the lecture notes for the examinations? We know one lecturer who tells her students that they will not pass their exams unless they are fully familiar with her lecture notes; we know of another who has put all his notes in outline on disk but tells the students that they must attend his classes to pick up the necessary details – and that the combination of both will provide all that is needed for the exams. In contrast other lecturers have emphasized the need for originality and have said that there is no point in attending a lecture unless it sets you thinking.

As we have already suggested, you will probably find it useful to **read up in advance** on the subject matter of the next few lectures so as to make yourself familiar with the main topics and key words and to prevent the spelling of new or difficult words from becoming a major problem. You could try writing a list of these words on a small piece of paper and have them near you in the lecture.

NOTE TAKING IN LECTURES

A good lecturer will normally write up new technical terms and the like either on the board or on an overhead projector sheet. If, however, for any reason, a lecturer is not in the habit of doing so, you can help yourself by developing **your own shorthand**. Commonly occurring words, such as *'compare'* and *'result in'*, and specialized words belonging to your particular discipline, such as *'hypothesis'*, *'monarchy'*, *'streptococcus'*, etc., can be represented by abbreviations or even by arrows, stars, and the like. It is important, obviously, that such shorthand expressions should not be so cryptic that you are baffled by them when you come to do your revision.

There is no point in wasting your energy in writing down the lecturer's jokes and asides; and if a student makes a conscious effort to distinguish the essentials from the incidentals then note taking, like reading, will become very much easier. We suggest that you aim to **jot down the key words** which represent the key themes of the lecture.

These key words can be represented in linear note form, with headings, sub-headings and points listed in order. Use *arrows* (->) and *stars* (*) to help emphasize points and *ampersands* (&) for brevity. You can then work vertically down the page, leaving yourself plenty of space. If you can make your notes look like the note pages at the end of Chapter 7 then there is every chance that they will be easy to follow.

As an alternative many dyslexic students have found the **'mind-map'** or **'thought plan'** method of taking notes very effective (**see note 9.3**). Here the main point is written in the centre of the page and the pattern of ideas works outwards from this; cross-links and cross-references can easily be added and the further expansion of ideas will continue outwards. For a full mind-map, it is easier to turn the paper sideways and work horizontally. The total pattern of notes can form a diagram which a dyslexic person may remember from its graphic rather than its verbal representation. Hence it may be easier to use for revision. In general, not so many words are used, which is easier both in time and effort!

The mind-map also makes you think in terms of concepts or key words rather than sentences which have unnecessary 'padding'. After a lecture, you can go over them and add colour, signs and symbols, even drawings. Some of our students use them all the time and find them really creative. There are, however, students who find that they cannot cope with them – they prefer linear notes. Some training and practice in mind-mapping is necessary so that you learn how to present the key concepts before filling in with details.

Mind-maps can be used for just part of a lecture and afterwards be built into linear notes. This again adds interest to the vertical linear pattern. An example of a mind-map summary of a biological lecture is given in Figure 1.

During the lecture itself we suggest that you **leave plenty of space** by writing on alternate lines and by leaving wide margins (compare also the section in Chapter 10 on 'getting across' what you want to say). This means that the relatively cryptic jottings which you might have made during the lecture can be expanded when you return to the subject during your own study periods.

If you find difficulty in spelling some of the words used by the lecturer it may be helpful to use *a pencil* or *different coloured pen* to indicate such words – or at least some approximate representation of them. If you are using a laptop you might put a * by them. If you

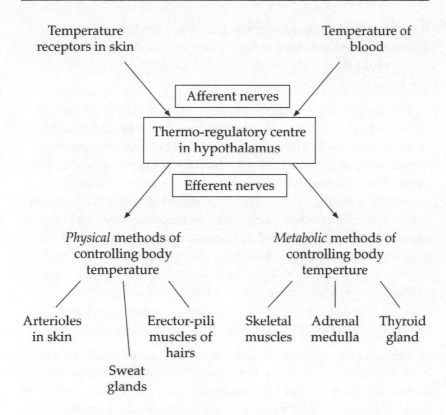

Figure 1 Notes in mind-map form from a biology lecture on the reflex control of body temperature

spend five minutes wondering if it should be 'Enistine', 'Einstine' or 'Insteine', you may easily lose the thread of the lecture, whereas you can sort out spellings at your leisure afterwards.

You should try to make use of the '**signposts**' provided by the lecturer. First of all, listen carefully to the first few sentences of the lecture: it is likely that in them the lecturer will state the purpose of the lecture and indicate his treatment of the topic. Similarly, listen particularly carefully to the end of the lecture where he may sum up the points he has raised. (This means that you should not be late for the lecture or start to pack up before he has finished!) Listen also for 'signposts' within the lecture when the lecturer may say, for instance: that 'There are three main aspects of . . .' or 'This can be developed in two contrasting ways . . . .' You can then number your points and subdivide your notes accordingly (or at any rate ask the lecturer for further help on where the subdivisions come if he has not made this fully clear).

It is also possible to *combine written notes with the use of a tape recorder.* Quite a few students now *tape record their lectures.* This has to be thought out carefully. You should first of all ask the lecturer if he will agree to it. Some may not – perhaps because it would make them feel uncomfortable or insecure, and obviously you must respect their feelings. If you use a tape recorder, invest in a good one with a strong microphone which will pick up voice only and not register all the background shuffling and coughing. Some students buy very strong microphones such as camcorder mikes. You will need to sit near the front of the class; and you will also need to have sufficient tapes and batteries. It is of course still useful to supplement the tape recording with your own notes, as this will ensure that you continue to concentrate on the lecture.

During the lecture you can **note down key words** which act as a reminder of the important points made. You can then reconstruct further details of the lecture by yourself, talking round the key words and recording yourself on tape. This procedure places emphasis, once again, on understanding rather than on the transcription as such. Indeed, if you find yourself unable to talk round the key words this may be an indication that you have not fully understood the main points of the lecture and should therefore try to obtain further help. In addition, if you are satisfied that you have recorded the lecture suitably you can then label the tape, store it, and bring it out again when you need to revise. If you have been doing a large amount of reading, then listening may be a welcome change.

Other means are also possible, though not all dyslexic students will want to make use of them. One is to **photocopy** another student's notes (unfortunately this can be expensive!), while another is to arrange to be given **a carbon copy** of the notes which he has taken. If a first year course has not changed very much since the previous year there may be useful material in the *notes of second and third year students*, who, as has been pointed out already, are often very glad to be able to help. In some colleges you may be able to find a *'buddy'* or a *note taker* to take notes for you. Also it is sometimes possible to claim the expenditure for all this through the Disabled Students' Allowance. In some cases the lecturer may be glad, if asked, to provide *a hand-out* or *copies of the OHP sheets* which he has used.

NOTE TAKING FROM TEXT

For the general approach to extracting material from text we suggest that you look at the section on reading in Chapter 8.

This is very much easier than taking notes from a lecture, since you can work at your own speed and return to a particular passage if you wish to study it further. The same general principles apply, however. First of all, again, think about **why you are taking notes**, whether they are background reading, whether they are to supplement lecture notes, or whether they are for an essay. It is particularly important that you should consider what information you are looking for. No useful purpose is served if you copy straight from a book without giving any thought to the subject matter – and for revision purposes you might equally have consulted the book itself, which will probably be more legible!

You should remember, too, that a mass of closely written material is likely to be daunting when the time comes for revision. It is therefore important that there should be **wide spacing**; and if all the notes are under **suitable headings and subheadings** it will be easier to pick out relevant points in the future. In particular, **key words** and – where appropriate – **key sentences** can be written down. Nearer examination time, some students may even like to transfer the key words on to postcards; they can then carry these around and refer to them at odd times, or leave them on the walls or on the mantelpiece for further scrutiny. If you leave spaces you will be able to add more notes from another book or piece of research, and you will also be leaving room for your own opinions and comments. Whenever you add extra points we suggest you do so in a different colour. You may also find that when you are taking notes from books mind-mapping may be useful.

In the case of *diagrams*, the *actual physical act of copying them* – if it is done with thought and not just mechanically – may help to fix the important details in the memory. Our students have often noticed that they remember what they have done themselves, be it diagrams or notes, better than they remember photocopies.

In note taking, as in reading, it is important that as a dyslexic student you should *use your strengths* in order to offset your weaknesses. It may be difficult for you to write down what a lecturer has just said while at the same time paying attention to what he is now saying, and you may equally find difficulty in locating a passage in a book or in finding the right name in an index. If, however, you use skill and judgement in the selection of relevant material – which is something which you can do well – then your relative limitations in the area of immediate memory and slow writing need not put you at too much of a disadvantage.

CONCENTRATION

Concentration is perhaps at the heart of coping with all aspects of study skills. Many of our students report difficulties with concentration, in lectures and in private study. It is a problem for all students, but perhaps dyslexic students have extra difficulty because of their limitations in short-term memory and their relatively slow speed of working. In the words of some of them, they have 'too many chasing thoughts'.

Poor concentration can be caused by worry and stress, by fatigue, by inactive or passive methods of studying (including note taking), and by negative, self-critical thoughts for instance, questioning the value of what you are doing and expecting not to do well.

Think positive. Think about the study skills outlined in the last two chapters. Concentration is helped if you:

• Choose times for working when you work best.
• Plan your work into manageable 'chunks'.
• Plan your allocation of time – taking breaks and deciding time limits.

- Avoid distraction; work in a place where you will not be distracted.

You should therefore try to:

- Deal with one task at a time – keep a list for 'floating thoughts'.
- Avoid looking too far ahead.
- Prioritize – forget irrelevant details.
- Have a clear desk – no clutter, since muddle can cause stress.
- Watch out for delaying tactics – get started!
- Work actively – when you attend lectures both listen and write.

When you are studying at home or in the library, become aware of your signs of fatigue or stress and make sure that you have a break during which you can relax. Do not forget the positive value of *doing things that you enjoy* when you are not working. You will then be better able to return to your work; and the happier you feel the more you will enjoy it!

Chapter 10

Essays and assignments

SOME OF THE DIFFICULTIES

We should like to suggest to college tutors the following penance: imagine yourself cooking the breakfast and finding that the milk is boiling over, that the toast is burning, that the telephone is ringing, that there is a knock at the door, and that several members of your family are simultaneously asking you questions. This may give you some idea of the problems confronting dyslexic students when they have to write an essay or carry out an assignment. Basically, there are too many things which have to be attended to all at the same time!

They will probably be well aware that it is necessary to **plan the essay as a whole**; yet there may be a dozen or more 'threads' or separate topics which have to be thought about and arranged in order. In addition, no progress will be possible until they have found the right words for saying what they want to say; and even when they have found them there is the danger that in typing or writing them down their hand movements may get out of step with their thinking. As if all this was not enough, they then have to check whether the words are correctly spelled and whether there is correct paragraphing and punctuation. Our experience is that many of them have not, in fact, been taught punctuation; and since it involves learning to name and use yet another group of symbols – the full stop, the comma, the semicolon, the colon, the question mark, etc. – it is easy to see why they failed to 'pick it up' at a younger age, when all their energies were directed towards writing and spelling.

Many of the essay-writing skills are 'second nature' to the non-dyslexic. If he wishes to write a word he does so; in most cases the word 'just comes' and he does not need to think about its spelling. There is no danger in his case that words or phrases will come out jumbled up or in the wrong order; and even if he has not received special teaching he may well have acquired the essentials of punctuation without conscious effort. As a result, he is free to concentrate his energies on the subject matter of the essay and on the construction of fluent and easily readable sentences.

It is small wonder, therefore, that the written style of a dyslexic student suffers in comparison. With so much else to think about he may forget what he wrote a moment earlier. The result is sometimes a very staccato and jerky style as he struggles to express a large number of ideas briefly before he loses track of them. Alternatively, he may sometimes go to the opposite extreme and write long convoluted sentences as though he did not know when to stop. In general, so much is being demanded of him at the same moment that he cannot monitor it all efficiently.

The result of all this is illustrated by a tutor's comment which criticized a dyslexic student's 'inability to sort out and organize his main ideas despite a keen understanding of the subject'. The essays of dyslexic students may, in fact, appear to have a relatively low level of analysis or abstraction. They sometimes appear packed with detail which is not sufficiently related to key concepts or presented with adequate generalizations.

Most dyslexics find it useful to **break down complex material into its component parts** and **deal with these parts one at a time**. It is widely agreed that for dyslexics the best way to remember a six-digit telephone number is to break it down into two groups of three, or even three groups of two. The same principle applies if you need to remember items in series, such as the months of the year; and similarly if you need to spell or write longer words it is often helpful to break them up into smaller parts (compare the suggestions on spelling in Chapter 12).

Similar strategies will almost certainly be helpful in essay writing. **The different components of the task need to be considered separately, one at a time**. *'Reading the question'* is a different activity from thinking about how to answer it; planning the essay as a whole is a different activity from considering how best to get across what one wishes to say, while questions of paragraphing and punctuation are different yet again. If you try to attend to all these things at once the result may be chaos: you may well be told that you have 'failed to answer the question', that the essay 'lacks coherence', that 'the style is immature', and that your punctuation is all wrong. If you have experienced such criticisms we suggest that you work on them one at a time!

In what follows there will be sections concerned with:

- what is expected in a college essay;
- reading the question;
- reading for and planning the essay as a whole;
- getting across what you want to say;
- preparing the rough draft;
- setting out references;
- checking what you have written.

Questions of grammar and punctuation will be discussed in Chapter 11 and questions of spelling in Chapter 12. We recommend that you read the present chapter in small doses.

WHAT IS EXPECTED IN A COLLEGE ESSAY?

Essays at college are not normally set with the purpose of making you 'write down all the facts'. Rather, you *are being given the chance to examine a problem* and to show that you can *formulate ideas* about that problem – thus presenting a debate or an argument. As an essay writer, therefore, your purpose will not normally be to describe events or 'tell the story', but to **analyse, discuss, and interpret** them. You will therefore need to arrange your ideas in a **logical order** and to produce **evidence** from the relevant literature in support of your argument.

If your department has a *front of assignment marking sheet* or any kind of handout which sets out the way written work is graded, you should look at it carefully. It may say, for example, that marks

will be given for your understanding of the subject, for the quality
of your argument, for your use of evidence, and for the way in
which you express yourself.

READING THE QUESTION

The first essential, before you embark on an essay, is to *read the
question carefully*. You should then spend time considering what the
question means and what precisely you are being asked. This will
ensure that all aspects of the question are covered in the answer.

A question set in a recent English paper was: 'How successful is
Wordsworth in integrating the various strands of philosophy and
experience in *The Prelude, Book 1*?' All students discussed what was
meant by 'strands of philosophy and experience', while many
referred to the integration of the two; but there were very few who
dealt with the key words 'how successful'. The question might in
this case have been ringed as follows:

How successful is Wordsworth in integrating the
various strands of philosophy and experience?

The student would then be in a position to use the ringed words to
guide his answer. Thus, since there is a ring round *'How successful'*
he is immediately led to thinking about the notion of 'succeeding',
while the presence of a ring round *'integration'* reminds him that it is
not enough to consider each of the components separately. Rings
round *'philosophy'* and *'experience'* are further reminders that the
meanings of these two key terms are by no means self-evident.

In the case of many essays it may be helpful to experiment with
changes in the wording ('Does it mean this?' or 'Might it mean that?'),
since such changes may help to clarify what is and is not relevant
and may open up new ways of treating the topic. It is important,
too, that you should make full use of the information which has
been given in the title; this can be done in particular if you check
that you have paid **attention to all the key words**. Indeed there are
some words which are likely to keep occurring both in essays and in

examinations – for example *'compare'*, *'contrast'*, *'assess'*, *'analyse'*, *'discuss'*, *'outline'*, *'evaluate'*, and *'summarize'* (**see note 10.1**). These words call for careful thought, and you should make sure that you completely understand their meaning.

Above all you should spend time considering what is implied by **the title of the essay** and what are **the important issues** which it raises. Ask yourself: 'What exactly is the argument to be debated here?' 'What are all the implications?' 'What debate does it raise?' From these basic questions further questions will arise. Write these questions down on a sheet of paper – in the form of a 'mind map' if you wish – or on your computer screen. (An example of a 'mind map' is given on p. 83.) If you do this, then there is a good chance that you will genuinely be answering what you were asked and will not be sidetracked.

If you are still unsure about what the essay is about, then it may be helpful if you go to see your tutor. You should do so, however, only after you have gone through this initial stage of analysing the title, so that she can see that you have already given thought to the topic.

READING FOR AND PLANNING THE ESSAY AS A WHOLE

It is at this stage that you should be aware of your objectives; in particular you should ask yourself as far as you can:

1 What are the main things which I want to say?
2 How can I arrange them logically?

You will then need to do some *preliminary reading*. You may like to look again at the section on reading in this book (Chapter 8). It is a good idea to start by reading a short book or chapter which gives you an outline or overview of the topic. It is also important that you should be clear as to what information you are looking for so that you are not wasting time on irrelevant material.

At the end of the chapter we make suggestions as to how you can keep track of all the references that you need. One possibility is to keep them on your computer, while another is to keep them on small separate cards; either way you will be able to arrange them easily into alphabetical order when you have finished the assignment.

At the same time as you do your preliminary reading you should provide yourself with a *master sheet* and develop the *main outline* of the essay on it. For this purpose you could use a mind map, as you will then be able to extend ideas across and down the page and subsequently recognize the relationships between them. Figure 2 is an example of such a master sheet. We have in fact chosen a topic from the history of education, but the same principles would of course apply to essays on most other subjects.

Let us suppose, then, that you have been given the following title for the essay: *Assess the changes introduced into British state education by the comprehensive system*. Your first move should be to put the title in a central box from which arrows can emanate in a variety of directions. You should then consider each key word in turn and write notes on each. 'In turn' is important; if you try to think of all the points at once you may well forget some of them and become confused. (One advantage of a mind map is that if a point does occur to you you can put it down somewhere on the page and consider later where exactly it fits in.) The end product might look like that shown in Figure 2.

Once you have understood the central theme of the essay it will be easier for you to ensure that all your reading is purposeful and that you select only material which is relevant.

Think about what you are reading. Try if you can to organize your material by giving it *headings* and *subheadings*; these can then be linked to your master-plan. Some students prefer to use cards rather than ordinary paper for this purpose: they are stiffer and therefore easier to organize, and there is the advantage that cards of different colours can be used for different topics. If all cards are numbered this will save time when you come to re-read them. Some students use A5 sheets (or A4 sheets torn in two) as they are smaller

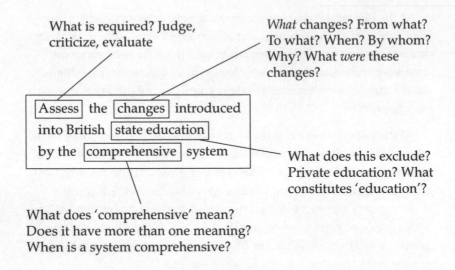

What is required? Judge, criticize, evaluate

What changes? From what? To what? When? By whom? Why? What *were* these changes?

Assess the changes introduced into British state education by the comprehensive system

What does this exclude? Private education? What constitutes 'education'?

What does 'comprehensive' mean? Does it have more than one meaning? When is a system comprehensive?

Figure 2 Example of a master-sheet

and therefore more manageable. You should write on one side of the page only; then, if necessary, you can cut pieces out or add them.

If you quote from the books which you have read, check that the quotation is relevant and makes the point that you wish to make – and for future reference make a note of the page number! Also make clear that it *is* a quote and that the words are not your own; otherwise you are guilty of *plagiarism* (see below).

Some students prefer to plan as they read and put all their notes straight on to the computer, moving and editing at the same time. Others choose to put everything on to the screen and then move the material around. The difficulty in the second case is that you can see only a limited amount of material at a time and it can therefore take you quite a long time to search for relevant sections. However, you can use bold or italics to indicate where certain parts belong. There are computer programs which help you to plan essays (see Chapter 14). You can also use a scanner; this allows printed text to be transferred on to your screen. You should be careful, however, that you do not put this material into your essay without analysing or paraphrasing it.

While you are reading you may suddenly be struck by a new idea, and in that case you should be prepared to explore it. For this purpose you may find it useful to keep a page where you write down notes for future use: these can include opinions, questions, agreements, disagreements, etc. about which you will later need to examine all the relevant evidence.

Keep your mind receptive and *keep asking questions*. Some of what you are reading may not fall easily under a particular heading, in which case it may be better to put off classifying it until you have read further and made the necessary planning.

It does not matter at this stage if the pages are filled in a seemingly haphazard way as long as all relevant material is included (and you may need to refer back to the title in order to make a decision as to whether a particular topic is or is not relevant).

You can next look back at your master plan. This will help you to organize your notes and jottings into a coherent order. Numerals written against each jotting can be useful; these will give you an order in which the different topics can usefully be discussed. Try using fluorescent markers or different coloured pens to circle related topics, and, as we have said, you can if you wish cut up your pages into strips so that the different topics can be clearly distinguished.

Finally, while you are making notes, be careful not to copy large chunks directly from the original. You may in that case be faulted for what is called 'plagiarism' – that is, stealing other people's ideas and passing them off as your own. It is best if you paraphrase, using your notes as brief summaries. You should, however, copy down any useful words or phrases which will improve the style of your essay.

In lighter vein we should now like to quote a passage from Dickens's *Nicholas Nickleby*. Mrs Nickleby's conversation provides an admirable example of how not to write an essay, since she 'rambles' instead of passing from one point to another in a logical way. Dickens's portrayal is a masterly one. Here she is, talking to a Mrs Wititterly:

I think there must be something in the place,' said Mrs Nickleby, who had been listening in silence; 'for, soon after I was married, I went to Stratford with my poor dear Mr Nickleby, in a post-chaise from Birmingham – was it a post-chaise though?' said Mrs Nickleby, considering; 'yes, it must have been a post-chaise, because I recollect remarking at the time that the driver had a green shade over his left eye; – in a post-chaise from Birmingham, and after we had seen Shakespeare's tomb and birth place, we went back to the inn there, where we slept that night, and I recollect that all night long I dreamt of nothing but a black gentleman, at full length, in plaster-of-Paris, with a lay-down collar tied with two tassels, leaning against a post and thinking; and when I woke in the morning and described him to Mr Nickleby, he said it was Shakespeare just as he had been when he was alive, which was very curious indeed. Stratford – Stratford', continued Mrs Nickleby, considering. 'Yes, I am positive about that, because I recollect I was in the family way with my son Nicholas at the time, and I had been very much frightened by an Italian image boy that very morning. In fact, it was quite a mercy, ma'am,' added Mrs Nickleby, in a whisper to Mrs Wititterly, 'that my son didn't turn out to be a Shakespeare, and what a dreadful thing that would have been!

An essay which imitates Mrs Nickleby can be reasonably sure of a low grade!

In contrast, before you start to write your rough draft, you should again scrutinize your master plan, examining all the *questions which you have raised*. You should then write them down in a **logical order**, checking that each point follows on from the one before. You may sometimes find that there is material which now seems irrelevant and that you can get rid of it. However, there may also be new ideas which you have derived from your reading, and these should be written down. You will probably end up with a series of questions or points arranged in a logical order. These can then be numbered, and you can sort out your notes into numbered piles which correspond. Then you will be able to expand in detail on each of the numbered points.

GETTING ACROSS WHAT YOU WANT TO SAY

Many dyslexic students are able to talk about difficult concepts with fluency and yet when they have to express themselves in writing they are unable to 'get across' what they wish to say with anything like the same level of sophistication. A group of dyslexic students recently had an interesting discussion of an essay written by a physics student on the theme of 'Nuclear Power Stations'. What was particularly noticeable was the maturity and complexity of their spoken language in contrast with the immaturity and apparent naivety of the language which they used when they tried to summarize the argument in writing.

Having to write the words down seems in some cases to affect fluency and spontaneity. The extra effort needed adds an unwelcome complexity, and the result may be that some students come to doubt whether they will ever be able to find exactly the right word. If, in addition, they are worried about making spelling errors they may conclude that the best response to all these pressures is to choose a simpler word, even though it may be a very much less effective one.

This is the kind of situation in which a tutor can be of considerable help. He can discuss the use of *alternative words and phrases* with the students and call their attention to nuances of meaning. We often find that our students offer key words and phrases orally, which the tutor then writes down. (In fact one of the most common comments made by our students is, 'Did I really say that?'.) Where appropriate this discussion can be recorded on tape and the student can be asked to summarize it in writing. The tutor can sometimes offer key words which trigger off further relevant phrases from the student.

A similar technique is that suggested by Dr Alex Main (**see note 10.2**). Main suggests that students struggling with written expression should select a passage written on a specialist topic. He first reads it with them, and they select key words from each paragraph. The student then rewrites the passage using these key words as a basis for the reconstruction: 'This exercise, repeated several times with different passages, if necessary, builds up the student's critical awareness of his writing style, and increases his confidence in seeking different ways of expressing himself' (p. 48).

It may also be helpful if you consider the use of *illustrations and diagrams* as ways of 'getting across' your argument, and in some contexts *graphs*, *histograms*, *bar charts*, and *pie charts* can also be useful for this purpose. The great advantage of all these devices is that they often convey information more succinctly and clearly than is possible by means of verbal explanations. If they are used, however, it is important that they should be well presented: it is best if they are drawn on a blank page which can then be mounted into the main text of the essay. Scanners and graphics packages are of course invaluable here.

Careful thought should also be given to the question of whether and how to define technical or unfamiliar terms. In the first place there are some situations where it can be assumed that the reader has the required knowledge. This is true, for example, of many mathematical or statistical terms, such as 'correlation coefficient', and of standard physical or biological terms such as 'impedance' or 'monozygotic'. Secondly, however, there may be terms which call for explanation, either because one cannot assume that the reader is familiar with them or sometimes because there is genuine doubt as to what they do mean, as in the case, for instance, of 'romanticism' or 'phenomenology'. When any unfamiliar term is explained it is often useful to give one or more examples of situations where it is being correctly used. What is unsatisfactory is to introduce the word without explanation – which may baffle the reader – and then several lines later try to explain its meaning. Good examples can in fact be useful both in illustrating the meanings of words and in clarifying the intended argument.

We also believe that dyslexic students should be encouraged to do plenty of reading, even though some of them find it hard work. One reason for this is that if you pay attention to the ways in which the writer is expressing himself you are likely to achieve a more mature written style yourself. It does not, in fact, take all that much effort to set oneself to read for, say, ten or fifteen minutes each day, and the choice of material can be guided by your personal interests. As with other kinds of reading it is important that this reading should be carried out purposefully, and we recommend that a dictionary is available for looking up unfamiliar words and that a notebook is available for writing them down.

We have found that many dyslexic students have never heard of a *thesaurus*. Once they have been shown how to use it, however, they have found it a very valuable form of support in written work (**see note 10.3**). Surprising as it may seem, dyslexic students are often interested in synonyms, etymologies, shades of meaning, and the like – perhaps because these are aspects of language which are intellectually challenging. In the same way, dyslexics – and others – can become very interested in advanced mathematical concepts even though they find the mechanics of calculation difficult and tedious. It is important for the tutor to try to give students the confidence to exploit these *new interests* in their written work. In addition, group discussion of *synonyms* and *shades of meaning* may help to make them aware of distinctions which they would not otherwise have noticed.

We have also found that students can be made more aware of style if they are asked to analyse some of their own work under the tutor's guidance. It is important in that case for the tutor to call attention – as tactfully as possible! – to imprecise or immature language and discuss ways in which it can be improved. This is best done on a one-to-one basis as the tutor's initial criticisms may unavoidably have to be somewhat negative. Such an exercise may demonstrate to a student the greater power of expressing himself which he can achieve if he examines shades of meaning with care.

Part of developing a good style involves *thinking about the reader*. As we pointed out at the beginning of the chapter, some students write in a very jerky or abrupt style. It gives the impression that they have the knowledge but cannot be bothered, or are too impatient, to explain it thoroughly. They seem to assume that the reader knows what they are talking about. Thus seemingly illogical leaps occur and it is not always easy to follow their train of thought.

We encourage students to see essays as *a dialogue with the reader*. This ties in with what we said earlier about the purpose of essay writing, namely to show that you can analyse and discuss the question set. The term 'intelligent layman' helps the student to visualize the reader, and indeed a Support Tutor is often a layman, dealing with essays from every field of learning, most of which he knows little about! You should assume that the reader is unlikely to be aware in advance of how you are going to treat the subject, and therefore you should 'lead' him through the essay step by step. We sometimes suggest to our students that they should imagine themselves 'creating a dialogue' with the reader.

Now a 'dialogue':

1 introduces;
2 explains;
3 analyses;
4 assesses;
5 discusses;
6 links up;
7 summarizes.

If you think in terms of a dialogue it helps you to be clear as to your own train of thought and it also helps the reader to follow the chain or pattern of your ideas. This dialogue can comprise introductory or concluding sentences within paragraphs or it could comprise whole linking paragraphs.

At each stage therefore it is important to check that the reader is being given a **sense of direction**. For this purpose, suitable **'signposting'** is very important – it makes explicit to your reader the logical links between one sentence or paragraph and the next. Also you should take special note of words such as 'nevertheless', 'but', 'however', 'on the one hand . . . on the other hand', 'consequently', 'likewise', 'thus', etc. The function of these words is to mark a variety of relationships, including contrasts, similarities, alternatives, and results. Even the use of the familiar words 'this' and 'that' can help the flow of ideas within an essay. To *check that* *these connecting words are being correctly used* is important for any writer, since such checking forces you to consider where exactly the argument is leading; without it there is serious risk that the essay will lack direction. We ourselves provide our students with a list of such words and an account of their functions.

WRITING THE ROUGH DRAFT

This is the most important part of the writing stage. The rough draft is where you think, question, alter, move text, cross out, revise, and re-edit. If all the work is done at this stage, the final writing up should be a fairly mechanical copy of the result of what has been done on the rough draft.

You should take heart from the fact that almost all writers struggle with this stage of drafting – not just dyslexics!

If up to this point you have planned your essay by hand, you should now turn to the word processor. The advantages are that moving text, re-editing, etc. all become very much easier. However, since there are some students who prefer to write their essays by hand we shall refer in this section to both ways of working.

If you are writing by hand, it is sensible to put the rough draft on one side of the paper only, since this means that passages can be rewritten or reordered without other passages being thrown into disarray. You can cut sections off and add them on elsewhere (which is why this facility on your word processor is called 'cut and paste'). It is also a useful precaution to write the essay title in pencil at the top of each page; if this title is attended to there will be less risk of writing things which are off the point. It may also be helpful to summarize the main points in the margin; and for this reason you should allow wide margins and plenty of space between lines and at the end of paragraphs. This will also enable you to make corrections. Stinting oneself on paper is a false economy.

If questions and problems crop up as you write, it is useful to have a piece of paper at hand on which you can make a note of them. Alternatively, you could put them in the margin of your script in pencil or a different coloured pen. The kind of comment you might write in could be: 'check reference', 'more needed here'; 're-phrase'; 'is this OK?' Some students may like to have a tape recorder handy into which they can talk their comments.

All this is easy on the word processor. If there are things about which you have queries you can write them in italics or in bold. You can do the same with your comments; it might be useful to put some stars (***) at the start and at the finish (***) of any comments that you make. If you move text, have some way of indicating where you are going to put it and where you have taken it from. It can involve some time searching through a document; and stars are again useful. If you are not sure whether you want to move a piece or not, or if you want to move it somewhere to get it out of the way of the section you are working on, then, again, you can put it in 'bold' to indicate that it needs attention.

Some students find it difficult to know *how to start an essay*. In fact, you do not need to write the introduction until you have written the body of the essay. In many ways the introduction is rather like the conclusion. There is no one set way of writing an introduction, and the suggestions which follow should not be followed blindly. However – depending on the topic – you may find some of the following suggestions useful.

1 Say something about the **key terms** in the question.
2 Indicate how you are **interpreting** them.
3 Tell your reader **what the essay is going to be about**, i.e. how you are going to treat the topic and what will be your lines of argument.

Similar principles apply to the **ending** of the essay. This should be a brief summary in which you draw all your points together and make the overall position clear. It is useful when you write your last paragraph to look back to the introduction. There are a number of expressions which can usefully occur in it such as 'in conclusion', 'to sum up', 'it therefore follows', and 'finally'; and you will need to judge which of these is appropriate for the purposes of a particular essay. No writer of essays can afford to overlook the wise words attributed to a preacher who was asked for his advice on how to preach a good sermon: 'First', he said, 'tell them what you are going to tell them; then tell them; then tell them what you have told them.'

PARAGRAPHING

When you are writing the essay, you should divide your topics into **paragraphs**. We have found that students can benefit considerably from instruction in paragraphing. Every paragraph needs to be thought of as a unit, each in succession contributing to the unity of the essay as a whole. There need not necessarily be subheadings at the start of each paragraph since this would be cumbersome; but you may like to 'think' or imagine them to be present (or even write them in pencil for your own use). You will then be in a position to check that every sentence within the paragraph is relevant to its main theme and that the paragraph as a whole is relevant to the main theme of the essay. Once you have grasped the significance of paragraphing you are likely to become clearer in your own mind as to what are the central points which you wish to make in the essay, and as a result you will be better able to organize them in the most effective way (**see note 10.4**).

Although we do not advocate writing to a 'formula', the difficulties experienced by some students in shaping a paragraph led a group of us to devise a procedure which could be of help to others. A paragraph might contain:

1 a general opening statement indicating the theme or topic of the paragraph – and perhaps its link with the previous paragraph;
2 a discussion or elaboration of this;
3 evidence to support the argument;
4 discussion of evidence;
5 conclusion.

The students worked out their own mnemonic for this. ODEDC – '*often dogs eat dirty carrots*' (there was a reason for the carrots – someone's dog had just done that, and been sick!). This 'formula' has sometimes been found useful in writing answers to examination questions.

OTHER TYPES OF ASSIGNMENT

We do not propose to discuss at any length the writing of laboratory reports, research projects or dissertations, since the guiding principles are, in general, the same as those for essay writing. Usually each department will issue its own guidelines for these more specialized types of writing, and if there is a rigid formula you can put it on your computer. You should keep in mind your central objective and check that everything which you write is relevant to it. If you are reporting on some research which you yourself have carried out you should remember to include full details of your procedure; it is very easy to assume that the reader will know what you did – but he has not got second sight and you must *tell* him!

In the case of dissertations it may be necessary for you to use more headings and subheadings than in the case of essays (since a dissertation is, in effect, an essay 'writ large'), but the same kind of 'master-sheet' is likely to be useful, and it is particularly important that the logic of your argument should be clearly 'signposted' (**see note 10.5**).

SETTING OUT REFERENCES

Projects and dissertations (and usually essays too) should include a list of references. Here you record the books and articles which you have used as sources or from which you have quoted. (Do not, of course, make the piece simply a series of quotations; otherwise the result will be what some tutors rudely call a 'scissors-and-paste' essay.)

One of the most important functions of the list of references is to enable the reader to evaluate the credentials of claims made in the essay. For example, if you have used expressions such as, '*it has been shown* that *x*', it is important to indicate how *x* was shown and who was responsible for doing so. You should imagine the marker writing, 'How do you know?' or 'Evidence?' over every statement that you make.

Some students find it difficult to know how to introduce

references. To some extent this will depend on the 'style' of your department, but at many colleges the Harvard system is widely used. In this system the name of the author and date of publication are put in the text, and the full reference is given at the end of the essay or book. Books and names of journals are put in italics; in the case of books the town and publisher are given at the end, while the titles of journal articles are put in plain text, followed by the name of the journal in italics, followed by its volume, number, and pages. Thus in the case of a book you might write, Bloggs, J. (1993) *My Friends the Owls*. London: Aviary Press, while in the case of a journal you could write: Bloggs, J. (1995) The owl in ancient Egypt. *British Journal of Owl Behaviour*, 27, 1, 39–43 (**see note 10.6**).

We in fact encourage our students to look in their own texts to see how writers present their references, and we have also drawn up a list of useful phrases such as:

• Brown (1994) states that . . .
• Brown (1984) points out that . . .
• Brown (1978) describes how . . .
• This has been shown by Brown (1989) who . . . .

If one refers in the reference section to a book or article this is, in effect, an undertaking that one has read the work in question. If, as sometimes happens, one has to rely on secondary sources – for example, a textbook which asserts that Brown pointed out such and such in an article in an untraceable journal dated 1870 – the correct procedure is to quote the textbook, since this carries no claim that one has read the original paper.

It is also important to check that the style of the reference list is consistent. What is irritating to the reader is to find that the year or place of publication is given in some cases and not in others or that some references to journal articles carry page numbers and some do not. Advice on the most appropriate style for the references can readily be obtained from the tutor. We must emphasize again how important it is when you are doing the initial research to keep a record of all the references which you consult. One can spend many tedious hours trying to find them again!

WRITING OUT THE ESSAY

When writing in rough there is no need to spell out each word in full, since nobody has to recognize what is written except you yourself. If you feel doubt about grammar or spelling you can always put a cross or some other mark over the words in question and return to them at leisure. Similarly, if you are not immediately able to produce the exact wording that you want, you can again indicate this and return to the passage when your mind is fresher. If you start worrying about such things at the time there is serious risk that you will lose track of your arguments and forget what you were trying to say.

When you have completed your rough draft you will need to spend considerable time in checking it. The crucial point in such checking is that you should make sure that what you have said reflects adequately what you *meant* to say (compare also what is said in Chapter 17 when you come to sit your examinations). As we have already indicated, there is a tendency on the part of dyslexic students to take too much for granted on the part of the reader: they may not appreciate that the details of their argument need to be 'spelled out' (an interesting and significant metaphor) if someone else is to understand it. They may, in fact, genuinely believe that they have made themselves clear when all that the reader finds is some cryptic utterances which in themselves do not amount to an argument at all.

A useful device is to read aloud onto tape what you have written and then play it back. This will provide the opportunity for *listening* rather than *looking*, and the result may be that inadequacies in logic, presentation or style are easier to detect.

The following are some further points which need to be checked: (1) Does the essay answer the question? (2) Does it contain irrelevancies which should be excluded? (3) Does it maintain a logical sequence, and does the use of 'connecting' words or expressions such as '*therefore*' or '*in contrast*' contribute to showing the direction of the argument? (4) Are the *sentences complete* and are they of the most suitable length? (5) Can the things which you have learned about *style, grammar, punctuation, and spelling* (see Chapters 11 and 12) be put to good use?

This checking or editing will need to be done at least three times, as it is extremely difficult to read for sense and style, for punctuation, and for spelling simultaneously. We suggest one check for sense and style (which should include a check that the essay reads coherently), one for punctuation, and one for spelling.

It is often helpful if you can allow a gap of several days between the completion of your rough draft and its re-reading. After this interval you can come to what you have written with a fresh mind, and it is easier to imagine yourself as someone who is looking at the essay for the first time. You may find it helpful to think of yourself as a tutor whose task is to make critical comments – which in a sense you are! You can then mark these in in pencil or with a red pen. We, ourselves, wearing our hats as tutors, have often found it helpful to say to students, 'From now on you do not need me to make these critical comments.'

Some of our students have written their essays out three or four times. This is very conscientious – but it is unwise! It is not just that there is increased risk of misspellings and of omissions and other errors of transcription; more importantly, it does not constitute the best use of the time available. Copying out is a purely mechanical task, and time can much better be spent on self-criticism. It therefore seems to us preferable not to write out a whole fresh draft but to 'patch up' the existing one. The end product may be full of crossings out, additions, caret marks ($\wedge$), sentences written sideways in the margin, and the like, but this does not matter because all these things can be put right at a single copying.

Finally, it will help the person grading your script if your work is well presented. It is best, therefore, if you type with double spacing or use wide lined paper, writing on one side only. Remember to number all your pages. On the front cover you should include:

1 your name;
2 the name of your course;
3 the year or module number;

4 the name of your tutor;
5 a clearly written title.

You should include a bibliography or reference list in accordance with the department's style, and it is useful if you 'package' your essay in a plastic envelope or folder. Do not put every page in a separate envelope, as this means the marker has to pull each one out in order to read it, and this is very time consuming!

Chapter 11

Grammar and punctuation

INTRODUCTION

To large extent this chapter is addressed to the tutor: we have found that it is difficult for students, dyslexic or otherwise, to teach themselves grammar. Computer grammar-checks vary in their complexity and we have found that, even when these are used, students work better with a tutor to explain the terms which come up. Many tutors who work with dyslexic students are language trained; we have therefore simply indicated the type of approach needed and the main difficulties faced by dyslexics.

Some dyslexic students have improved their written language considerably as a result of help with grammar. In the past students were taught parsing and clause analysis (learning about the parts of a sentence and how they fit together); but in the last few decades these have largely gone out of fashion. We believe, however, that their importance has been underestimated. They may in fact be coming back into the classroom as a more grammatical approach to language develops through the National Curriculum.

Words are *precision tools*, and the person who has a thorough knowledge of how they function may be compared to a craftsman who has a wide repertoire of skills or to a cricketer or tennis player who has a wide range of shots. In our view, all students – and dyslexic students in particular – are likely to benefit if they are made aware of the rules of basic grammar; without good written skills it can be difficult to express ideas clearly and effectively.

In the case of dyslexic students, it is important to go slowly, since it is impossible to study grammar without using at least a few technical terms, and these may be somewhat daunting. A tutor who, without adequate explanation, introduces words such as 'adverb' or 'conjunction' may confuse the students. It is possible, however, to make clear to them that in learning about grammar and punctuation they are embarking on an intellectually challenging discipline, namely, a systematic study of certain aspects of human verbal communication.

Some of our students ask specifically for 'grammar lessons' and seem to find them stimulating. Once they recognize that technical terms are unavoidable in such a study they will feel happier about trying to learn them.

If students come forward asking for help with grammar, it is a good idea to look in advance at some of their written work and analyse their errors before you actually meet them in a tutorial. This is likely to be less demoralizing for them than having to listen to criticism the moment they arrive! We also ask them to develop their own awareness by noting down any difficulties which arise when they are writing.

In general, a thirty to forty minute session is enough. Over a period of time the tutor can collate the points that are discussed in the tutorials and give them to the student as a personal grammar book. This can be supplemented by relevant texts and exercises (**see note 11.1**).

THE SIMPLE SENTENCE

The most useful way to start is to introduce the idea of a simple sentence. This is the basic unit from which eventually to expand into more complex sentences. It can also be used to introduce key grammatical terms. We try to make the teaching a joint exercise as far as possible and we also try to keep it subject-related; we therefore extract a sentence or two from the students' work or ask them to give us one orally.

Here are two examples of such sentences:

> Three sorts of grass grow abundantly on Bird Island.

and

> We marked out the same number of plots in each sward (**see note 11.2**).

SOME KEY GRAMMATICAL TERMS

From such sentences certain key grammatical terms can be introduced (**see note 11.3**), while at the same time you can make them aware of the implications for spelling.

These grammatical terms are:

- subject; object; noun; pronoun;
- verb; tense;
- adjective; adverb.

An understanding of tense will help the dyslexic student with the '-ed' ending. Using *marked*, you can show the student that most past tenses end in '-ed'. The effect on sound can be discussed: in some cases the 'e' which comes before the 'd' is sounded ('*acted*', '*hurried*', etc.) while in other cases it is not ('*groaned*', '*crammed*', etc.). As in *marked*, the ending may have a 't' sound, and though in most cases the '-ed' spelling is retained, there are a few words where the letter 't' actually appears in the spelling, as in 'wept', 'crept', and 'smelt'. We have often met misspellings such as 'happend', 'determind', and 'gatherd'. Although these represent what is heard, the writing of 'd' in place of '-ed' is evidence that the writer has not fully appreciated the past tense ending (**see note 11.4**).

Learning about adverbs helps students to understand the '-ly' ending. They can then see the function of '-ly', work out the original word, and add '-ly'. This helps with the spellings of words such as 'likely', 'safely'. We have been surprised how few of our students knew this rule.

A tutor should take care: (1) not to introduce too many of these terms in any one session; and (2) not to use any of them without indicating the job which each one does. For example, one would not simply introduce the word 'adjective' out of the blue; rather, one would ask the student to think about ' *green* grass', 'a *large* island', and '*different* sorts' and then to consider what 'job' is being done by the words 'green', 'large' and 'different'. The logic of class membership is perfectly intelligible to a dyslexic student, and in this context the need for the word 'adjective' becomes obvious.

If you expand the simple sentence, you can then introduce the comma and perhaps provide a checklist of its uses. The student might add more adjectives, using commas to separate them, or add a separate phrase:

• The grass was long, green, red, and salty.
• In a study of Bird Island, for example, three sorts of grass were identified.

WRITING COMPLETE SENTENCES

'But how do I know whether or not it is a sentence?' This is a frequent wail! Many students – not only dyslexics – write combinations of words which do not form a complete sentence, such as:

• To analyse this topic.
• Starting with the first example.
• Attlee, a Labour Prime Minister.
• In a very short time.
• Who served under Elizabeth I.

When these non-sentences are seen outside their context, it may seem clear that none of them is properly formed, but this may be far from clear to dyslexic students who are struggling to put their ideas down on paper.

One way of getting a student to recognize a non-sentence is to provide combinations of words, some of which do *not* form sentences. Thus it will be easy for him to recognize that on Bird Island grass

is not a sentence since the words in that order do not make sense.
Moreover, even if the word order is changed, and we say, or write,

grass on Bird Island

the result is still not a sentence. A useful way of explaining why this
is so is to point out that a sentence should answer a particular
question – for instance the question, 'What kinds of grasses are there
on Bird Island?'– but that these words fail to do so. The student
might then come to recognize for himself that there is **no verb** in the
sentence.

Another useful way of helping dyslexic students to see that a
sentence is not complete is to get them to realize that it is a 'stand
alone' unit. Sometimes their minds race ahead of what they are
writing: they mentally link one 'sentence' up to another without
realizing that the full stop is a complete break. For example, the
following combinations are wrong because there are *not* the breaks
which are suggested by use of the full stops:

Because many conifers grow on mountain sides. Drainage is
easy. There being many natural streams. Which flow downhill.

It is useful to have strips of card to isolate the non-sentences and to
highlight the real unit of sense; this enables the student to realize
what is happening. It should then be possible for you to work out
jointly the criteria for a complete sentence. These are:

- It must make sense.
- It must answer questions such as 'who', 'what', or 'when'.
- It should have a subject and a verb.
- It must start with a capital letter and end with a full stop.

All this can be quite difficult for dyslexic students. It can be good
training for them to learn to read their work aloud, seeing each
sentence as a separate unit. They may sometimes be able to
recognize the non-sentences from their own intonation.

Once the simple sentence is understood, it is useful to look again at punctuation. A common error is to end a sentence with a comma, not a full stop; and as a result the student strings would-be 'sentences' together separated only by commas. This is a fault among many students, dyslexic and non-dyslexic alike. It should be made clear to them that the full stop is used to mark boundaries between sentences; if they are careless about the use of this particular mark, the sense of their work can be affected:

> We studied the marshland, although it was raining, there were many geese there.
>
> (Where does 'although it was raining' fit?)

It could again be that the dyslexic student's mind is moving on to the next sentence. In this case, the important thing is to know that after a complete sentence there has to be a full stop. Faulty punctuation may reflect faulty logic.

If students are encouraged to listen carefully to passages which are read aloud to them they may notice that when the reader's voice falls and he makes an appreciable pause he is almost certainly indicating a full stop; in contrast, if there are minor pauses these will be represented in the written version by commas. We have found that students can detect faulty punctuation fairly well when they read their work aloud or when it is read aloud to them; sometimes we work off two photocopies: the tutor reads the work aloud while the student follows with a pencil in his hand and marks what seem to him to be the punctuation errors.

The colon and semicolon can next be introduced: these are particularly important for academic writing. They are useful for those dyslexic students who tend to write long involved sentences, since these sentences can then be broken up.

The *colon* can be regarded as a sign that some kind of expanding statement or list is about to be introduced', as in 'There are various ways in which this can be done: . . .' (followed by an indication of what these ways are) or in 'You should take with you the following: . . .' (with an indication of specific items).

In contrast the *semicolon* simply divides the full sentence into two distinct sub-sentences with a closely related meaning, for example:

> the Saxons invaded the south of Engand; the Danes invaded the North.

COMPLEX SENTENCES

In the case of complex sentences, dyslexics in particular often have difficulty in writing clearly and succinctly. They can often be helped if they are shown ways in which sentences can be expanded. It is important therefore to explain what job is done by a conjunction. Discussing the meaning of the word 'junction' helps here; and the whole idea is easier to grasp once the student understands what a complete sentence is. We have found it helpful to start with *'and'* and *'but'* and build up from there.

It will be necessary to explain that a conjunction can occur at the *start* of a sentence but that a full sentence needs to follow. Students who start a sentence with words such as *'because'*, *'although'* or *'whereas'* can often fail to complete it. This point can more easily be detected if the sentence is read aloud.

Sentence length

In general, dyslexic students tend to make errors of two opposite kinds. The first is to write what comes out as a series of sharp staccato sentences. The second is to go to the opposite extreme and write long, involved sentences which try to compress too many ideas within too short a space. In that case the student does not see the sentence as a pattern; each new idea is added as it occurs to him, and the sentence becomes unconnected and disjointed. As a result, it is difficult for the reader to understand the overall meaning.

Golden rule 1

One main idea in one sentence.

Golden rule 2

Never start a sentence without knowing how you are going to end it.

A sentence which rambles on should be broken down into shorter sentences, with the logical links between each being made clear. If sentences are too short, however, the student should consider how they can be made to flow more easily; in particular, the introduction of longer sentences containing words such as 'when', 'because', etc. may convert what seemed like isolated and unexamined ideas into a coherent logical argument. We suggest that if students are prone to writing very long sentences they make a 'physical' check on the page and mark where the full stops occur. We have had some fun colouring in sentences with different highlighters to indicate varying sentence length; this can be done in study groups. We have also found it useful to invite students to comment on each other's work from the point of view of sentence construction and length, though this should be done only if there is good rapport between members of the group. Thirdly, there is:

Golden rule 3

Think of the person reading the essay.

Students should be reminded of the fact that this person needs to *understand what they have written* – but yet *cannot ask them questions*.

In our experience teaching sentence structure in a fairly formal way can be beneficial for a number of reasons. Not only can students be taught a more fluent style, but, perhaps more important, they are made aware of the sentence as a unit which can be shaped and modified so that it expresses as effectively as possible the writer's message.

SOME COMMON FAULTS

One reason, we suspect, why the written style of some dyslexics seems cramped or stilted is that they produce these short, staccato-like combinations of words without making explicit the logical links between their different ideas. Thus what the writer may have meant in the *'Attlee, a Labour Prime Minister'* example, was: *'My next topic is to discuss the achievements of Prime Ministers since the Second World War, and I shall therefore begin with Mr Attlee.'* In this sentence the word *'therefore'* has an important job to perform and should not have been omitted. There are plenty of occasions where, implicitly, the arguments in the script of a dyslexic student are perfectly logical; where he may need help is in making them explicit. Once again he should remember *'Golden rule 3'*: **think of the reader**.

A common error is to write sentences with unrelated parts. Thus if a student were to write:

Working on the marshland it was raining.

one could point out to him that this is a clumsy sentence and in particular that it fails to indicate *who* was working on the marshland.

Even worse, it is sometimes possible to present a distorted picture which implies something that one does not mean. Thus:

Walking down the road my hat blew off.'

suggests by implication that my hat was walking down the road! One can avoid this kind of mistake by working out who is the subject of the sentence and adjusting the verb-form accordingly. Thus:

Walking down the road I was overtaken by John.

is correct, since the sentence makes clear that I was the person walking down the road.

Alternatively one can put things right by the use of conjunctions. For example:

> While I was walking down the road my hat blew off.

is also correct.

In addition there are times when the presentation can be made more logical simply by changing the order of the words. Thus in the case of

> We will be pleased to see you, if you will call together about your problems.

the movement of the words 'about your problems' so that they follow 'pleased to see you' is clearly an improvement. The wording then becomes:

> We will be pleased to see you about your problems if you will call together.

Similarly:

> He remembered that he had forgotten his girlfriend's birthday while shaving.

can be corrected if the words 'while shaving' are put after the word 'remembered'. This example can also be used to illustrate the correct placing of commas. Thus:

> He remembered, while shaving, that he had forgotten his girlfriend's birthday.

is acceptable, as is:

> He remembered while shaving that he had forgotten his girlfriend's birthday.

What is unacceptable is:

> He remembered while shaving, that he had forgotten his girlfriend's birthday.

This violates the 'two-commas-or-none' rule: there are many sentences which are acceptable both when there are *two* commas and when there is *no comma* but not (as in the last example) where there is *one* comma (**see note 11.5**).

Subject/verb agreement can be confusing in some contexts. Thus, if one is being strict,

> a group of scientists are working on this theory,

is wrong; the subject of the sentence is 'a group', but it is easy to be misled by the word 'scientists'. The sentence should read, ' a group of scientists *is* working on this theory.' Similarly

> many studies of this topic has shown . . .

is wrong since '*studies*' is the subject of the sentence and therefore needs the plural verb '*have*'. Dyslexics (and others) need to remember, too, that '*data*' is a Latin plural: thus '*these data show . . . .*' is correct; '*this data shows . . . .*' is wrong.

For the sake of logical accuracy the student should be encouraged to think of the correct placing of words such as 'only' or 'even'. These should be put immediately before the word or phrase which they refer to. Thus

> This is only allowed if . . .

is wrong, while

> This is allowed only if . . .

is correct. Similarly

> He only discovered some old rubbish

is wrong, while

> He discovered only some old rubbish

is correct.

In the case of 'even', '*He could even do it better than Smith* is wrong, while '*He could do it better even than Smith*' is correct. Mistakes over commas and over the words 'data', 'only', and 'even' are of course not limited to dyslexics.

SCIENTIFIC WRITING

In a scientific paper, it has been normal practice up to now to write impersonally, and some departments do not allow the use of 'I' or 'we' in scientific papers. In that case one cannot say, 'I did this' or 'We did that'; instead the passive form has to be used and one says that this or that *was done* or that *it was decided* to do this or that.

However, writing in an impersonal scientific style can be very difficult for dyslexic students since it involves the construction of longer sentences. Simple exercises converting active to passive can be helpful; and there are some useful books on scientific writing, with some telling examples, which the student may like to consult (**see note 11.6**). It is possible that in the future the impersonal style will no longer be insisted upon (**see note 11.7**).

Chapter 12

Spelling

WOULD TUITION BE HELPFUL?

Not all dyslexic students will wish for help with spelling, but in our experience quite a number of them worry about it; and it is therefore important that help should be available for those who feel the need for it.

Spell-checks on word processors are of course useful, but they have their difficulties which can sometimes contribute to extra stress. For example, they are of value only if the student knows the *approximate* spelling; they may throw up a bewildering list of alternatives. Also, they cannot detect a correctly spelled word used in the wrong situation, such as 'there' in place of 'their' or 'they're'.

We have found that quite a few students do in fact benefit from spelling help and that if the student is made **more aware of spelling patterns** considerable improvement is possible with relatively little expenditure of effort. For example – and this of course depends on the severity of the dyslexia – we would expect a well motivated student to benefit from about three or four sessions of suitable tuition.

WHERE TO OBTAIN HELP

The first step is for you to find someone who can help. In some colleges this could be the Support Tutor. Otherwise you can make enquiries in various quarters – through the college Counselling Service, through the welfare section of the Students' Union, through

the local Dyslexia Association (if there is one), through the Adult
Literacy Scheme, or sometimes through the student's own
department. It is sometimes possible to use post-graduate students,
particularly from departments such as Linguistics and Education
where there may be an interest in dyslexia. It is sometimes possible
for a student to tap into a 'buddy' or student mentor scheme, and, if
payment is required, it may be possible to draw on the Disabled
Students' Allowance.

Since, at this level of spelling, willingness to co-operate is a more
important qualification than formal training, it is always possible to
ask for help from a sympathetic friend. Indeed, one student whom
we taught was lucky enough to become engaged to a fellow student
whom he described as *'an excellent speller'*. We are tempted to adapt
the saying about 'marrying money' to: 'Do not marry good spelling
but love where good spelling is!'

The help which you receive from a friend or tutor will depend to
some extent on what form of spelling training you have had in the
past and on your particular needs. It is likely that volunteer tutors
may be somewhat uncertain where to start, and, in what follows, we
will make some suggestions which can be adapted according to
individual needs.

It is probably best, in the first place, if you – the student – give
your tutor a sample of your uncorrected written work in advance of
any teaching session. The tutor can then examine and classify the
types of mistake that you are making and afterwards discuss them
with you. There may also be helpful suggestions in your assessment
report.

You may also like to consider whether you have any preferred
'sense' (e.g. vision or hearing) which makes spellings easier to
remember. For example, some students actually close their eyes and
picture the spelling (**see note 12.1**); others try to *say the letters aloud*,
while others again will *write the word down and look at it*.

REGULARITIES IN THE ENGLISH SPELLING SYSTEM

A particularly effective way of helping is for the tutor to demonstrate the **regularities** or '**patterns**' in the English spelling system. For example it is regularly the case that *past tenses end in '-ed'*; and if the student is made aware of this it is a principle which he can apply in many different contexts.

We recommend that the sessions between tutor and student should be short, perhaps half an hour at most, and that not more than two or three spelling patterns should be taught at a time.

Although it is possible for the tutor simply to correct words that are misspelt this is unlikely to produce any result of permanent value unless both you and he think about the correction and try to work out where you have gone wrong.

It is often useful if you work together on a laptop or word processor, since this means that parts of words can be moved around on the screen and combined and re-combined to form the correct spelling. This can sometimes be an exercise in 'proof reading', that is, in detecting spelling errors. It is possible in that case to discuss the spellings as you make the corrections, and in some cases we have noted down the correct spellings in categories or groups as we have gone along. Another advantage of working on the screen is that spellings can be corrected without the student feeling that he has 'lost face'.

If you use someone to proof-read what you have written it is easier if you hand her your disk rather than the hard copy; this is because there is still the risk of error in copying on to disk from the corrected version.

As was pointed out in Chapter 1, it is a basic weakness in most dyslexics that they cannot simultaneously hold in mind more than a limited number of disconnected symbols or remember the order in which they have to be arranged. Moreover it is obvious that for all of us a combination such as 12–12–12–12 is much easier to remember than a succession of eight isolated digits; and the reason why dyslexics have trouble with series such as the days of the week and the months of the year is undoubtedly because there is no special logic to them – the components are isolated units which simply have to be remembered in a particular order (**see note 12.2**).

In the case of spelling, however, there are all kinds of regularities; indeed the English spelling system is far more logical than many people realize. This means that if you can identify particular patterns you will be able to *deduce* what letter to put next instead of having to rely on your uncertain memory. It follows that, if you have not been taught this already, you should be made aware of the correspondence between the letters which we write and the sounds which we make in speech. This will immediately give you a way of deducing spellings instead of having to remember them. In that case even your misspellings will be intelligible from the phonic point of view, and in most cases your reader will be left in no doubt as to what word you intended.

There are certain regularities which you should make every effort to learn. You should notice in the first place the difference between long and short vowels: thus *hat* has a short vowel sound while *hate* has a long vowel sound. (This long sound in fact coincides with the name of the letter.) Let us now suppose that letters are added so as to make longer words, for example *'hatter'* – one who makes hats – and *'hated'* (strongly disliked). You will notice that where there is a *short* vowel the consonant which comes next is *doubled* and that where there is a *long* vowel the consonant which comes next remains *single*. Here are some examples:

- saddle–cradle
- nibble–bible
- hopping–hoping
- Jimmy–slimy

Similarly one normally writes '-*tch*' or '-*dge*' after a short vowel (as in *fetch*, *ledge*, etc.) and '*ch*' or '-*ge*' after a long vowel or pair of vowels (as in *teach*, *saga*, etc.). Also, when there is a '*k-*' sound one writes '-*ck*' after a short vowel (as in *back*, *luck*, etc.) and '*k*' on its own after a long vowel or pair of vowels (as in *make*, *speak*, etc.).

There is a further rule which states that the letters *'c'* and *'g'* are hard before *'a'*, *'o'*, and *'u'* and soft before *'e'* and *'i'*. There are exceptions to these rules but they are rare (**see note 12.3**).

There is even a logic in some of the easily confusable short words if one looks for it. Thus if we wish to say *'belonging to you'* we add to the word *'you'* the letter *'r'*, so that it changes to *'your'*. It follows that if we wish to say *'belonging to them'* we start with the word *'they'* and again add the letter *'r'*. Since, however, the letter *'y'* often changes to *'i'* in the middle of a word we write, not *theyr* but *'their'*. There is therefore no need to confuse the word with *'there'* which has the same pattern as the other two *'place'* words, *'where'* and *'here'*. For ease of memorizing the following diagram may be useful:

OWNE R

OU R

YOU R

THEI R

A pictorial diagram of an *ear* may also be of help to students who are liable to confuse *'hear'* with *'here'*.

If you continue to have difficulty with these short words, then they can be written out on cards or posters and placed above your desk. Some of our students keep recurring spellings on cards in a filing box and get the relevant ones out when they need them. It is useful to **highlight** the difficult parts in **colour**, so that they stand out.

MNEMONICS AND OTHER AIDS

Mnemonics, even though they may seem childish or silly, can sometimes be helpful; for example a student who is confused between *'piece'* and *'peace'* can think of *'a piece of pie'*. There are similar mnemonics for longer words; for example those who have difficulty over the spelling of the word 'necessary' should remember the maxim: *'Never Eat Cake: Eat Salmon Sandwiches And Remain Youthful.' 'Please Say Yes'* starts *'psychology'*. *'Pete Hates You'* starts *'physics.'* If *'because'* is a problem try *'Big elephants can always understand small elephants.'*

It is always possible to separate out the difficult parts of words. To return again to *'necessary'*, the hardest part is likely to be *'-CESS-'.* (If it helps, you can think of CESS as 'one collar and two socks'). Once you have isolated CESS you can try:

acCESS

proCESS

sucCESS

It may also be useful if you isolate – or get someone to isolate for you – the part of a word which is difficult to spell. For example in the case of *'stimuli'* you would isolate *'i – u – i'*; in the case of *'colour'* you would isolate *'o – l – o'*; while in the case of *'conscious'* you would isolate *'s – c – i'*.

Similarly you may like to think of certain letters going in *pairs*

–NM

–LY

–WH

–OO

In the case of *'NM'* you may like to put them together on a poster as the core of 'enviro*nm*ent'; *'LY'* is a useful combination because adverbs end in these two letters; the two letters *'WH'* start words which ask questions, for instance *'when?' 'where?'*, *'why?'*, *'which?'*, *'what?'*), and in the case of *OO* you might say to yourself, 'The two *O*s in *TOO* are *TOO MANY*' or 'There is one *O* and another *TOO*')

You may also like to note the combinations *SCI* . . . and . . . *OLOGY.* 'Sci . . .' is the start of the words *'science'* and *'scientific'*, and the same root occurs in *'conscience'* and *'conscious'* – the original Latin word means 'knowledge' or 'awareness'. '. . . ology' is the ending of large numbers of words, e.g. *'biology'*, *'ecology'*, *'palaeontology'*, etc.

The 'log' part is derived from the Greek and means 'study of'; thus, since 'bios' means 'life', biology is the study of living things.

In the case of long words we suggest that you say them carefully aloud before trying to write them. One possibility is to speak them into a tape recorder and then play them back, while another is to ask a friend to say them for you. It is important that you should pay attention to small differences in sound between different words, since if you are not clear as to what sounds you are trying to represent then the chances of representing them accurately in your spelling will of course be very much less. You could ask your tutor to go over the pronunciation very carefully with you, particularly in the case of technical or scientific terms.

Another possible exercise is for the tutor to listen to the pronunciation of her students. This needs to be done carefully and tactfully, or perhaps as a lighthearted exercise, as was possible in the case of the student who confused 'Bradley' and 'Baddeley' (see p. 4). One student whom we knew continually used to say 'persific' in place of 'specific' ('persific gravity'), while another confused 'conscious' and 'conscience'. We have in fact been surprised at the number of mispronunciations which we have noticed over the years (compare p. 4); and sometimes it is possible as a result to recognize the reason why particular words have been misspelt. Students should be encouraged to say very carefully the sounds of the words which they misspell, e.g. 'environ ment'.

It is also a good idea to break longer words down into segments or syllables and, if possible, to recognize the *root* of a word. (For example the word 'contemporary' has the same root as the word 'temporal' – the basic idea being that of 'time'.) We regularly give our students a list of prefixes and suffixes with their meanings. Thus *'recrimination'* contains the familiar prefix *'re'*, the familiar suffix, *'-ation'*, and two straightforward middle syllables, *'-crim-'* and *'-in-'*. Provided you do not feel under pressure of time you need have no difficulty in writing these segments separately and then arranging them in the correct order. It may also help if you say the word carefully and then tap out the number of syllables.

Another possibility is to use a pencil to mark the boundaries between syllables or to use pencils of different colours to mark familiar prefixes and suffixes. Let us take as an example the word 'readily'. If you inspect this word you will probably recognize both its connection with 'ready' and its '-ly' adverbial ending. You may also recognize the 'ea' pattern which also occurs in 'bread', 'instead', and the like, and we have already mentioned how 'y' usually changes to 'i' in the middle of a word. The 'read-' will then take care of itself; the '-ly' adverbial ending is already familiar, and all that remains is to change the 'y' in 'ready' to 'i'. To take a few extra seconds to work out the spelling logically is far better than making a wild guess; and it should be noted that what is involved is a succession of deductions and not the memorizing of these different points simultaneously.

TECHNICAL TERMS

A device which may be helpful for some students is to make a list of technical terms and then obtain information, either from a tutor or with help from a dictionary, about their derivations. Here are some examples:

1 'Ped' and 'pod' are derived from the Greek word for 'foot': hence 'biped' (= two feet) and 'tripod' (= three feet).
2 'Cephale' is the Greek for 'head': hence a 'cephalopod' is a marine animal with the foot modified into arms around the head.
3 'Zygote' is derived from the Greek word meaning a 'yoke' and thus implies two cells yoked together; and if you know this it will be easy for you to make sense of derivative terms such as 'monozygotic'.

You should perhaps note that in the case of prefixes derived from the Greek, such as 'mono-' (= 'single') and 'syn-' (= 'together') the doubling rule mentioned on p. 124 does not apply: as you can see, there is in these cases a short vowel followed by a single consonant. There were in fact many different influences on English spelling, which means that some generalizations, such as the doubling rule, have exceptions.

No comprehensive list of useful technical terms will be attempted here. However, you may well find it gives you a greater understanding of a word if you look up its derivation in a dictionary. You may also benefit from learning about the history of the language and the changes in it as it has developed (**see note 12.4**). You may also like to have a checklist of specialist words which you regularly need in essays but which you continue to find difficult. These can be put on posters or postcards. It is also a good idea to look at **textbooks**, **glossaries** and **indexes** before you write an essay and then compile a list of the most needed words. If you own a word processor the more unusual words and names can be entered into your spell-check.

AIDS AND REFERENCE BOOKS

Apart from offering assistance with actual spelling, your tutor can, of course, guide you towards helping yourself. There are many books and manuals on spelling which you may find helpful (**see note 12.5**) and you and your tutor may like to discuss together which one best meets your needs.

Whether or not you set about trying systematically to improve your spelling we strongly recommend that you buy your **own good quality dictionary** and get into the habit of referring to it as a matter of course. You may like to look not only at derivations but also at stress marks and other indicators of pronunciation. If you are unsure of the order of the letters of the alphabet you may like to write them on a card which you can keep available.

We have found that dictionaries designed for those learning *English as a second language* are often very useful to dyslexic students (**see note 12.6**) since both types of learner need the same structured and patterned approach. These dictionaries often give the spellings when new parts are added to a word. For example:

> *run*, running;
> *dine*, dining, dined, diner

Other dictionaries containing specialist technical vocabulary may also be useful to students concerned with that particular specialization (**see note 12.7**).

Besides a full-scale desk dictionary you may also find *pocket spelling dictionaries* very useful, since they provide a quick and easy way of checking spellings (**see note 12.8**).

What many dyslexic students find invaluable are the *pocket electronic spellmasters*. They contain spell-checks, offer alternatives based on sound and meaning, and are very easy to use. There are various types of these and you can usually can find one to suit your needs (**see note 12.9**).

In addition you may like to build up what is in effect *your own dictionary*. For this purpose an alphabetically divided index book is probably best but you can use an address book. In it you can enter specialist vocabulary, important names, short words which cause difficulty, confusing letter combinations, and the like. Many students have found these 'personal' dictionaries very easy to use and very helpful, and in many cases they have taken pride both in adapting them to their needs and in giving them an artistic appearance. You may occasionally find it difficult to look up a word in a dictionary because you are unsure of its first letter, and once these words have been identified they can be placed in a separate section at the front. Words which you are likely to need regularly in an essay or dissertation can be put on cards which can be kept ready for consultation during the editing stage.

Finally, we should like to emphasize once again that the priority in essay writing is the flow of ideas. For this reason it is important that you should not worry too much over problems of spelling. If you are not sure of a spelling you can always write something in pencil and carry out a check later or use your spell-check. Meanwhile you are free to concentrate on the important thing, namely the writing of the essay, with this particular source of anxiety removed. One of the advantages of spending time on spelling during the early months in college is that you may reach a level where worries over spelling no longer divert you from the subject matter of the essay.

ADVICE TO A TRAINEE NURSE

A few years ago we were approached by someone wishing to obtain help for a trainee dyslexic nurse who was having major difficulty with her spelling. Not only did the nurse herself feel uncomfortable about this; more seriously, those in charge of her training course took the view that spellings as poor as hers would cause patients and their families to doubt her competence and perhaps, by association, the competence of the hospital where she worked.

We began by asking her for a list of the words which she found particularly difficult. Some of these were non-technical words, for instance *unnecessary, insufficient,* and *acclimatization;* however her particular problem lay in the long technical terms which were used in her job. With the aid of a friend she gave us a list which included the following:

carbenoxolone	
sucralfate	bretylium
dicyclomine	mebeverine
peroxisome	disopyramide
arginine	zymogen
acinar	osteoclasts
reticulocyte	agglutinogen
megakaryoblast	agglutinine
sarcolemma	myelogenous
oligodendroglia	aneurysm
thalamencephalon	syncytium
telencephalon	cholinergic
cimetidine	synchronization

These particular words are highly specialized, and few readers of this book will need them. However they illustrate *general principles,* and if readers *generalize* from what we say here they may be able to use similar principles in devising ways of remembering *any* complex word.

The advice which we gave was divided into six sections, as follows:

1 general principles: dividing longer words up into smaller units and using a multisensory approach;
2 some common letter combinations;
3 the 'c' and 'g' rule;
4 words derived from the Greek;
5 'silly' mnemonics;
6 going through the list.

1 General principles: dividing longer words into smaller units and using a multisensory approach

'The words on your list will be very hard to remember if you try to write them 'all at one go'. Sub-divide them and concentrate on the parts separately. Do not try to remember more than about four letters at a time. We will try to give some guidance in section 6 as to how to divide them up. This can often be done in a logical way; and if there is a logic in the way one letter follows another you will not be in the difficult position of having to learn all the letters separately. (In what follows we will refer to these 'bits' of words as 'word parts'.) When you are sufficiently familiar with the word parts on their own try, very slowly, to say them one after the other so as to make up the whole word, for instance 'di – cyclo – mine'. When you hear a long word tap out the number of syllables, and if possible get someone to check that you have done so correctly.

It is widely agreed that, if dyslexics are to learn to spell, 'multisensory' methods are needed. This means: *listen* to the word carefully; *say* it carefully, paying attention to your mouth movements as you do so; *look* carefully at what is on the page, and pay attention to your *hand movements* as you write. Take plenty of time, and don't 'fudge' by slurring over the word as you say it.

2 Some common letter combinations

You will have come across many of these in your normal reading, but we would like to remind you of some. Some words end in '-ine' ('*arginine*' is like '*mine*' and '*fine*') and some in '*-ium*' (for instance *valium*). In breaking words down look out for common letter combinations.

3 The 'c' and 'g' rule

The letter '*c*' has a 'hard' sound (like '*k*') if it is followed by '*a*', '*o*', or '*u*' (as in '*cat*', '*cot*', and '*cut*'); it has a 'soft' sound (like '*s*') if it is followed by '*e*', '*i*', or '*y*' (as in '*centride*', '*cimetidine*', or '*di cy clomine*'). The letter '*g*', with a few exceptions, also has a 'hard' sound before '*a*', '*o*', and '*u*' (as in '*gap*', '*gorgon*', and '*gut*') and a 'soft' sound before '*e*', '*i*', and '*y*' (as in '*gem*', '*gym*', and '*gypsy*') (compare '*arginine*').

4 Words derived from the Latin or Greek

(This section is optional, but you may find it interesting, and it may help you to remember certain combinations of letters.)

* *sucr* – connected with sweetness
* *ethyl* – connected with ethane
* *acinus* – grape
* *gen* – producing (note the 'soft' '*g*')
* *zyme* – ferment
* *clast* – breaking (compare *iconoclast*)
* *reticulum* – a net (network of fibres)
* *cyte* – a cell (note the 'soft' c)
* *myelos* – marrow or soft white substance
* *mega* – large
* *karyon* – nut
* *sarx* – flesh
* *lemma* – sheath
* *syn* – together
* *oligo* – little
* *dendron* – tree

- *encephalon* – brain*
- *chole* – bile[†]
- *chron* – time[†]

* Note: that there was no '*f*' in classical Greek; therefore when the '*f*'-sound occurs in words derived from the Greek it is written as '*ph*'.
[†] also note that in words derived from the Greek '*ch*' has a 'hard' sound, as in '*chemistry*,' '*Christmas*', etc., not a 'soft' sound as in '*chain*'.

5 'Silly' mnemonics

Although dyslexics can do much to help their memory by noting logical patterns, it may also be useful, at least as a fall-back, to invent 'silly' mnemonics. These, oddly enough, are memorable precisely because they are silly! You will be able to invent your own, but I will make a few suggestions in section 6.

6 Going through the list

Here are some suggestions, based on the points which we have been making. In particular, (1) break the word up, (2) tap out the number of syllables, (3) bring in speech and writing as well as looking and listening, (d) learn to identify common combinations of letters (for instance '*zyme*'). We strongly suggest you take this list in small doses!

- *carbenoxolone*: what about car – ben – oxo lone? Ben is a lonely person in a car and wants some oxo.
- *sucralfate*: sucr (common combination) and Alf ate some!
- *dicyclomine*: di – cyclo – mine ('cyclo' has soft 'c'; 'mine' is a common combination of letters. Or think of Princess Di on a cycle that is mine!
- *peroxisome*: I suggest per – ox – I – some (with long 'o' as in 'dome') – again phonetically regular.
- *arginine*: ar – gin – ine (or ar – gi – nine).
- *acinar*: affecting the acinus. The Latin 'acinus' means 'grape'; presumably it is thought to be like a grape in shape. The 'c' is of course soft.

- *reticulocyte*: reticulo = net, 'cyte' a cell (note the soft 'c').
- *megakaryoblast*: I suggest 'mega' (= big, as in 'megaphone'), then 'caryo' which means 'nut', then 'blast' which means 'grow' or 'sprout'.
- *sarcolemma*: sarco – lemma. 'Sarx' means 'flesh'; 'lemma' means a husk or membrane.
- *oligodendroglia*: oligo – dendro – glia.
- *thalamencephalon*: thalam – encephalon. You already know 'thalamus', and 'encephalon' means 'brain' (see above). So it is really quite logical – and where there is a logic it will save you having to rely on your memory.
- *telencephalon*: tel encephalon ('encephalon' again).
- *cimetidine*: cim (soft 'c') – eti – dine. You can dine on it!
- *bretylium*: I suggest bret (which is regular) – yl – ium (which is a familiar combination of letters).
- *mebeverine*: meb – ever – ine. All the parts are phonetically regular.
- *disopyramide*: I suggest di – so – pyra – mide (five syllables). By the way, you use 'dys' with a 'y' only when it means 'difficulty with' something, as in *dyslexia*; 'dis . . .' often means 'not', as in '*disquiet*', and sometimes 'di' implies cutting into two, as in *dissect*.
- *zymogen*: 'zyme', a ferment, and 'gen' = producing.
- *osteoclasts*: osteo – clasts ('osteo' = 'bones'; 'clast' = 'breaking').
- *agglutinogen*: perhaps start with 'glutin' (= antibody). As with many words, such as 'abbott' and 'attend', the consonant doubles after the 'a'. Note that in some words such as 'alexia' and 'ataxia', where the 'a' implies some failure or difficulty, the next consonant does *not* double.
- *agglutinine*: take out 'glutin' as before – and the rest is straightforward.
- *myelogenous*: 'myelo' = marrow, 'gen' = producing.
- *aneurysm*: according to my dictionary 'aneurism' is also OK; 'ism' is easy to remember, and 'eurys' is the Greek for 'broad' – hence the word means a widening or broadening.
- *syncytium*: most of the words that you will meet with the sound 'sin' will; in fact be spelt 'syn'. The Greek 'syn' means 'together', as in 'synthesis', 'synopsis', etc. If in doubt I suggest you put 'y' rather than 'i'. The 'c' before the 'y' in 'cyt' is soft, as usual; and you know the combination '-ium'. Take these points separately,

one by one – say the word slowly and carefully, as it will be more difficult to say – and spell – if you go too quickly

- *cholinergic*: cholin – ergic (with the 'g' soft before 'i').
- *synchronization*: 'syn' as usual; you know words such as 'chronic' (another example of the 'hard' 'ch' as in 'chemistry' etc.) and then there is the '-ation' ending.

In the case of *'unnecessary'* we gave her the 'silly' mnemonic (see p. 125). In the case of *acclimatization* we said: 'you can do '-*ation*', in this case with '*iz*' before it. You also know the word '*climate*'. With the short '*a*' at the start the '*c*' must double, so it is '*acc . . .*' and you then have to write the rest of '*climate*', dropping the '*e*' before '-*ization*'.

This story has a happy ending: she passed her examinations and is now a qualified nurse.

Chapter 13

Mathematics and statistics

DYSLEXIA AND MATHEMATICS

Most dyslexics are likely to have struggled with certain aspects of mathematics. The difficulties are basically of two kinds.

In the first place there are problems over *calculation*. In particular a very high percentage of dyslexics have found it difficult to learn 'times tables' and quite a number are slow in carrying out simple addition, subtraction, and division (**see note 13.1**). It seems that they have fewer immediately available 'number facts' than do non-dyslexics; for example, they may not know 'in one' that $8 \times 7 = 56$ or that $15 - 8 = 7$, and if no calculator is available they may need to spend considerable time in working the answer out. This is not normally due to a lack of understanding of how the number system works – they know what working needs to be done. The trouble appears to be that these basic number facts do not easily become automatic (**see note 13.2**).

In the second place, dyslexics often need extra time before they become fully aware of the significance of a mathematical symbol. Any symbol such as '+' or '=' is difficult at least for younger dyslexics; and often it is helpful if the teacher can begin the lesson not by writing a lot of symbols on the board but by **doing things** (physically adding two blocks to three blocks, for instance). Symbols such as '+' can then be introduced as *descriptions of what is happening*. This kind of introduction to mathematical symbols may be of help even to dyslexics of student age (**note 13.3**).

Careful attention to basics is particularly important in the teaching of algebra. There are many dyslexics who find algebra difficult – and there is a personal friend of one of the authors who teaches other branches of mathematics but refuses to teach algebra because he 'finds it impossible'! The point is that if a symbol conveys nothing then despite his high reasoning powers the dyslexic will have nothing for these reasoning powers to work upon – and he may mistakenly conclude that mathematics in general is too difficult for him. However, once the function of the various symbols has been grasped, his reasoning powers will have the chance to show themselves, and tiresome 'chores' such as carrying out calculations can be done by calculator. It is important for dyslexics to know enough about the number system to enable them to tell *approximately* what the answer should be – and, when they use a calculator, they need to be careful not to press the wrong button! Otherwise, however, the calculator can be a great time-saver (**see note 13.4**).

If you wish to take a course which has some mathematical content (for instance physics, engineering, or a course which requires statistics), you should not *necessarily* be deterred by the fear that you are 'no good at maths'. If you really feel that weakness at mathematics is going to be a problem it might be wise to get some training in the basics before your course actually starts – so that if the worst happens you could consider a change of course. However, we have found in many cases that dyslexics have simply 'missed out' on the significance of a particular piece of notation and that this is something that they can learn. We suspect that the dyslexic mathematics teacher, mentioned above, who said that he found algebra 'impossible', was never taught it properly.

DO NOT BE PUT OFF BY SYMBOLS

Many different symbols are used in mathematics; and the important thing from your point of view is that you should learn the function of the symbols that you need. (Some dyslexics have reported difficulty in learning the symbols used in chemistry; but these, too, can be learned if one goes slowly enough.)

There are plenty of symbols which you already know – for example the symbols *1, 2, 3*, etc. which stand for particular numbers. You probably also know quite a number of the symbols which tell you what to *do* with numbers, for instance '+' which means '*add*', '×' which means '*times*' or '*multiply*'. (If 3 children have 2 oranges each then there are 3 × 2, that is 6, oranges altogether; one can therefore speak of 'three *times* two', or 'three *multiplied by*' two.) In general, if there is a symbol whose meaning you do not know ask someone to explain it or go to a book (**see note 13.5**). When you do statistics there will be various *new symbols* whose meaning you will need to know – but once you have learned what job they do you will be quite as good as anyone else at operating with them.

You may find it interesting to think about numbers in general. There are all sorts of situations where we use numbers: in particular we use them for *counting* things and for *measuring* things. For example, we may need to know the *number* of children in a class, the *number* of cars which go past a particular road junction in a 3-hour period, the *number* of potatoes that you have planted in your garden, and so on. Similarly you may need to *measure* the *length* of carpeting needed in a room or (if you suspect you are ill) *your body temperature*. In the first case you would use a tape measure, in the second a thermometer. In all such cases the result is expressed numerically, and once you have learned the symbols, '1', '2', '3', etc. you will be in a position to understand what this result means.

SOME MORE SYMBOLS: ALGEBRA

To make things easier for you we should now like to introduce you to some further symbols. If they are already very familiar you may like to skip; but, as we say, the important thing is that if you are confronted with any unfamiliar symbol it should not be too difficult to **make yourself familiar with its meaning**.

You have probably already met the algebraic symbol, *x*. If someone has difficulty with this symbol it may be helpful to show him a simple subtraction sum with the aid of bricks. If you have five bricks and take away three bricks you will have two bricks. This operation can then be written down – we write it as '5 – 3 = 2' – and it applies to bricks, pencils, paper clips, and all kinds of other things.

Let us now ask the question, 'Five take away *how many* leaves two?' Let us suppose that this 'how many' refers to an *unknown* number – but one whose value we can work out. We then write this unknown number as 'x', and this means we can then write '5 – x = 2'.

This group of symbols (which contains the '*equals*' sign) is called an *equation*, and if we then work out the value of x this is called *solving the equation*. The equation 5 – x = 2 is an easy one to solve – the answer, of course, is that x = 3. However, once you have solved a few easy equations then there is no need to be terrified by the more difficult ones: they will take you longer and you will need to proceed carefully step by step, but the symbols 'x', '=', etc. need not themselves be off-putting. Remember, of course, that 'x' in a sense means '*any* number' and that in different equations its value will be different.

In some cases you may have two unknown numbers, in which case it is customary to use the symbols 'x' and 'y', whilst if you need a third number you would write it as 'z'.

STATISTICS

As was indicated in Chapter 2, a knowledge of statistics is necessary for a number of different disciplines: these include psychology, education, economics, biology, agriculture, and many others. It would be a great pity if any students were deterred from these courses because of fears over their competence at statistics.

If you are doing statistics you will need the symbol 'X' – that is, capital X, as opposed to the lower case x which is used in equations. Suppose John has scored 10 points on a test, Mary 8 points, Elizabeth 11 points, and Tom 9 points. We can then say that these four numbers, 8, 9, 10, and 11, are different values of X. We could put them in a column, like this:

10

8

11

9

and we might say that $X1_1$ is 10, X_2 is 8, X_3 is 11, and X_4 is 9. We can also note that the average score in this case is 10 – that is, the *sum* of the different Xs divided by the *number* of Xs. This average is known more technically as the *mean*; it can be written as $\bar{X}$ (pronounced X-bar). The sum of the different Xs is written as ΣX (pronounced as 'sigma-X'). Then, if the number of Xs in the sample is written as 'N' we can describe the working out of the average by means of the following notation:

$$\bar{X} = \frac{\Sigma X}{N}$$

or, in words, X-bar equals sigma-X over N.

We realize that you may still feel alarmed by symbols; but, once again, if you **think positive** we believe you will be able to understand the ones that you need. They are merely ways of describing what you are doing – which in the above example was adding numbers together and taking the average. Our advice is simply that when you are introduced to new symbols you go slowly and make sure you fully understand what each symbol stands for.

In due course, if you continue in your study of statistics, you will be introduced to further symbols. These include χ^2 (pronounced 'chi-squared') and the alphabetic letters *t*, *r*, and *F*. It is beyond the purpose of this chapter to explain these different symbols to you, but there is no reason to think that learning their different functions will be any more difficult for you than was the learning, say, of the '=' sign.

THE USE OF COMMON SENSE

We indicated earlier that you might have difficulty in adding up a column of figures. The interesting thing about statistics, however, is not that it involves adding up but that we need to use our **reasoning** in deciding **how to interpret the results**.

As an example let us take the following column of figures:

45 +

49 +

46 +

4
___

In this case it would be possible in principle to carry out the same procedure as we did in the case of the test scores of John and his friends – that is, we could take the average. But if 4 children earn respectively 45p, 49p, 46p, and 4p one does not have to be good at *addition* to recognize the absurdity of saying that the *average* earning is 36p. The skill called for here is that of statistical reasoning, and we have met many dyslexics who are brilliant at this even though adding columns of numbers at speed may be difficult for them.

In brief, if you want to do a course which requires a knowledge of statistics do not be put off by the fear that you are 'no good at maths'. If you proceed *systematically and slowly* you will find that statistics is not all that difficult.

Chapter 14

Information technology

WHAT ARE YOUR NEEDS?

Since the first edition of this book appeared in 1986 the position with regard to technology has changed dramatically and continues to change.

Although we shall at times be referring to various items of software, we shall not in this chapter be naming individual computers. This is for three reasons. In the first place, changes are occurring extremely rapidly and any information presented will therefore soon be out of date. Secondly there already exist specialist groups who regularly produce updated information bulletins and hold conferences (**see note 14.1**). Thirdly, there is no point in recommending equipment if it is *incompatible with what is already used in a particular college or department*.

Many of the new developments are likely to be of particular benefit to dyslexic students; and those who receive the Disabled Students' Allowance will be in a position, within limits, to buy much of what they need.

If you order equipment in this way it will be necessary for you to obtain advice, written costing, and a statement of needs. These can normally be obtained from your computer laboratory, from the college information services, or from your own department. You may also wish to consult fellow students. Your Local Education Authority may suggest that you go to a specialist ACCESS Centre (**see note 14.2**).

Some of the equipment is expensive; and in this case it may be best purchased by the college to supplement its existing resources. Colleges which do not do so should perhaps consider setting up a special needs resource base.

Some of the equipment which is used by hearing-impaired or visually impaired students can be of help to dyslexic students – and vice versa. We suggest that you find out what information technology facilities are available for use within your department and in the college generally.

PORTABLE EQUIPMENT

First, however, you may like to consider some of the small portable electronic pieces of equipment which we have referred to in earlier chapters (see pp. 31–8). These are usually available in large stationers or stores or in office suppliers.

There are *electronic organizers*. Some of these are multifunctionary and include graphics, calculator, dictionary, word processor, and in some cases a schedule and diary facility. It may even be possible to link them up with a personal computer and printer. If you simply want an organizer, a dual-function machine with names, numbers, dates, schedules and clock will probably be sufficient.

There are also various *electronic diaries* which can be set to bleep at appointed times. It is also possible to get pocket memos or notepads. A more sophisticated version is a *voice organizer* into which one speaks one's ideas or appointments. These could be very useful for a new student having to cope with the complexities of the early days at college.

Note pad and *pen pad* are electronic diaries which recognize writing and turn it into type. At present these are fairly expensive, but they could be a great help for dyslexic students because someone else can write the necessary information on them, for example, names and addresses – and even maps. The information is then turned into type and stored alphabetically. They can be plugged into a personal computer.

Many students carry calculators around with them, and there are now talking calculators and large-digit calculators (**see note 14.3**). For spelling there are various pocket-sized spelling aids, such as the whole Franklin range, with *Spellmaster, Language Master* and *Thesaurus*. There is now a speaking Language Master (**see note 14.4**). Many students find these indispensable; this is because they are easy to use and carry around and are much simpler than computer spell-checks. They have a 'sound alike' and thesaurus program, which means that you can tell the difference between words which sound alike, such as *'they're'*, *'there'*, and *'their'*, by being given the various meanings.

We have referred to *dictaphones* throughout the book and have indicated, in particular, how useful they are for taking lecture notes or for recording what one reads into them from an overhead projector sheet. There are also voice activated or variable speed recorders – you can use the latter if you want to transcribe notes. It is also possible to have a 'slow' pedal attached to a dictaphone so as to help you to keep up with the transcription of notes.

WORD PROCESSORS AND NOTEBOOKS

The majority of dyslexic students nowadays use a *computer or word processor* of some kind. Some students, however, particularly mature students, still feel frightened of word processing. We therefore quote some of the points made by Colin Wilsher, who was one of the dyslexic contributors to the 1986 edition of this book. Although the position with regard to word processors has changed considerably in the interim we believe these points to be still relevant. This is what he wrote:

Technical advantages

Word processing machines offer several technical advantages over handwritten and typewritten methods of communication.

1 Unlike traditional typewritten text, mistakes can be corrected immediately and will never be seen by the outside

world. In normal typing the paper becomes messy with correcting fluid. With WP the student does not have to 'print out' until he is satisfied with his 'input'.

2 WP allows revision of ideas via an 'editing' mode. Whole pages can be seen and revised. This includes not just retyping words but moving sentences and paragraphs about the document. This is particularly useful to a dyslexic who may initially put down ideas out of order, and upon re-reading may wish to change the sequence.

3 Editing of your work can be done by others, or you can edit the input of others. This allows dyslexics to use other people as mediators between themselves and the written word. A proof reader can correct a student's mistakes directly on to the disk.

4 Some microcomputer WP software packages contain a spelling checker that corrects spelling mistakes.

5 Some programs have a glossary of words that are commonly used by a computer user. This is activated by the use of a code; for example instead of typing the word 'statistical' during input the operator would use a code such as Control key plus the letters STA. The computer will always print the word 'statistical' when it encounters that code.

6 WP programs can be commanded to search for a word or phrase in the text. Unlike a tape recorder, WP is an 'intelligent' way of recording words that can recall exactly what you want. This is particularly useful if some 'Key Words' are used in each paragraph.

7 Dyslexics are thus enabled to present to the world written material of a first-class standard. This is particularly useful for dyslexics with very poor handwriting. This ability to produce a polished, finished article is extremely rewarding.

8 The operator can use parts of existing documents to create new documents without entering any new material. For instance, a series of letters (with similar content) to several different people can be rewritten by the computer by only changing a few words for each recipient.

9 If the operator becomes proficient with the WP system he

can 'skip' the pencil and paper preparative stage and go
straight to entering his ideas directly into the computer.

10 From my own experience I am convinced that practice with
a WP system helps spelling ability. This is because every
word has to be spelled out and it gives practice at phonetic
breakdown of words.

The advantages which Colin Wilsher cites are therefore very
numerous.

However, if you use a word processor it is important to consider
the *physical effects* of long hours spent working on the keyboard and
in front of the screen. We recommend that you think carefully about
what type of chair to use, about the way in which you use your
hands and forearms (we have two students suffering from repetitive
strain injury), and that for the sake of your eyes you take a ten
minute break from the screen every hour. You could also dull it
down, change the colours on it, or put something in front of it so that
you are not always looking at it.

In general, therefore, you should **plan your time on the computer
carefully**. You will need not only to use the keyboard but to follow
the various menus. If you become physically or mentally tired
mistakes can very easily occur and you can do silly things. This
happened recently when a student pulled a plug out so as to boil a
kettle late at night – a moment's thoughtless action, and she lost
everything that she had done over several hours. You should make
a habit of 'saving' your material each time you pause for a break.

If you have not learnt *keyboard skills* at school or college, you will
need some *instruction* to help you to get going. Computer manuals
are dense and very difficult to access and it is better to be taught
personally. Your college will probably run courses, and in addition
there may be evening classes locally which cater for people with
different levels of word processing ability. If you go on a short
course you will find that you will be given simplified hand-outs for
each stage. There are also some advantages in learning touch-
typing, but this is not essential and in fact many dyslexic students
say that they spell better if they look at the keyboard. If you are

interested, however, it is possible to obtain software for touch-typing; and there is even talking software which helps people to become more familiar with the keyboard. There are also simplified, clearly set out, portable manuals which explain all the necessary processes for basic computing and word processing (**see note 14.5**).

We have observed that certain students actually perform *worse* on a keyboard than when they write by hand. It seems that they are somehow *drawing* the spellings when they write and can therefore perceive the patterns more clearly than when they type. Some students also make many typing errors, and if they are poor spellers these may go unnoticed.

There are students who need only dedicated word processors, since their work involves just essay and report writing; these are becoming cheaper and more efficient. Other students will need computers with spread sheets, statistics packages, graphics software, CD ROM and so on. It is useful to get an integrated package which might come under the name of 'works' or 'office'. A multimedia facility whereby the computer can perform several functions at the same time can be very useful.

Note book (or laptop) computers are small portable computers which vary in capacity. It is possible that you may need a small straightforward notebook for taking notes wherever you go (**see note 14.6**), but such machines have a limited memory and do not always take software. There are, however, notebook computers with a range of facilities, such as statistics and graphics, and multimedia machines with sound systems and graphics which work at high speed. Most are the size of an A4 pad and are about two inches thick. If you plan to carry them around it is important to consider their weight – most weigh about six to seven pounds and you should also consider for how long a time they can run on a set of batteries. You will need a carrying case (to protect your note pad), spare batteries, a battery charger, and a separate transformer if you have to run it off the mains. Many of our students have found a track ball easier to use in lectures than a mouse. You will obviously need to have a notebook which is compatible with an easily accessible printer.

Note books are likely to be useful for note taking in lectures; in addition, they can be taken into the library and, indeed, can be used wherever you decide to work. They are also useful because they allow you to work side by side with a tutor or an amanuensis, since together you can move text around and alter spellings. They are also easier to take home for the holidays. It is, of course, important to look after them carefully to ensure that they are not damaged or stolen; and if you are the owner of any expensive piece of equipment it is advisable to take out an insurance policy.

Whether you are using a word processor or computer, you will probably find that icon-based programs with a mouse are easier to use than those which involve control keys on the keyboard. A large-print facility both on the screen and on the hard copy can sometimes be useful, though it is also possible to obtain a magnifier or view-scan. You may also like to consider whether there is the facility to select the most suitable font (some students find Ariel or Courier difficult). A number of our students have been able to buy colour printers, and these have helped them particularly with note taking and with the planning of essays.

SPELL-CHECKS AND OTHER SOFTWARE

If you need a *spell-check* (as most dyslexic students do) we suggest that you look at the type of program which is provided, how the spell-checking is presented on the menu and how easy it is to use. For those with poor spelling, spell-checks are by no means easy. We have found that students normally prefer to have the alternative spellings presented in a vertical list rather than across the bottom of the screen, since it is easier in that case to pick out how the word starts.

Sometimes a good thesaurus facility can be of more use than a spell-check: if you cannot find the right alternative on the spell-check one possibility is to choose a simpler word and then use the thesaurus to find a better one. In that case, hopefully, the word which you originally intended will come up. For example, if you wanted to say 'manufacture' and could not spell it you could write 'make' and then look up the alternatives – and with any luck you would find 'manufacture'. Dave Laycock of the University of Westminster suggests that students get on better if they build their own spell-checkers from scratch (**see note 14.7**). It is possible to put in one's own subject-specific words and names from a flatbed scanner. A read-back facility can help to indicate bad spelling. This seems to work more effectively than with a print-out, as you can then listen with a pencil in your hand to mark the errors.

Grammar programs are useful to a limited extent. A disadvantage is that their advice is given using grammatical terms, which means that a tutor is usually needed to provide explanations. However, they also show the sentence with the mistake highlighted; and as a result they will detect non-sentences, faulty agreements (for example a singular subject with a plural verb), and incorrect endings to a sentence. They may even pick up the wrong use of 'their', 'there', and 'they're'.

Software which may be of help to dyslexic students is increasingly being produced. What you choose is very much an individual matter. Thus there are some students who prefer to work out their thoughts on paper and use a word processor only when they are ready to write the rough draft, whereas others are happy to do their thinking at the keyboard. A particular piece of software may be suitable for some students and not for others – and if there is sufficient computer capacity in the college or support unit a tutor could keep a suitable supply of software for students to borrow or try out.

There is software for all of the following:

1 *Planning essays*. There is, for example, a 'think sheet'. This is a planning program which enables students to organize notes under topic headings, as if they had a pile of notecards; the ideas can then be rearranged to form a mind-map.
2 *Spelling practice and tuition*.
3 *Grammar practice*. (As we noted above, some programs use grammatical terms and are best used with a tutor.)

4 *A practice program for grammar and punctuation* ('perfect copy')
 which uses editing techniques.
5 *Mathematics packages.*
6 *Graphics packages* – 'draw package', quick sketch, autosketch.
7 *PAL – predictive adaptive spell-check.* This predicts from context;
 you type in the beginning of a word, and your word will be
 predicted.

There have also been considerable advances in *synthetic speech
feedback*, although there are still some difficulties with clear and
understandable speech production; for instance British students find
the American pronunciation difficult to follow at times.
Nevertheless, the digitization is improving and the voice can in
some cases be modified. The use of sound obviously makes text
accessible to people with reading difficulties and it can alert the
student to the use of the wrong word and quite often to the wrong
grammar. It also will also show up a wrong spelling since it cannot
read an incorrectly spelt word, and in this respect it can therefore
sometimes be better than a spell-checker. Its disadvantage is that it
can be quite slow and time consuming.

It is also possible to have a *screen reader*. This may help with
proof-reading. Also some students may benefit from scanning texts
from books and listening to them through screen read. In that case
they will need a scanner with optical character recognition software
and a text-to-speech system. Scanners save a great deal of time for
the student; they can transfer photographs and diagrams into the
text. The main danger is that students are liable to incorporate
chunks of text into their essays instead of summarizing or
paraphrasing.

Other possibilities include *file reader*, and *Kurzeil reading edge*
(which can read a book in nine different voices and recognize
photographs and diagrams).

A particularly exciting advance is the use of the *voice recognition
system* (such as Voicetype) whereby the software enables the words
which you speak to be entered into a word processing program
which you can then edit and print out. This is still fairly

experimental, although one university is using it with quite positive results (**see note 14.8**). The software is expensive and it takes some time for the computer to recognize the speaker's voice. Dyslexic students who use this system will need the help of a tutor or mentor so as to ensure the correct input of vocabulary.

Finally *CD ROM* offers a multisensory approach to study with sound, music, colour, static text, and moving images. It can be an excellent way of providing a general background to a subject and, for dyslexic students in particular, it is opening up the study of literature and history. There are in fact encyclopaedias on CD ROM but they are very expensive.

Thomas West (**see note 14.9**) has shown the power of the computer in enabling dyslexics to become freed from the hard graft of writing. It seems that the developments in computers are moving towards the greater use of a multimedia approach, and we can expect dyslexics to derive immense benefit from this.

It is also likely that in the near future computers will be used for the early identification of dyslexia (**see note 14.10**) and perhaps for the screening of adults before they undergo further testing.

Chapter 15

Examination provision and its administration

ADMINISTRATIVE ARRANGEMENTS

If dyslexics are to have special provision in a way which is fair and is seen to be fair, a number of administrative issues arise.

Ideally, each student's case should be treated individually and based on his specific needs. These should have been pinpointed in his assessment, with the report indicating which parts of the examination are likely to put him at an unfair disadvantage (for instance writing speed). A Support Tutor or academic tutor can also make recommendations. The means by which a candidate normally presents his work should be taken into account, as should any provision which he has previously had – in GCSE, A-level, BTEC or GNVQ.

As far as dyslexic students are concerned the Examining Board will almost certainly require a dyslexia assessment certificate supported by relevant facts from the student's tutor.

Many students with a permanent or semi-permanent 'special need' will already have had examination provision at school and will therefore have a fairly clear idea of what they can expect at college.

In some cases the assessment certificate will set out clearly the recommended special provisions; the psychologist will have based these upon the student's performance in the various tests and upon the measure of the speed and accuracy of his reading and writing. She may have discussed them with the student. Sometimes a tutor may have gained an extra insight into the student's performance and may then submit a request for provision which was not mentioned in the assessment report.

Setting up special provision for examinations is time consuming from the college's point of view. Colleges vary in their procedure. Some have a clearly stated policy which is set out in their regulations (**see note 15.1**). What quite often happens is that the student goes to the examination office with his list of courses or modules and his assessment certificate and checks with the Examinations Officer what arrangements have been agreed. At Bangor we recommend that if examinations are being held in May or June the process of negotiation for examination provision should be started no later than February or March.

If you leave your request for provision (or even assessment) until the very last minute you will probably find that the Examination Officer is working under extreme pressure and there is the risk that he will not be able to comply completely with all your requests. You should bear in mind, too, that there are many other students with special examination needs – not just dyslexics!

Finally, it is easy to understand how the examination period is a time of tension not only for students but for tutors and administrators also. Whatever reassurances have been given, some dyslexics may still feel that if they receive special provision they are being treated 'differently' in some uncomfortable sense, and tutors and administrators should realize that to be in this position may not be easy for them. Quite a number of our students have in fact found themselves torn in two directions: on the one hand they want to be examined in the same way as everyone else, yet on the other they know that they will not do themselves justice unless they allow themselves to be treated as 'special cases'. Those in the examinations office, where the students will go to arrange their provision, should be aware both of the tensions that the students feel in these circumstances and of the need for confidentiality.

We have occasionally found, too, that there are tutors who react with hostility, for example by accusing the student of 'looking for an easy way through the system'. This may well be because they themselves are under pressure and do not want any extra hassle with complicated or time-consuming arrangements. Things are made worse if dyslexic students do not realize the general pressures that there are on academic and administrative staff at examination times and become over-demanding of their 'rights'. Empathy on both sides is very important.

COMMON PRACTICES

At present the most common practices are:

1 allowing candidates *extra time*;
2 allowing candidates during the examination to *dictate their written answers* either into a *tape recorder* or to *a typist*;
3 the same as in (2) but with the dictation taking place shortly *after* the completion of the examination;
4 providing someone to *read the questions aloud* to the candidate or allowing questions to be *read on tape*;
5 *oral examination*.

We should like to comment briefly on these five procedures and on the ways in which students can make the best use of them.

1 Extra time

It is common policy nowadays to allow extra time to dyslexic candidates. As has been pointed out already (Chapter 1) there is in fact good evidence that 'slowness of information processing' is an inherent characteristic of the dyslexic adult and that speeding up is possible only to a very limited extent. Someone who is slow at information processing is therefore at a disadvantage which is irrelevant from the Examining Board's point of view (compare Chapter 18).

It is usual to offer *ten* to *fifteen minutes* per hour. This can be adjusted, however, in the light of the candidate's assessment. If, for instance, a candidate has a particularly slow handwriting or reading speed it is not unknown for more time than this to be allowed.

Whenever extra time is offered, we suggest that the candidates in question should enter the examination room early rather than leave it late, since the noise of other candidates leaving the room is likely to be a serious distraction, whereas the chance to look at the questions in detail before other candidates have arrived may lessen the sense of being under pressure of time. There is the further advantage that they will be less noticeable to the other candidates. Some institutions may provide *a special room* for 'extra time' candidates though not all dyslexic students will wish to use it.

2 Dictating answers during the examination

If this provision is used, it is very important to practise well before the examination and to establish a correct code of practice. *Only certain kinds of communication between candidate and scribe are permitted.* Guidelines are available which set out what these are (**see note 15.2**); for example, the candidate has to make clear when he is thinking aloud and when he wants the scribe to write something down. A post-graduate student in the candidate's department is sometimes employed as scribe.

3 Dictating answers after the examination

The same principles will apply as those mentioned under (2).

4 Providing someone to read the questions aloud or having the questions put on tape

Not all dyslexic candidates need this or would ask for it. However, as has already been pointed out, a dyslexic candidate may easily misread the examination paper, and the risk of error is minimized if someone else does the reading.

5 Oral examination

If the rules of the Examining Board allow it, this can often be a useful source of additional information for the examiners, though, as will be seen in Chapter 18 (p. 188), it is not invariably the right answer. If a candidate is going to be examined orally, then, as with interviews, it is important that he should practise in advance.

SUGGESTIONS FOR FURTHER PROVISION

There are various extra provisions which Examination Boards may wish to consider. Not all dyslexic candidates will need them, but the case for permitting them is that *some* of them may do themselves better justice as a result without there being any risk of endangering relevant standards.

These suggested provisions are:

1 that *coloured* examination papers, *coloured* answer papers, and the use of *coloured filters* should be made available;
2 that a *second copy* of all examination papers be made available;
3 that dense or complicated examination papers be *magnified* or *enlarged*;
4 that a *spare answer book* be permitted for rough work.

With regard to (1) the cost would be minimal, and even if only a small number of candidates found reading easier the measure would be justified. Clearly the ability to read without eye strain is not something on which a college Examination Board would wish to grade its candidates.

With regard to (2), duplicate copies of examination papers would enable the student to have both sides of the question paper in front of him at once. The point here is that a dyslexic student can very easily lose his place when moving from one question to another in a complicated exam paper.

The advantages of (3) are self-evident.

In the case of (4) it is not always appreciated how much time dyslexics have to spend looking for rough notes which they have written in a different place in their answer book. If there were a second answer book this would ensure that such rough notes are easily accessible. Examining Boards which ask for all rough work to be handed in could continue to do so.

USE OF WORD PROCESSORS

Here we can write only about the position as it exists in 1995. As technology advances, the situation may change radically. Thus the introduction of 'voice-type' would mean that the student could dictate directly on to a machine. We already have a growing number of students doing their examinations on word processors or notebooks. This will increase as those dyslexics who have grown up with laptops come through to higher education – one student recently said to us of his laptop, 'It is my biro.'

Examination Boards will need to draw up *regulations* concerning the use of word processors. Colleges vary in the number of computers, computer rooms, and technicians or supervisors available, and the regulations which they adopt will depend on the facilities at hand. Points that need to be considered are:

1 *What type of equipment may be used?* Will there be a 'standard' college machine or will the student be permitted to use one identical to his own? (He will have been using his own for revision, and if he has to use an unfamiliar one this will need practice.)
2 *What is the policy with regard to hard disks?* Presumably (unless attitudes change) they will need to be wiped clean; but in that case there is the question of how material can be saved for future use.
3 *What is the policy with regard to the use of the facilities on the keyboard, such as editing and spell-check?* Does it, for instance, give candidates an unfair advantage if they have editing facilities? Is there any relevant difference between candidates who cross out or remove text by machine and those who do so by hand?

4 *What time allowance should be made for saving and printing?*
5 *Should the candidate be allowed to look at and edit the hard copy?* (For example, a Board might rule that additions of substance were not permitted but that typically 'dyslexic' errors such as writing words in the wrong order could be put right.)

These are all questions which are currently being discussed. The results will affect the future of all students, not just dyslexics; but the fact that dyslexics have distinctive combination of strengths and weaknesses brings the issues into particularly sharp focus.

At the time of writing, only a small number of students use word processors in examinations, and their request for this facility usually has to be supported by the tutor or by the psychologist in his report. There is a debate among tutors and students, dyslexic and non-dyslexic, as to whether and how far this might offer dyslexic students 'unfair advantage'; this is because many students nowadays are accustomed to doing all their work on computer and find handwriting a chore. In the future, perhaps, every student will be examined on computer, in which case the dyslexic students will need only the facility of extra time.

Chapter 16

Preparing for examinations

INTRODUCTION

For a large number of students, whether dyslexic or not, examinations are a strain. In particular, many mature students may never have done any exams for twenty years or more and they will seem a big hurdle to them.

The right approach and the right kind of planning, however, can help to make the whole process of preparing for and taking the examination much less stressful. In this chapter, we shall look at ways in which you can make the best use of your memory; and we shall discuss the application of this both to long-term planning and to the intensive period of revision just before the examination. We shall also talk about examination techniques.

LONG-TERM PLANNING

One final year student told a group of fresher students, '**Start thinking about the exams in the first week of term!**' They were quite shocked, but the advice was good. The dyslexic student needs to plan well ahead for examinations and if possible start at the very beginning of the year or semester in which they are being taken. You cannot afford to find yourself in a position where a large amount of revision is needed and there is only a short time in which to do it.

It is most important to obtain a copy of the *syllabus* early in the course so that eventually you can plan your revision around it; and if there is any difficulty in obtaining one it is perfectly reasonable to ask a tutor. In addition, lecturers who have mentioned large numbers of books and articles during their lectures are usually willing to provide guidance as to which are the most important ones. We suggest that you try to read these as early as possible: if they are library books they are more likely to be available when other students are not competing for them; and, more important, it will save you from trying to find them for last-minute 'skimming'.

It is also useful if, as early as possible, you can obtain copies of *previous examination papers*. They are often kept in the library. This will give you an idea of what lies ahead. You may be able to detect themes which crop up over and over again and to deduce how closely the questions set are related to the material given in lectures. You will also become familiar with the layout and rubric of the papers.

You should work on your notes throughout the year. Lecture notes and the notes which you have taken while you were reading should be reviewed regularly and, if you have time, expanded so that you have a coherent body of material to revise from. As a dyslexic student you will find it very difficult if you try *both* to read up new material *and* to revise – all in the last few weeks before the exams. You will need to prepare your notes so that you can learn from them. We think it is best if you do this preparation as you build up your notes over the year rather than when you start to revise.

USING YOUR MEMORY

To help you with your revision we should like to offer you a simple (and not very scientific) analogy (**see note 16.1**).

Let us say, then, that our memories are like a food cupboard! We put food into it and store it until it is needed. If we put our food into the cupboard in a certain order, keep the shelves organized so that the different tins and packets are in separate parts, label them clearly, and every now and then check to see that they are there, then it should be fairly easy to find whatever food we want when we open the cupboard. In contrast, if the cupboard is all jumbled up, it is much harder to find the food – we have to rummage around for it and often cannot find it.

When we revise we are, as it were, putting everything we learn into the food store – large amounts of it. We need, therefore, to organize our material and ideas so they are easily found when we want them. We need to label them so that we can retrieve them quickly and efficiently. It is important to work out what helps us to remember things so that while we are building up the memory store we are also ensuring that there is easy access.

PREPARING LECTURE NOTES FOR REVISION

Most dyslexics have difficulty in learning things by heart: they cannot easily get things 'off pat' and recite them mechanically. Memorizing can be made much easier if the right *strategies* are used.

The discussion which follows makes use of dyslexics' *strengths*, and in particular of the fact that most dyslexics are good at logical reasoning. We are going to suggest ways in which you can organize your notes so that, like the food cupboard, they will be easy to use. The techniques are in some ways similar to those which you will have already used in learning to spell.

You need to think about *how* you remember material that you have learnt. Do you see a picture of it? Do you remember the lecturer's voice? Do key words stay in your mind? There is evidence which suggests that individuals vary in this respect (**see note 16.2**), and it is therefore important that you should work out what suits you best personally. Here are some suggestions.

1 Make sure that you *understand* everything. If you find a section of your notes to be really difficult, do not just memorize the words: try to work out what the words mean or ask someone else to explain them to you. We remember things that we know about far better than blindly learning something that we do not understand. Seemingly separate ideas will become easier to remember if you

look for logical links between them and indicate these links in your notes.

2 Use *colour, shape and pictures* to help you remember your notes. Write introductions in one colour, main points in another. Use felt pens to underline things with. If it helps, draw pictures in your notes.

3 Add *shape* by making *mind-maps*. Make them interesting and lively. Colour them in as much as you can.

4 *Summarize important points* on postcards or posters: these will be key words which will 'trigger' off your memory. (For an example of a revision card, see the end of this section, p. 165.) You can develop a set of cards which you can carry around with you. Make *large, lively posters* (not too many) and put them on your wall and on your ceiling. Keep looking at them – think how we subconsciously absorb the material displayed in advertisements.

5 *Number your points*. You may well find that numbers trigger the memory. If you know, for example, that a gas has *six* properties, you can use 'six' as a memory jogger and will not feel that you are confronted with an indefinite list.

6 *Create mnemonics*. These can be really silly, or very rude. (We know that medical students specialize in very rude mnemonics. We have a list of them but they are not fit for publication!) If you are studying English and need a mnemonic for the four 'big' Shakespeare tragedies, you have HMOL – *Her Majesty's Off Licence* (*Hamlet, Macbeth, Othello, Lear*). Tests have shown that capital letters are good memory joggers (**see note 16.3**). We took up this idea by asking our students the capital cities of various European countries; few knew any of them, but when we supplied the first letters they were able to recall them quite easily.

7 A very helpful way of learning, if it suits you, is to *put your notes on to tape*. Many of our students listen to their tapes on personal stereos or, if they commute into college, on the car radio. Some of them get their friends to read parts of their notes so that their own voice does not become too tedious. Several have put music on to their tapes as a background and have found that it is an aid to memorizing. Others revise to the sound of music, always using the same tunes for the same topic. Eventually, what you hear can be linked with its visual equivalents on the cards and on the posters.

8 You may like to try *'pegging'*. According to Buzan (**see note 16.4**), 'a peg system can be thought of much like a wardrobe containing a certain definite number of hangers on which you hang your clothes'. Basically pegging involves making associations or links, so that what you want to learn is linked (or 'pegged') to something. For example, you could visualize a room and 'peg' your notes about the Industrial Revolution to different features of the room:

- *door* – machinery
- *fireplace* – raw materials
- *rug* – factories
- *lamp* – transport
- *bookcase* – coal
- *armchair* – steam
- *settee* – cities
- *coffee table* – population

The best way to do this kind of thing is to create your own system.
9 You may also like to try *aroma therapy* that is, the attempt to memorize things by associating them with particular aromas or smells.

Not long ago one of us (DEG) was confronted with a tearful student facing page after page of narrow-lined A4 paper, packed with closely written words. There was a solution! The notes were worked on with coloured felt pens and fluorescent markers; headings were transferred to postcards and to posters which were pinned on to walls; names and lists were read into the tape recorder; mnemonics were devised, and diagrams and flow charts with cartoons, pictures, stars, etc. were created.

What we need to remember is this: written material on its own, particularly when it is closely packed, can be very daunting. In contrast a 'multisensory' approach (*looking at* colours, *listening to* sounds, *writing* with a felt pen, and *moving* about the room) may make things much easier.

A REVISION CARD

Try putting key words on to small cards. These key words may then trigger off other points. You may well be amazed at how much you can remember! Here is an example of such a card.

Industrial Revolution

1 machinery
2 raw materials
3 factories
4 transport
5 coal
6 steam
7 cities
8 population
     8: M R F T C S C P

There are eight points here, which can be represented by the eight letters; and here is a sentence for remembering them: *My Red Fat Tom Cat Soon Catches Parrots!*

THE PRE-EXAMINATION REVISION PERIOD

It is not possible to specify an ideal time for starting revision. If you are in a modular system you may have lectures almost up to the exam period. Much also depends on how well you have done your background reading and sorted your notes out. This revision period is under *your* control.

Try to **get yourself organized** before you start. Buy plenty of coloured pens and get hold of as much scrap paper as you can. Some cardboard, postcards and A3 size paper are also useful. Check that you have blank tapes on to which you can talk your notes. Think, even, about your food – some students plan out their meals for the week ahead. Decide which is the best place to work.

If you are living with people who are not doing exams at this time make sure that they do not disrupt your revision. If you live away from college it may be worth finding out when the local library is open as it will probably have a reading room where you can study. Plan your time off – you will need breaks.

Back to one of our previous adages – **think positive!** There is a good probability that you will pass for the simple reason that very few candidates fail. If you approach the exam period negatively, this may discourage you from studying. The obvious thing, in any case, is that you should try to do as well as you can.

Structure your work. If you have not done so you should organize your notes, so that you will be able to learn from them. You will probably find that you have to start working in more detail on them – making condensed notes, producing short summaries, and drawing up lists of relevant points as introductions to a subject. By writing summaries and lists you are in effect reconstructing the subject matter of your course.

Even though some examining boards may not penalize poor spelling, there will probably be *essential words* which it will pay you to learn. You could isolate two or three a day and work out ways of remembering them; you should then consolidate your learning by writing them down and saying them over to yourself. Be careful, too, of words that are similar to each other in both sound and appearance, such as *'clarify'* and *'classify'* – the difference is important!

Make sure that your revision time is suitably **planned**. Try writing a list of topics and making a revision timetable. Make plans for the revision period *as a whole*, and then break them down into weekly plans and daily plans. Think back to what was said about organizing your study time in Chapter 8 – allow plenty of time off and do not set yourself impossible tasks. Some time off is necessary each day and there should be one day a week when you have a complete break. Watch out for the habit of putting off work by constantly revising your timetable!

Check at this stage that you have plenty of *old examination papers* to work from. You should make a detailed list of *topics* (rather than questions) that are likely to come up. We do not recommend deliberate 'question-spotting' since this practice encourages the view that to every examination question there is a single 'right' answer. In many examinations the obtaining of a high grade almost invariably depends on the ability to think and criticize. If you develop a 'topic bank' you can work on the material for these topics; and once you know this material you can then apply it to any question that may come up. How you are graded will often depend on how you handle it.

Another method of examining (used mainly in science departments) is to set very short questions which demand rapid recall. For these questions you will need to use the memorizing techniques which have already been discussed. It is particularly important to practise multiple choice questions as these can be quite difficult to work out. Some of our students have worked together in groups on this type of examination paper and pooled their ideas on how to approach it.

If you know at this stage how long each examination paper lasts, how many questions you have to answer, and what marks or grades are allocated for each question, you can then plan out a time schedule. In the case of marks it is worth calculating how many minutes are available for each mark to be earned, how much time should be spent on the first question, at what point you should have answered half the questions, and so on.

YOU ARE NOW GOING INTO THE LEARNING PHASE

As has already been pointed out, it is very important that you should not find yourself in a position where you have to carry out a large amount of rote learning in a short time. You may see some of your non-dyslexic friends flinging themselves into all-night revision sessions, but you will almost certainly find it difficult to 'speed up' more than a limited amount. If you work against time, the stress of fighting for precious minutes may cause you to go blank or be unable to think clearly. Your writing and spelling may deteriorate and you may find that you cannot concentrate.

Without proper sleep and rest periods you may find the situation worsening. For these reasons we have constantly advised dyslexic students to work slowly and steadily. The tortoise gets to the winning post eventually even if he does not run as fast as the hare; and if other students try to behave like hares that is no reason for trying to imitate them.

You should plan out your schedule in such a way that at some times in the day you are doing really hard memory work while at other times you are reading or practising examination papers. If you vary the type of revision this may help to prevent you from becoming stale.

Work actively. Do not just 'read it through' without thinking about it! We suggest that there should *always* be a pen or pencil in your hand so that you are continually writing down relevant points. (If it suits you, talk to yourself – sing – walk around the room – do anything as long as you are *active*!) In particular, ask yourself questions and write down your answers. Make a question bank and use it every day. Take your cards or tapes out with you and use them if you have to wait for a bus or have some spare time. Learning is most effective if it is continually being tested. In other words, you learn more by going over what you have learned.

Above all, practise, be active. **REVISE, RECALL, REVIEW**.

As you get nearer the time of the examination, think of yourself as '**going into training**' so that you are in the best possible shape for answering the questions.

When you return to previous examination papers and use them for practice your first step could be to take a question and *map out an answer in the form of notes*. These notes should contain an effective introduction which brings in the *key words*; they should indicate the way in which the answer is to be presented and the way in which the different threads are to be gathered together in a conclusion. You should remember that tutors are normally very willing to give help both when you are revising and at other times; and you may like at some stage to check whether the notes which you have produced seem to the tutor to be along the right lines.

If you have any special examination provision, such as a scribe or the use of a dictaphone, or if you are doing your exam on a word processor, you will need to check that the arrangements have been completed and to practise the necessary techniques. If you are using a word processor it will be worth 'going into training' on the keyboard so as to improve your speed and to enable you to work out how much you can type in a restricted amount of time. If a word processor is not permitted, make sure that you *practise your handwriting*, particularly under timed conditions.

A small number of dyslexic candidates have been allowed to dictate their answers to an amanuensis and have opted to do so. If you are planning to do so, it is wise to check that you are familiar with the correct pronunciation of scientific terms and the like (see below).

Attention to what one is writing may also be an aid to memorizing. Eventually you should attempt a full-length answer in timed conditions (without coffee breaks and the like!), and, after that, a full-length paper. If the examination is one in which you have to write short answers on the printed paper, make a photocopy first and use it for practice; you may like to check, for instance, whether you can fit your answer in the space provided. It is also a good idea to practise diagrams, again trying to fit them into the space. One lecturer gives the following useful tip to his students: when they write a practice essay they should do so not on every line but on *every alternate line*. Then, when they come to check what they have written, they will be able to write in on the blank lines the details which they had missed out. The essay can then be written out over again.

Working on previous examination papers not only helps you to get your timing right; it also enables you to get used to different rubrics (*'Answer two questions from Section A and two from either Section B or Section C'*), so that you are not bewildered by these when you meet them in the actual examination.

Finally, you are unlikely to do yourself justice in examinations if you are tired or under pressure. It is therefore particularly important that you should have *plenty of sleep and plenty of fresh air* and that you should eat properly. We have already said that it is more important to relax if you cannot sleep than to become tense worrying about the fact! It is also worth while thinking about possible ways of combating stress – for example you may like to practise relaxation or deep breathing.

Bear in mind also that stress can be 'catching'. Do not therefore be misled by horrific stories which you hear around the time of the examinations as to how much or how little revision your friends have done. Remember, too, that there may be all kinds of rumours circulating at examination times which it is usually best to ignore. All these things are matters of common sense, but we have found that if a student is under stress common sense is sometimes forgotten.

Chapter 17

Sitting the examinations

SUGGESTIONS FOR THOSE WHO FEEL ANXIOUS

Sitting an examination is quite a different experience from revising. The revision period may have seemed like an endless jog along a long road; the examination, in contrast, is like a short intensive race, run at sprint speed. If you can, you will do better if you approach your exams methodically and with a positive outlook.

To some extent they are a test of nerves. There are indeed people – not just dyslexics – who are highly skilled and highly intelligent but who nevertheless seize up when faced with a written exam paper. It is therefore not surprising if you as a dyslexic feel anxious. If, however, you *prepare yourself for exam conditions* and *practise exam techniques* during the run-up period you will be better able to take the examination itself in your stride.

If it seems like a real ordeal, you might discuss the whole process of examining with your tutor or your fellow students. It could be of help if you try to visualize what lies ahead – by **imagining yourself waiting to start**, looking at the paper, and coping with the students around you (**see note 17.1**). It might be worth going to see the room in which the examination is being held if you have not already done so; then you will know what sort of a room it is and may even be able to visualize where you will sit. Some colleges allow dyslexic and other 'special needs' candidates to sit their examinations in a separate room; if this applies in your case it is worth finding out where this room is.

CHECK ON WHAT PAPERS YOU ARE TAKING, WHERE, AND WHEN

An obvious point – but one worth mentioning – is that you should make sure that you turn up in the right place at the right time! Although we all make such mistakes from time to time, a dyslexic person – at any age – is likely to be more 'at risk' on such matters; for example it is not all that difficult to mistake 'Tuesday' for 'Thursday' or to mistake 1400 (i.e. 2 o'clock) for 4.00 (i.e. 4 o'clock). Those who have problems over punctuality need to make a special point of not being late since none of us can produce our best work if we are feeling flustered.

You should check that you know:

1 the name of each paper that you are taking;
2 its reference or code number.

This is especially important if you are in the 'special provision' room, since there will not be complete sets of papers there but only the papers for the candidates who have been allotted to the room, and you may not be with anyone else from your course.

DO NOT BE PUT OFF BY WHAT OTHERS SAY

At the time of the examination you may come across students who tell you in detail about every topic which they have revised. There may be some who say that they have learned everything – and others who boast they have done no work at all! Comparing notes on the way to the exam room seems to us unhelpful, and you may find it better to keep to yourself in the moments before the exam starts. It is important to approach the exam in a calm frame of mind, and this means avoiding any situations which could give rise to panic.

Many students have asked us about last minute revision. This depends on you: you should *not* be learning new material immediately before an examination, but if you feel easier in your mind you could refresh your memory by looking over your cards, posters and tapes.

KEEP A CHECKLIST OF WHAT YOU NEED FOR EACH PAPER

We strongly advise you to keep a checklist of what you need for each examination paper. You are likely to need some of the following: pens, rulers, HB pencils, pencil sharpener and rubber (for multiple choice questions), and – for some subjects – a calculator (make sure that there is a spare battery). As a precaution put everything in a pencil case. (We know of one student who washed his denims with his calculator in the pocket the night before a mathematics paper!) If the examination is being held first thing in the morning then, to avoid panic, you should attend to all these things on the previous evening – and check, too, that your alarm clock is working!

LOOK AFTER YOURSELF!

Writing examination answers takes up energy. It may therefore help if you have a good breakfast on the day of the examination; and, if it is allowed, why not consider taking glucose sweets or barley sugar into the examination room? (However, make sure they do not have crackly paper, or the other students will not thank you!)

IN THE EXAMINATION ROOM

In the examination room, again keep calm. If you have to sit and wait for people to settle try deep breathing as a way of helping you to relax. If you go in early for your extra time, be prepared for some disturbance when the others come in – but if possible continue writing. It is also important that you should train yourself not to be distracted by what other candidates are doing in the examination room. Your concerns are yourself, the exam paper, and the clock. The other students may appear to be writing faster; they may even leave the examination room early. If you, however, as a dyslexic candidate try to write too fast your mistakes may increase dramatically; and if others leave early there is not the slightest reason for you to feel under pressure to do the same.

The first few minutes of an examination are perhaps the most stressful. Be aware, therefore, that this could be when you will panic and make silly mistakes. It is particularly important that you should take *plenty of time and care* over *reading the instructions* (rubric) at the top of the paper just as you did in your 'mock' exams. Use a pencil to ring the key instructions; and if there is more than one section make sure that you have checked how many questions need to be answered from each and which questions are compulsory.

Where this is applicable, look at the *marks awarded for each answer* and work out *how long* you should spend in proportion to the total time allocated. In some science papers the first section is of the 'short-answer' variety, whilst the 'heaviest' section usually involves the writing of an essay; and since this section is likely to carry most marks make sure that you allow yourself sufficient time to write it. It is also very important to work out the *timing per section* and *per question*. For example, if you are sitting a three-hour paper in which you are required to answer four questions, it is probably wise to allow at least 20 minutes for reading the instructions and deciding which questions to answer; this will leave 160 minutes, that is, 40 minutes per question. If you have been allowed extra time you can adjust your calculations accordingly. As a precaution, you should check your arithmetic and make sure that you do not misread your watch!

Be careful not to spend more than your allotted time on one or two questions to the neglect of the others. If you really run into trouble over time, most examining boards will give you some marks for brief outline notes in place of a full answer, provided you make clear that you could have written at greater length if you had had the time (see below). But we suggest you use this remedy only in emergency!

It is important to *read through the whole paper at the start*. If there is a choice of questions we suggest that you decide immediately, if you can, which ones you are going to answer. If you then put a tick against them this will save you having to re-read the paper later. You may like to write down at any stage things which you think you will need for answering other questions, for instance names or formulae; and if an idea for a different question occurs to you while you are writing, it is a worthwhile jotting it down somewhere so that you do not forget it. (Rough work should eventually be crossed out, as most examining boards expect this.)

We suggest that you *start with the question which you think you can do best*. This will give you confidence and 'ease' you into the exam. When you have chosen a question, read it carefully more than once, *ringing the key words*. Errors may creep in, and it is essential, for example, that you do not overlook the word 'not' or misread 'greater than' for 'less than', 'important' for 'unimportant', or, like one examination candidate, 'Henry IV' for 'Henry VI'. In at least some subjects the question will probably require very careful analysis; and for this reason it is essential to be on the look-out for shades of meaning which have to be recognized if the full significance of the wording is to be grasped.

When you underline or ring the key words, look out in particular for the 'logical' words – *'necessary'*, *'possible'*, *'always'*, and the like – and to check after every paragraph that what is being written is still relevant. You should also think carefully about the words with which the question starts – words such as *'discuss'*, *'examine'*, *'explain'*, *'compare'*, and *'analyse'*. These words help you to understand what you are expected to do.

In most examination questions there will almost certainly be more than one key word. Indeed, there is a risk that if the student relies on a single key word – for example the word 'intelligence' in a psychology paper– he may produce the kind of answer which tutors rudely call a 'write-all-you-know-about' answer; and this is scarcely likely to gain high marks. To think to oneself, 'Wow! Here's the question on "intelligence". Off we go!' is no way to proceed if some highly specific question about intelligence has been asked. In general, the examiner is asking you to discuss a particular issue; and you should attempt the question only if you are clear as to what this issue is and have something to say about it.

It is also very important to think before you write and to plan each answer carefully. The plan which you make need not be long, but it will be your guide through the question. Many students have found it useful to take two answer books (if this is allowed) or at least two separate sheets of paper so that they can plan their answer on a sheet which 'travels with them'; if this is done the plan is still available when they turn over a page and they need not waste time or become confused in having to look back for it.

If you find that you are absolutely stuck for something to write, you can at least take the question, discuss it, and analyse its implications. This might help if you 'blank out', which is something which dyslexic people dread. If this happens, you should try to write *something*, even if it is not very good – you can always cross it out, but at least it will keep you writing. Another possibility is to leave the question that you were working on and move on to another one about which you know you have something to say. We have seen students sit for many minutes not writing, and we suspect that the longer you sit the harder it is to get going again.

If you find yourself short of time near the end of the exam, it is wise to get *something* down on paper as a way of indicating how you *would* have answered the question had more time been available. This is likely to be a series of headings, arranged if possible in a logical order and containing a small number of key concepts or key names. You should consult in advance with your tutor in case information is available as to the Examining Board's view of such 'answers'; in our experience at least some credit is likely to be given and the penalties for not writing at full length are unlikely to be heavy if the rest of your work is good.

Some dyslexic students are allowed *extra time*. This is unlikely to be much in a short exam, but could be as much as forty-five minutes in a three-hour paper. You will probably find it very tiring, and quite difficult, to write solidly for almost four hours; and our advice is that you take time off between questions so as to allow yourself to think, to clear your mind, and perhaps to check what you have written. We once had a dyslexic student who would put her head down on the desk and relax for five minutes in between questions – rather a risk to take, but she found it worked (and she got Upper Second Class Honours in History!).

If you are dictating your answers it is advisable to make some written notes before starting to speak and to have a pen and paper handy in case you wish to stop and organize your thoughts in the middle of an answer. You will need to indicate to your amanuensis when you want her to write, when you want her to stop, and when you are thinking aloud but do not want her to write. As we pointed out earlier, you will need to be able to pronounce accurately any names or technical terms with which she may be unfamiliar.

DO NOT WORRY TOO MUCH ABOUT CORRECT SPELLING

It is important that you should not let any weakness that you have at spelling become a major concern. If you do, this may make you lose track of where you have got to in your answer. If you find yourself worrying about a word you should remember that some misspelled words are relatively unimportant, whereas a 'rambling' answer matters a great deal. There may be scientific words which have to be exact, e.g. *chlorine, chloride, chlorate,* and you should be particularly careful over words which sound similar but have a different meaning, such as *'clarify'* and *'classify'*. Your best plan will probably be to leave some words misspelled (and perhaps mark them with a query so that if you have time you can return to them) and make sure that the flow of your argument is maintained.

'SHORT ANSWER' QUESTIONS

As has already been said, it is possible, particularly if you are doing science, that you will be given some *'short answer'* questions, involving only a small number of words. In most examinations the requirement is that you have to answer *all* of these, usually by writing on the exam paper itself. If there is a blank space for your answer, as there normally is, you will be able to deduce from it how long your answer should be, and, as the marks awarded for each question are usually shown, you will also have an idea how many specific points need to be made if you are to get the maximum mark. These sorts of question call for immediate recall rather than discussion and you need to move rapidly. We suggest:

1 that you answer first the questions that you know you can do – in any order;
2 that if you cannot do a question you do not waste time worrying about it but move on to one that you *can* do;
3 that you do not spend time re-writing the question; you should simply give the answer;
4 that you bear in mind that sometimes three words may get you three marks (but check in advance with your tutor whether full sentences are required).

It is quite useful to imagine the examiner ticking your paper: ask yourself if you have provided enough answers to enable him to make the right number of ticks!

In the case of 'multiple choice' examinations you are given a set of questions and a choice of possible answers, from which you have to select the correct one. For this you normally require an HB pencil, and you will need to find out from the instructions if answers may be rubbed out. There are advantages for dyslexics in this type of examination in so far as it saves writing and avoids problems over spelling. Nevertheless, you should take care because some of the words may well have fine shades of meaning which have to be distinguished; in addition there may be complications such as double negatives – 'it is not the case that such and such *never* happens'.

As the questions can be answered in any order, we suggest you start by looking through all of them at a reasonable speed and then *do at once all those to which you know the answer*. If you are in doubt, you may find it helpful to cross out the options which you are sure are wrong and then study carefully the ones which are left. As in other types of examination make sure that you watch the time: it may sound obvious, but if you have to do fifty questions in an hour, it follows that you will need to have done twenty-five in half an hour!

ORAL EXAMINATIONS

If you are given an oral examination (or 'viva') you should remember that *the examiners are on your side* and are not there for the purpose of catching you out. Memories of unsympathetic questioning during schooldays may return, and if this happens in your case it is understandable. However, it would be totally unprofessional for any member of an Examining Board to try to victimize a candidate, nor would other members of the Board permit it. It is important in this connection that you should not mistake friendly or neutral questions for hostile ones. You should take the first two or three questions very cautiously; that is when you are likely to be at your most nervous and when you could rush into an answer and say something inappropriate.

Examining Boards may wish to use oral examinations for a variety of reasons. One of the most common is that if they examine you orally they are giving you the chance to clarify or expand on points which you have made in your written papers. It may simply be that the written answer was somewhat cryptic and that the Board wishes to check that you have genuinely understood the point of what you have written, or it may sometimes be that they wish to check further on your originality or creativity. A great advantage of the oral examination, from the point of view of dyslexics, is that it gives them the chance to display the quality of their thinking without the effort of having to write things down on paper.

Finally, it is generally understood that whatever a candidate does in an oral examination he cannot actually be marked *down*; and if you are able to relax and to recognize that the examiners are on your side there is a good opportunity, whatever the standard of your written work, for you to show the high quality of your thinking.

Chapter 18

Discussion points for moderators and Examining Boards

SPECIAL CASES

Virtually every college now employs a system by which Examining Boards are permitted to treat particular candidates as 'special cases'. A student may be a special case for a variety of reasons. Some of the more common reasons are illness or accident shortly before or during the examination, illness or death of relatives, or, indeed, any painful or adverse circumstances which in the Board's opinion may be going to affect or have affected the candidate's performance. We hope that as a matter of policy all Examining Boards will be willing to treat dyslexic candidates as 'special cases'.

However, it may still be asked: 'Given that this candidate is dyslexic, what do we do about it?' Such a question raises all kinds of policy issues to which there are no easy answers. The purpose of this chapter is not to make specific recommendations but rather – in the light of our personal experience of dyslexic candidates – to raise points for discussion.

As was pointed out in Chapter 15, when the Board is considering a particular candidate it will normally be in possession of an assessment report, coupled with a recommendation from his tutor, suggesting certain types of provision. The Board is then empowered, if it so wishes, to put these provisions into operation or, if the application is retrospective, to revise the grades which were originally allotted. The disadvantage of not operating some such system is that, without it, there is serious risk that some dyslexic students will be incorrectly graded.

We have sometimes asked ourselves whether, as a matter of logic, a statement that the candidate is dyslexic can have any relevance to the awarding of a grade or degree class. Thus if one were examining candidates on the ability to run 100 metres in quick time one might feel sorry for a physically disabled candidate who failed the test but that would be no reason for pretending that he had passed; and it is arguable that there is a comparable problem over a dyslexic candidate: if he possesses the requisite skills he should be graded accordingly; if he does not, no amount of 'sympathy' over his dyslexia can justify giving him a higher grade than he merits. We have met not only examiners but, indeed, candidates who have been troubled over this point. Only a very unscrupulous candidate would want 'concessions' (see note 18.1) in the sense of extra marks over and above what he had earned, and many students have emphasized to us that they are anxious not to seek any kind of 'favour' from the Examining Board. As we saw in Chapter 1, to say that a candidate is dyslexic is to imply a constitutional limitation which is not his fault; but if the candidate lacks certain skills, is a causal theory as to how he came to lack them in any way relevant?

On reflection, we believe that it *is* relevant, and this for three reasons.

In the first place, if the fact that a candidate is dyslexic is not known or not taken into account there is serious risk that he will be marked down for lack of skills which from the Examining Board's point of view are *irrelevant*. This is a point to which we shall return shortly.

Secondly, Examining Boards often wish to look at a candidate's record and (whether or not the candidate is dyslexic) at how much effort he has put in. In that case it is open to them, if they wish, to distinguish a candidate who has tried very hard and whose shortcomings are the consequence of a constitutionally caused limitation from a candidate who shows similar shortcomings through not having taken enough trouble.

Thirdly, a large amount is now known about what to expect from dyslexic candidates – for example that clumsiness of expression may conceal all sorts of good ideas. A certificate to the effect that a candidate is dyslexic may alert examiners to this possibility and may therefore result in more careful marking.

For these three reasons we believe that it is proper for Examining Boards to take a candidate's dyslexia into account and that it is proper for dyslexic candidates to request this; in doing so they are not asking for any favour but simply collaborating with the Board in trying to bring about the fairest possible assessment (**see note 18.2**).

THINGS WHICH CAN GO WRONG

The essential point for an Examining Board to bear in mind is that in a written examination the dyslexic candidate is being asked to respond via a medium – the written word – which creates special difficulty for him. It is possible, therefore, that he may have plenty of good ideas which in the conditions of the examination fail to appear in his script. He may be a brilliant computer programmer, for instance; he may devise a new technique for zoological or botanical research or have grasped some new principle in economics; he may show in discussion that he is a brilliant creative chemist or may make a highly original contribution to the appreciation of *Macbeth*. In the script which he presents to his examiners, however, none of these things may come through! The position was tellingly summarized for us a few years ago by a science student who said to one of us (TRM) 'When we had the practical classes during the year I always had to explain to my partner what we had to do. Yet after the examination she was offered Honours and I was not.' One must assume in this case that the candidate's script did not demonstrate that he had the requisite knowledge and that his Examining Board did not check by other means whether this knowledge was present.

Examples such as this, of course, strengthen the case for basing part of a student's overall grade on coursework – a policy which is now becoming common practice.

One of the curious things which we have noticed over the years is that the dyslexic student often assumes that he has made his points clearly and logically and that the reader will immediately pick up what he wanted to convey. In tutorials one can sometimes say, 'I think what you mean is . . .', wishing to help him with his formulation; and one sometimes gets the reply, made with genuine surprise, 'But isn't that what I have said?' when he is very far from having said it! In the stress of examination conditions all such weaknesses become exaggerated, and, because of his difficulty in expressing himself in writing, his thoughts may totally fail to keep pace with the words which he is putting on the paper or on the screen of his word processor. Potentially there may be a valid and interesting argument, but because of his difficulties with the written word the force of this argument may not come through to the reader. If he then decides to slow down he may panic because he finds he does not have enough time to complete the paper!

This brings us to a problem which regularly confronts the dyslexic candidate in examinations – the problem of determining the best trade-off between speed and accuracy. If time were unlimited, and he did not feel under pressure, there would be the chance to check whether what he wrote in his script was really what he wanted to say. If such checking takes him a long time, however, he will find himself in danger of leaving much of the paper unfinished, and for this reason he may decide to forfeit accuracy in the interests of speed. A student whom one of us met some years ago said his tutor had noticed that he tended to attempt those questions which had the shortest wording rather than those which on other grounds might have been easier (**see note 18.3**). We will discuss the issue of allowing extra time later in the chapter.

A further difficulty for the Examining Board is that the performance of dyslexic students may vary from one day to another. On a 'good day' the putting of ideas on paper may be very much easier than on a 'bad day'; and there appears therefore to be an element of chance in their performance which adds to the difficulties of correct assessment (**see note 18.4**). It is, of course, true that any of us may seize up or 'go blank' on occasions, but the dyslexic person is particularly at risk in this respect; and if a student goes totally blank during one examination and has a 'good day' during another, the spread of his marks is likely to be considerable.

There is also a problem of awarding a suitable grade if the student misreads one of the key words (as in our earlier example of '*clarify*' for '*classify*'). It is also possible for a student to misread the rubric and fail to answer the appropriate number of questions from each section. There is often no easy answer to these problems. In the next section, however, we shall make some suggestions which Examining Boards may like to consider.

ON WHAT IS THE CANDIDATE BEING EXAMINED?

The fact that one has to examine a candidate who is dyslexic – in the words of Dr Johnson – 'concentrates [the] mind wonderfully'. It forces one to consider what precisely are the things for which the candidates are being awarded a high or a low grade. Examining Boards are, of course, right to insist on their own autonomy. For that reason it would be inappropriate for the present authors to say simply that, for instance, poor spelling or poor handwriting should be disregarded. What we can do, however, is to help Boards to ensure that they do not unwittingly mark a candidate down for lack of skills which they would agree on reflection to be irrelevant. Thus if a Board is concerned to determine a candidate's knowledge, his ability to reason logically, and his powers of creativity and originality, one can point out that, as a matter of logic, it is bad examining if the marker of the script allows himself to be influenced by poor spelling or poor handwriting.

When this matter is considered it will probably be found that in some contexts a particular grade in an examination is simply a certificate of achievement. In that case the Examining Board is saying that, no matter what the candidate does in the future, he has at this moment reached a particular level of competence. In other contexts, however, and particularly in the case of qualifying examinations, achievement is taken into account only because it is assumed to be a good predictor of whether the person will display and maintain certain standards in the future.

For most examination candidates this assumption is justified. Thus it is perfectly proper to argue that a person who lacks knowledge in certain areas should not become a dentist, a nurse, a teacher or whatever it may be. There are in fact further safeguards in the system – in particular interviewing and the taking up of references – by which unsuitable people are excluded from such jobs even though they have passed the requisite examinations. What is needed, as far as dyslexic candidates are concerned, is that there should be safeguards in the other direction. If they are downgraded in their examinations for lack of skills which are not relevant to dentistry, nursing, teaching, etc. then they are deprived of the opportunity of doing such jobs even though they would in fact be entirely suitable. In view of what is now known about the unusual balance of skills in dyslexics (see Chapter 1) this may be a tragic waste.

Similarly, when Boards are examining for Honours and need to make a decision as to the candidate's degree class, they will probably decide that their primary concern is to indicate the candidate's achievement not to try to predict his future progress (**note 18.5**).

In this connection there is a serious risk that an examiner, particularly if he has large numbers of scripts to mark, may unwittingly be misled into awarding a dyslexic candidate a lower grade than he deserves; after all, it is very easy to suppose if a person cannot spell and has immature handwriting that his thinking is therefore immature. As was indicated above, the certificate reminding the Examining Board that a candidate is dyslexic is a useful safeguard.

In the case of non-dyslexic candidates there are certain things which can be taken for granted – for example that they will have no difficulty in reading the question, in writing the answer, or in carrying out a simple subtraction sum. These skills may be components of the end product which is required of all candidates, but it is for the Board to decide which of these components are to be regarded as important. If reading print at speed is not thought to be important, for example, then as a matter of logic candidates who do not possess this skill should not be penalized. Indeed, if they were so penalized, the Board would be committed to explaining why the same penalties are not exacted from blind candidates.

Difficult problems of marking can sometimes arise if a candidate has written enough to lead the examiner to suspect the presence of some good ideas but insufficient to show that he has fully grasped the point of what he has said. Since, as we have seen, the style of a dyslexic student may be stilted and his script may contain some awkward and ungainly expressions, the examiner sometimes has to make some kind of guess as to how the candidate might have elaborated his argument had he been given the chance. Has he, for instance, simply dropped in one or two names or mentioned one or two key concepts without having understood them, or has he understood them perfectly well and simply expressed himself somewhat awkwardly? And at what point does stylistic inelegance – a relatively unimportant matter – turn into failure to explain oneself – a weakness which clearly an Examining Board must take seriously?

Issues relating to new technology have already been discussed in Chapter 15. All kinds of decisions need to be made as to what should or should not be permitted. In his book, *In the Mind's Eye* (**see note 18.6**), Thomas West has suggested that many of the traditional literacy skills – those, in his words, of the 'medieval clerk' – can now be performed by computer, and he suggests that when dyslexics are free of these 'chores' there will now be a greater opportunity for their talents to flourish. This certainly raises important issues for Examining Boards. In particular they should perhaps reconsider what value they place on memorization skills. If these are regarded as important then those dyslexics who find memorization difficult (as most of them do) will obtain lower grades. As against this, it is arguable that nothing is gained by insisting that candidates should hold in mind information which for the remainder of their lives they will be able to obtain by pressing a button on a computer. Similarly, it is arguable that coloured paper and the like should be provided for any candidate on request, as suggested in Chapter 15, since few Examining Boards would regard themselves as being in the business of giving higher grades to candidates who are unaffected by dazzle!

SOME SUGGESTIONS

Although it is for Examining Boards – and not for us – to decide what is and is not important, we should like to offer the following formula as a possible guide for those marking the scripts of dyslexic candidates: *it is important to look for evidence of creativity, knowledge and reasoning powers which are not apparent at first glance*. An untidy and seemingly 'scrappy' presentation can sometimes conceal important and original ideas.

There may also be difficulties if the candidate's performance is uneven; for example, if the examination comprises four papers he may do well on three of them and perform disastrously on the fourth. When confronted with his pattern of marks the Board needs to determine whether the performance on the 'weak' paper is genuinely due to lack of knowledge or whether he has failed to show the knowledge which he possesses. It will also need to decide whether failure to show such knowledge (a failure which may be repeated in the future) merits any appreciable penalty when the knowledge was in fact present.

Similar problems arise, as we have already noted, if the candidate 'goes off the rails' as a result of not following the rubric or misreading the question. Presumably the intention behind a rubric such as 'Answer two questions from Section A and two from either Section B or Section C' is to ensure that the student's knowledge covers a sufficiently wide area. It follows that if the Board can be satisfied on other grounds, for example on the basis of an oral examination, that the student's knowledge is sufficiently wide, then mistakes over rubric need not be too severely penalized. The same principle can sometimes apply when the question itself has been misread, as in the case, cited earlier, of the candidate in a history examination who wrote on Henry IV instead of Henry VI. If the candidate *could* have written about Henry VI this is highly relevant. It is unsatisfactory, in our view, to award no marks at all if the candidate misreads the rubric or answers the wrong question, since this places him on a level with those having no knowledge at all in this area; and if one argues that he should receive a zero mark 'because he ought to have been more careful' this assumes that such misreadings are serious academic faults.

In this connection it is worth noting that the mean (or what is popularly known as the 'average') can sometimes be a very misleading statistic. In the case of a dyslexic candidate the spread of the results may be unusually wide: there may be high marks in some papers while in others something may have gone seriously wrong. When this happens it need not imply that the candidate is simply 'weak' without qualification. Uncritical averaging of marks will almost certainly give a distorted picture.

One of the provisions made by most Examining Boards (see Chapter 15) is to allow dyslexic candidates *extra time*. There may still be situations, however, where, with or without extra time, the dyslexic candidate fails to complete the paper. One possibility here is that the Board should compare the work of such a candidate in timed examination conditions with his performance in dissertations, projects, etc. for which unlimited time has been allowed. If the marks are higher in the latter situation it is reasonable to infer that what they can do in timed conditions may not fully reflect what they can do in untimed conditions, and this is clearly relevant to the issue of grading. Not long ago a dyslexic student said to one of us: 'They thought that by allowing me extra time they had done all that was needed to ensure me a level playing field, but they didn't understand how my dyslexia affected my performance.'

In Chapter 15 we also mentioned the possibility that Examining Boards should allow dyslexic candidates to be examined orally. This procedure can either be used on its own or as a supplement to the information obtained from the written papers, and it can sometimes provide the Board with very useful information about a candidate. We have in fact met many dyslexics who are fluent orally and are therefore glad to be examined in this way. However, this is not an ideal solution for *all* dyslexic candidates, since on a 'bad day' some of them may become tongue-tied or find themselves unable to find the right words for expressing their argument.

We believe it could sometimes be of help to an examiner to consider what a good copy editor might have made of the script. A copy editor is in no position to query the ideas which an author wishes to express but he may well be able to help the author to make his points in a better or more telling way. We suggest therefore that candidates should not be penalized for something which a good copy editor could have put right. The Examining Board is in that case saying that it prefers a knowledgeable candidate whose script shows such blemishes to a weak candidate whose spelling and sentence construction are adequate; and this seems to us a judgement which most Boards would find acceptable.

In our experience there is greater risk of underestimating the dyslexic candidate than of overestimating him. The central question which needs to be asked, in our view, is this: has the candidate lost out through lack of skills which from the point of view of the Examining Board are irrelevant? If so, then there is a case for adjusting or revising his grade. Detailed thought is needed, however, as to what skills the examiners should be looking for.

Appendices

INTRODUCTION

As a postscript to the main body of the book we have included contributions from five adult dyslexics who have successfully completed college courses.

Colin Wilsher's paper, 'Study techniques for examinations', was an obvious initial choice, and we are grateful to Mrs Wendy Fisher, the editor of *Dyslexia Review* (now, happily, in print again) for permission to reproduce it. (In the interests of brevity it has been slightly edited.) Colin has also contributed a further appendix on 'Characteristics of successful dyslexics'. (Material from the appendix in the 1986 edition entitled 'Word processing and dyslexia' has been incorporated into Chapter 14.) Secondly, both of us had held discussions with Andrew Bullock over a number of years about study techniques for dyslexics of all ages, and a selection of the material which he wrote during this time has been included under the title 'Work organization, essay writing and examination techniques'. Contributions were also requested from Stephen Martin and Simon Batty. Their contributions are somewhat different from those of Colin and Andrew in that they were asked to write about their personal experiences rather than about study techniques as such. For the 1996 edition Stephen and Simon have supplemented their original material with some more recent news; and an important addition is an Appendix by Fiona Zinovieff who has described in considerable detail those study techniques which she herself found particularly useful.

So as not to disturb the personal style of the contributors we have done very little by way of editing. We have corrected a number of misspellings, since there seemed no point in retaining these unless some systematic study of the spelling errors of dyslexic adults was being attempted. In addition, Simon Batty's contribution, which was originally made on tape, has undergone some minor changes to make it suitable for written rather than oral presentation. In general, however, it has been our policy to let the contributors speak for themselves. Although this has, of necessity, involved some repetition of points made in the main part of the book we took the view that further editing would have made the writing less genuine and that, in any case, advice which is important could usefully be given additional emphasis.

Each contribution is different, and it will therefore be possible for readers to identify and select the techniques which suit them personally. It is also pleasing to us, the authors, to see how much the contributions supplement what we have written in the main chapters of the book.

APPENDIX I – STUDY TECHNIQUES FOR EXAMINATIONS

C.R. Wilsher, BA, PGCE, Ph.D.

The dyslexic's problems with note taking in lessons and lectures call for adopting several different strategies. The student may feel embarrassed or shy about admitting he has a problem, but unless he asks for help he is likely to become more and more confused. First, have a word with the teacher and see if he can slow down or provide a list of notes for you (he often has his own) or he can provide extra time for you to see him and catch up on what you have missed. Secondly, do not take the notes at the expense of understanding. It may be better to understand the lecture and write a few notes on what you understood than to write down every word but miss the meaning of the lecture. Thirdly, it is a good idea to adopt a policy of note taking that is economical (both on time and effort) and understandable. This should take the form of headings with brief notes, not whole sentences. Fourthly, it may be possible to circumvent direct lecture note taking by finding other techniques such as tape recording.

'Reading for meaning' is extremely important in both study and revision. There is a tremendous amount of reading to be done both at school and in further and higher education. The student is presented both with essential reading for the 'core' of his subject and with background (and supportive) reading. It is most important for the dyslexic that he makes a judicial choice of book. First, the book must be relevant to the subject being studied. Here the teacher will be of considerable help if he can give a priority list of the most helpful books. Next, the student should try to select the type of text he is most able to learn from.

Texts can vary, e.g. programmed texts, texts with scientific or literary emphases, etc. Also the amount and detail of illustrations and pictures must be taken into account. The student should ask himself, 'Do I understand this type of presentation?' It is useless plodding through thick, 'set' books deriving no understanding when an alternative book may be more revealing.

The method of reading can contribute a lot towards understanding. If the material is relatively short then it may be advisable to read through it once before re-reading it for meaning. However, if the text is long or complicated this may result in misinterpretation. The important feature of reading for dyslexics is to reduce the 'load' to be learned and remembered. In reducing the load we must focus in on the relevant information. It is important to use and understand the contents and index pages. By judicial cross-reference the exact location of relevant material can be found. The contents page also gives you information about the advisability of selecting the book. When viewing the contents page it is possible to categorize the areas covered by the author.

When the relevant pages have been found, the titles and subtitles tell us of the area being discussed. It is advisable at this stage to have pen and paper ready. The titles can then be written down as headings on the piece of paper. In scientific (or other structured textbooks) there are often summaries and conclusions. These should be read most carefully and 'key words' selected from these to place on your piece of paper. You should now be familiar with the area the author is discussing. Sometimes the summary and conclusion may provide information enough. When reading the text take one paragraph at a time and read it carefully and slowly. After reading it, ask yourself, 'What has it told me?' Here again, you can jot down the information received, in note form. This process takes a long while but is considerably more efficient than reading the whole article or page at a time. Although it is slow at first, the process of asking the meaning will become a habit and progress will be faster. It is also important that relevant and meaningful notes be taken. These can then be rearranged to form a 'checklist' of the important facts to be remembered. This rearrangement can be done in the light of: your notes; the summary and conclusion; and other relevant material on this topic. This checklist can then form the basis of a 'poster' for revision purposes.

One of the most important sources of help that a dyslexic can receive is from other people. Here interested and helpful individuals can act as mediators of the written word. A fellow student or friend or teacher could read the relevant text to you. This could be done directly or on a tape recording. However, it is important that the dyslexic student has the opportunity to discuss the text. Here the reader can distil the meaning which is all too obvious to him but which is sometimes obscured to the dyslexic. The helpful tutor will be so much more adept at: picking out key words; synthesizing the meaning; and having a general understanding of a large text. However, the tutor may not always be good at passing on this understanding. This is where question and answer and preparing your own notes will help your understanding.

Commit the bare essentials of a particular topic (or sub-topic) to a poster. The poster can be of any size of blank paper but must be of a size so as to hold all the relevant information. This means there is no sequencing of material from one page to another but an 'immediate' presentation of material. The student should use large headlines in bright colours (preferably using felt pens). All writing should be big, and important names should be underlined or have bright circles drawn around them. The student should follow his own layout, that is meaningful to him. A good idea is to make the essentials into numbered parts that descend the page even if they may not obey a left–right sequence. Not only can topics for revision be put on these posters, but actual prepared exam answers too. Also, essential spelling for particular subjects (such as chemical names for chemistry or kings' names for history) can be made into posters. The posters should be placed in a variety of different places on windows, on walls, on doors, on ceilings, inside cupboards, on mirrors, on furniture and even on the TV screen. The posters by themselves will not provide you with a good memory (although the time spent creating them will familiarize you with the information). Posters, just like familiar wallpaper, are easily ignored. It is important therefore that they be difficult to ignore and that they be used with a multitude of learning techniques. These methods rely upon active participation in the learning and not a passive reception of material.

These brightly coloured posters can be used in a 'multisensory' way. 'Multisensory' means using more than one sense. The reading of a book silently involves the eyes in a recognition task and little else is involved. However, if the book is read out loud the words are heard by the reader at the same time as seeing them. Here both auditory and visual means are being used. The learner can also use his tactile (kinaesthetic) sense by writing the information at the same time as saying it out loud and looking at it. It may be necessary to either rewrite the posters or to write something down on spare paper. This can also take the form of testing your ability at remembering what is on them. It is important in all methods of learning that there should be a great deal of repetition (over-learning). Over-learning means repeating the material to be learned, not just until it can be repeated once successfully, but going on to continue repeating it even after it has been learned.

Mnemonics (memory aids) are very useful in both increasing the amount to be learned and also improving the retention of material. Mnemonics may provide a 'conceptual leap' by providing a framework for understanding. This is where the student understands something formerly confused, because the mnemonic clarifies the logical pattern. Mnemonics can also act as memory increasers by providing a 'key' for recall. If a topic has a novel appeal it will be remembered for that novel device, whereas others may be forgotten. Mnemonic techniques should be used wherever possible with the poster techniques. The information on the poster can be recited several times, possibly making use of a rhyme or song. Little devices (such as cartoons on the poster) should be used to draw your attention to it.

When learning from the posters the student will soon be able to repeat half the poster with his eyes closed and then open them. This should promote immediate knowledge of results and immediate correction of any errors. Immediate knowledge of results is important for learning because any delay means that errors continue or are even learned better than the correct version. The student himself can control this by using the first line of a poster (or first word of a tape recording) as a cue to recall the rest. He should continue this learning in a distributed fashion. That is, not learning several hours of posters *en masse* but taking a few minutes' rest between posters and then retesting himself. If many posters of a similar nature are revised together, for a long while, the information will tend to interfere with other material. This will lead to a decrease in all things learned and also a possible muddling of several things together. For this reason it is better to keep subjects segregated and work on a system of many short study periods than one very long one.

Reducing interference is important when promoting the clarity of that to be remembered. Usually it is better to revise on one's own and away from distractions such as the television or a younger brother or sister. However, some people can revise better when they are surrounded by a wall of pop music. At first, this may seem to be an interference, but, for some, people this provides a masking effect which does not allow outside interference in. The student should find out which technique is best for him. (If you find yourself listening to the pop music it may not be a good idea.) Another good way of reducing interference is to commit material to memory either just before sleep or just after. Here a poster on the ceiling above the bed can be memorized before sleep or again in the morning. When the last thing memorized is followed by a period of sleep there will be very little 'interference' with it. However, repeating information just before sleep may promote sleeplessness (especially just before the exam) and the student should find out for himself the best methods.

Motivation is important, because if the student does not want to learn he won't learn. One can motivate oneself in different ways. First, the material can be made interesting and the approach novel. For instance, the words of a poster can be recited to a well-known pop song (I used to like 'Yellow Submarine'). Secondly, one can arrange one's own schedule of reinforcement. Hence for example, when a poster is recalled twice without looking at it you can have a cup of coffee. Having a cup of coffee before you work is not a good idea. Get something done (you set the target) before you have that cup of coffee or watch *Top of the Pops*. Sweets can be used as reinforcement, but I found the most effective was learning so many posters before going on a visit to my girl friend! It is also a good idea to extend the schedule of reinforcement as one becomes more competent (that is, increase the amount of posters learned before the cup of coffee). Also, of course, the satisfactory learning of a set of facts is in itself rewarding. It is, of course, important that the student 'plays fair'; if he cheats he is only cheating himself.

A very good idea I found was a small notebook (about five inches by two inches). It is important to use the same techniques as with the posters. First, it is immediate presentation of data (not sequential) so it covers a whole page (or two pages together) and must contain all the essential information on that subtopic. Again, it must be multicoloured and contain headings. This small book does mean that revision can be carried out anywhere and often. Finally, it is important to employ techniques of immediate knowledge of results, distributed effort, cued recall, high motivation and reducing interference.

A notebook is particularly powerful when used in conjunction with the following ideas. Tape recorders can be used as another novel way of repeating data. Here the same essentials as on the posters and in the books can be tape recorded. They can be repeated (at several differing volumes, at different pitches, and even using comical voices) several times on the tape, and, of course, the tape can be played back several times. When used in conjunction with the small book you can follow your notes at the same time as hearing the tape. The tape can be used for cue recall by starting a topic with a key word. You then switch off the tape and try to recall the whole topic. Play the tape and receive immediate knowledge of results of your performance. It is again important to join in with the tape and recite important data. This method is particularly useful in reducing interference. If the tape recording is played just before going to sleep there is less interference from other activities. If some parts of set books are important these can be recorded (perhaps by someone else) and can be played back whilst following the text. Useful spellings can be repeated by this method.

Compact disks or tapes can be bought of famous books (e.g. Shakespeare); hence you can follow the text while listening to the record. Again it would help to recite the work at the same time. A novel idea is to take the part of one character in the play and say his words. This is also an interesting way of repeating material several times. Motivation should be quite high as it is the only way to read a Shakespeare play in about two hours (not bad for a poor reader!). However, it is probably better to repeat small passages many times, and learn each one rather than the whole. Of course it is also a good idea to see the plays if you can.

Many dyslexics experience difficulty with some aspects of arithmetic, possibly due to their limited short-term memory. However, this problem with mental arithmetic does not mean that higher mathematics is not available to dyslexics. On the contrary, they may be very good at understanding and making proofs, but unable to do simple subtraction or may reverse the numbers in the answer. Here posters, booklets and tape recordings can be used to learn formulae, proofs, etc. The problem with subtraction may be due to the fact that the load is too great. Therefore we must look at ways to lessen this load. First, it is a good idea to break down all the sequences to be remembered; therefore 69713251 becomes 69–71–32–51. Do not be afraid to use paper when doing simple arithmetic. It is nearly always possible to use a piece of scrap paper to write down the numbers. If the calculation involves several items in a sequence it may be best to list these in descending order down the page. It is sometimes possible to set out the problem in a spatial manner on paper. This will involve the conversion of numbers to 'concrete' examples. In this way the number can be seen as a number of milk bottles or bars of chocolate. These can then be taken away from (subtraction) or shared out amongst the customers (division).

When the actual exams arrive, it is important to be sure of your strategy. All the revision you have done will be useless if it cannot be presented in the prescribed manner.

APPENDIX II – CHARACTERISTICS OF SUCCESSFUL DYSLEXICS

C.R. Wilsher, BA, PGCE, Ph.D.

Most clinicians will agree that intelligence is a great predictor of successful outcome in the case of dyslexia. However, a variable that I believe to be of equal, if not greater, importance is the personality variable. Here I refer to personality, but what I really mean is the attitudes, personal motivation, and self-image that the individual has.

Certainly intellectual level is very important, and I believe that a certain minimal level is necessary for a 'good' outcome. Also the greater the level of intelligence, the better the chances of progress. However, this intelligence will not be applied if the individual does not adjust to the situation of his handicap (for I view dyslexia as a handicap), and build up his self-image. The process by which an individual and his family (the family is crucially important) come to terms with this handicap is not unlike the process most individuals go through in resolving a trauma (such as a serious illness in the family). Obviously dyslexia is not such a devastating problem as a major illness, but the processes gone through are much the same.

First there will usually be a period of denial of the problem. The

child will not wish to think of himself as 'different' or 'strange', and
the parents will avoid facing the problem of a 'handicapped' child
(particularly when all outward signs say the child is normal).
However, acceptance of the condition is the most important step in
adjustment. In thousands of clinical situations the child and the
parents have been released from feelings of guilt and frustration by
knowing that the problem is diagnosable.

This leads to the second phase, which is to understand the
condition of dyslexia. Again both parents and children are freed
from the notion that they somehow 'caused' the reading handicap.
As far as we know dyslexia is not usually caused by environmental
conditions such as: not loving your child enough/loving him too
much; not disciplining him enough/disciplining him too much;
giving him the right vitamins or diet, etc. In fact there is some
evidence that dyslexia may be of constitutional origin, being caused
by an abnormal distribution of cells in the left hemisphere of the
brain during the 16th to 28th week of gestation. Anyway, most
presenting cases of dyslexia show very few 'barriers to learning'
(hearing and sight problems, inadequate school experience, poor IQ,
etc.). On the contrary, most cases show many positive signs of trying
to encourage reading (presence of books in home, help with
reading, etc.). Hence it is very unlikely that the child or his parents
'caused' the condition.

The next step for the child (aided by the family) is to learn to
judge himself independently of his handicap. That is, he must adopt
a system of self-worth that highlights the positive. It is important
that he values the things that he can do, rather than always being
presented with his failures. He must learn to judge himself by his
own standards rather than judging himself by the standards of
others. That is not to say that he should ignore his handicap but
rather put it in the correct perspective. After all, literacy is only one
small part of his total life. Much effort must be put into valuing
those things that he is good at.

The fourth step is to reach a situation in which the handicap is
somewhat resolved. This does not mean that the handicap goes
away but that the devastating personal impact of the condition is

reduced. This can be achieved by two routes. First, many facets of the handicap must be met by a 'head-on' confrontation. This would involve continued efforts to master literacy to the best possible level. The second method (not an alternative but an adjunct) is to develop alternative strategies for coping with the problems presented by this handicap. Here the dyslexic can use his strengths to overcome his weaknesses. I advocate not only using these strengths in the process of learning what is most difficult (i.e. literacy; see Appendix I) but also in developing radical alternatives to the problems themselves. By this I mean finding alternatives to the use of literacy (or methods that utilize very little literacy) to achieve the same end result, for instance the use of tape recorders, word processors, preparing 'posters' instead of reading from books, or listening to a problem (or seeing a problem in spatial terms) and resolving it either orally or spatially.

I have described the psycho-social process the individual and his family must go through to help resolve the effects of this handicap. Throughout that process the personal response of the dyslexic child is critical. It is important that he learns that he is otherwise 'normal' and that he is successful at other things; it is also important that he develops a method of looking at the world that protects/enhances his self-image. He must believe that literacy is only one part (unfortunately a very important part) of the world and that people are not judged by this alone. This does not mean that he should dismiss literacy as unimportant, but I feel it is far more important that he should preserve his self-image than that he should gain literacy skills. Admittedly, it is a value judgement of mine, but for my money I would rather have a happy, well adjusted dyslexic who was successful at some things and had no literacy than a child who was unhappy, had low self-esteem, and had not developed other skills, and was fully literate. Of course there is a compromise position which would hopefully capitalize on the best of both worlds.

Successful outcomes are usually seen when basic skills of literacy are brought up to at least a minimal level and where compensatory skills are maximized. In fact, many successful dyslexics never achieve a satisfactory level of literacy but their compensatory mechanisms have become so advanced that they gain notoriety in their chosen areas. The process should be viewed as a problem-solving one, in which the problem is the impact of the handicap. The resolution of these problems means that the individual is gaining important problem-solving skills that will stand him in good stead for any career in which problem-solving skills are pre-eminent over literacy skills. One might quip that non-dyslexics are at a distinct disadvantage because they enter the world of work without the benefit of advanced problem-solving skills.

APPENDIX III – WORK ORGANIZATION, ESSAY WRITING AND EXAMINATION TECHNIQUES

A.B. Bullock, BA, M.Ed.

> Trust wholeheartedly in God,
> put no faith in your own perception;
> in every course you take, have Him in mind:
> He will see that your paths are smooth.
> (Jerusalem Bible, Proverbs 3: 5, 6)

Work organization

In the planning of one's time, it should be remembered that several shorter stints of work are much more efficient than one longer session, as this will probably be counter-productive. Thus it is better to work for shorter periods, but each day. Even pauses of five to ten minutes can restore one's attention. However, if this does not work, there is little point in sitting over books in a dazed mood, not getting on with reading them. Hence, one could change and do something completely different, or even have a nap of up to an hour. It is also efficient to take a day completely off current work. (I am very active on Sunday but I set it aside for different activities.)

For many dyslexics, much of what they know will have been gleaned from listening to others. They have become astute at asking questions of others in order to learn. At university they may also learn a lot from lectures. These, however, may well be a waste of time unless efficient notes are taken; and unless they are well taken, re-reading them can be tiring. Yet it is possible to learn by having to organize one's ideas on to paper. It will undoubtedly be the case that each student will function differently, but I certainly learn more if I have made notes, even if I do not re-read them. Furthermore, having made a good set of notes, one can skim them and remind oneself of the contents of the lectures in a brief space of time.

Consolidation or further information will be attained from books. Some of these one will read once only, others one will wish to re-read. If they are one's own property, then one can mark the books in such a way as to bring out the important points. Thus one can make notes and underline in red, black, pencil or some other colour. Scoring through words or lines with a yellow highlighting pen makes the words stand out. One can later scan the passage and immediately be made aware of the key words.

The other very useful tactic is the use of filing cards. On these one can write the author, title, date and publisher for immediate reference. Card references may be made on books, articles, newspaper articles or simply useful ideas for filing. It is a good idea if the card has on it the main gist of the book, results and then one's own ideas. Not only does the card concentrate one's own interpretation of the work, making one think of the main points that the author wished to put forward or portray, but it also helps one to remember the facts. It is important that one should not include more than the bare essentials. If more is required, one will need to go back to the original. Later on one can easily go through all one has read and 'shuffle' (literally) the different points into a relevant sequence. Much of one's 'brain work' is thereby done through one simple expediency. One can look upon these cards as a tape store on a computer. They are not for very fast access, but one knows where to look for fairly quick, easy reference.

Having taken the information in and put it upon cards, one simply sorts it, reorganizes it and adds one's own part and then reproduces it. The last part may be what one calls 'essay writing'.

Essay writing

When I spoke with a group of dyslexic undergraduates they insisted that their problem was not so much the organization of their thoughts as the inability to convey the ideas in a way that reads well. Typical comments were: 'I know what I want to say but it never comes out on paper as I mean it to'; 'You know you are as good as someone else, but you always do badly on paper'; 'It's getting it down, that's the problem.'

My own hypothesis is that the writer may know what he wishes to say but that he may assume too much from his reader. He assumes that the reader knows the background or that he can guess it from a few words. One trouble with that is that those few words are not 'well picked words'. Thus for what a brilliant author can convey in one neat sentence the dyslexic will need a complete paragraph. Even then, his reader may not follow what he wishes to say. The situation may not be helped by incorrect spelling or grammar or even not quite the correct word. However, in reality, it may be more likely that the point is inadequately presented; that is, that it is in one short sentence without any surrounding explanation. The dyslexic assumes that the reader will 'understand'.

Sadly, misunderstanding is often the case. Letters come back saying, 'I did not quite see what you were getting at' – when you thought that it was plain. Essays are returned with comments such as 'Keep to the point.' Thus, to avoid the reader having to follow the dyslexic's mental acrobatics, almost everything needs to be 'spelled out'. New points in the argument must be introduced, and one needs to couch the idea in suitable language. While writing, one must constantly keep the idea in mind that the reader does not know what one is talking about. Some idea which may never have occurred to other people may be pertinent to the argument. Putting it down in the middle of an essay will not convince anyone, even if they can understand it. The idea may even need a separate paragraph. This is a tedious way round the problem, as writing is taxing enough without having to insert even more 'useless sentences'. However, it really is the only way to make others understand. (I have only found it possible to follow this dictum through typing and instead of having adverse comments on my essays, I now have compliments!)

So the planning needs to be done in order that all the relevant points are included in the most appropriate order. It has been suggested that one might use a tape recorder in the process of essay writing. Having tried this method very briefly, I have doubts as to its usefulness. It is not easy to 'see' what has just been said and it is not easy to turn back and forth through what is written. Furthermore, it is slow to transcribe.

However, having once drafted out one's work, it may well help one to see where it is lacking in explanation by reading it on to tape and then listening to it.

In preparing an essay it is helpful to take a rough sheet of paper and jot down in a list all the points that may be worth including. They naturally come out in a haphazard order and thus need sorting. To do this one must either use letters or numbers to group ideas which should be included in the same section. Then the ordering of sections needs to take place so as to give a coherent essay. As one thinks about what is involved so one will think of more good ideas. With this system these may easily be added right up to the place of the section being written. If one does not plan but simply writes, new ideas will become a clumsy insertion, which can be difficult to justify or rearrange neatly. To number pages as they are written is helpful.

Having written it out once, one would go through it, correcting as one feels fit. One could then ask a friend to go through to correct spellings and grammar or to make other suggestions. It will then need rewriting. This may happen two or three times, in order that it may read properly. Even experienced authors may do this when writing books. This, naturally, is where word processing is of extreme value, as it is so much quicker.

Examination techniques

In the following section some of the special problems encountered in exams will be discussed. Having to choose quickly which questions to answer; a lack of time to prepare one's answers; not being able to rewrite what one has written; and then the time pressure – all contribute to make exams difficult, especially when important outcomes are dependent upon the results. Thus exam technique is quite different from normal essay writing. In the group of dyslexics studied, worry was not necessarily a problem, though, had it been, that would be very understandable. What is important is to get on with the task in hand, without letting one's mind wander, due to the plethora of decisions to be made, and so waste time.

Should the exam be an internal one, marked by tutors from the department, then it is important that one should become acquainted with the tutors. Attendance at tutorials is important so that, the tutors become aware that, although the answers may not be neatly expressed, the thinking behind them is probably very logical. Hence, they will give one the benefit of the doubt, knowing how one would reply should they ask for further explanation.

Thus before starting one should allow oneself time to read the whole paper through completely. Exams often come in sections. The examinee is requested to answer so many questions from each section. It is important to follow this request, as otherwise, if too many questions are answered from one of the sections, no marks will be gained from those not required. One must then either think which questions one can most easily answer – or which one knows least about. In order to decide which remaining questions should be tackled, one may take a minute to allow one's thinking to examine how to tackle a reply, thereby allowing an idea to germinate. The process will continue without effort while answering the first questions. When one comes to the time of deciding which to answer, if two questions appear equally challenging simply pick one, forget the other, and get on with one's choice. This procedure may be usefully practised prior to the exam by taking a question from past papers – and going out on a boat or punt or into the country to consider how one might best answer it!

Before answering each question try to plan out your answer. Use a scheme similar to the one for writing a formal essay, but naturally abbreviate it by cutting the time on each part of the execution of the plan. Thus jot down ideas for an answer (remembering that trying to cover too much will result in a poorer answer), and order the ideas so as to make a logical sequence. If further points occur to one, it would probably be best to forget them unless one includes them in a skeleton continuation of a reply. One must then write out the answer. It may be appropriate to allow time to draft out, for the examiner, an account of how one would see the writing continue should one have had more time. It is important to allow time to read through the replies. Some glaring errors may be spotted and it can be pointed out, through some correction, that one has at least been aware of them.

While in the middle of the exam, or any other work, concentrate upon the reply undertaken at that moment. Much valuable time can be expended by allowing one's mind to wander to a later question to be answered. Should, as often happens, some good idea occur, write it down in two or three words on a separate note. It will then be a reminder of one's thoughts when one comes to that point. In the meantime one has not become distracted by this alien thought!

Finally, enjoy life at all times – even when waiting for your exam results!

APPENDIX IV – DYSLEXIA IN MY LIFE

S.J. Martin, B.Sc., Ph.D.

Discovery of dyslexia

After failing my O-level English Language for the second time my mother forced me to go to private lessons in an attempt to improve my English. I needed English O-level to enter university. After some weeks had passed, and little improvement in my English, my private English teacher after reading an article on dyslexia in a popular woman's magazine realized that I shared many problems that dyslexics have. She then talked to my mother and then my school to see if it was possible for me to be tested for dyslexia, but the headmistress refused, saying that I was just lazy and not trying hard enough. So through a series of friends we contacted the local Head of Education and he agreed to arrange a series of tests at school. I then spent a full day doing little games and tests with the conclusion that I was dyslexic. I was nearly 18 years old. So now I realized why nobody could ever solve the crossword I used to make for the school magazine.

Sixth form

Even after I was confirmed dyslexic, little changed at school and some teachers still considered me lazy and that I now used dyslexia as an excuse. This image wasn't helped by the fact I took a lot of time off from school to study local nature and go climbing. On the third attempt I passed my O-level English mainly through luck as I had to write an essay on 'Your experiences with nature' and I had lots of them. My A-level Examination Board informed the school that no concessions would be given to dyslexics, except they would re-mark my paper if I was borderline between pass and fail. I was the only student to fail General Studies; this I attribute largely to not reading books or newspapers as I found reading difficult and always lost interest. In my other exams – maths, chemistry and biology – I managed to write very little and instead used lots of diagrams, equations and formulae to explain things; this is possible to a large degree in science subjects. Much to my headmistress's surprise I managed to get the required grades to enter university (Bangor) as well as having a very enjoyable sixth-form life.

University: the first two years

I welcomed the freedom that university offered but as the workload increased I began to have difficulties in keeping pace with the other students. I had to spend a lot of my spare time in my room re-writing notes I had taken that day in lectures, as my notes consisted of only a few key words, often illegible after a day or so when my short-term memory was lost. This filling out of notes was a time-consuming task which I did for my entire university life. I thought I was doing OK until my first set of laboratory reports came back with my words floating in a sea of red ink. Some even had 'you must be dyslexic' printed on them; many students found this very amusing. I didn't say anything and kept on trying harder and harder but my marks got no better, while other students appeared to do very little to get respectable marks, which I found difficult to swallow. Then I received a small brown envelope in which a small piece of paper informed me that a small group of dyslexics were meeting, and would I like to join them. So with nothing to lose I went along one evening to find other normal-looking students all having similar problems at college. The meetings were informal affairs, mainly talking about problems and ways in which they could be solved. This resulted in my talking to my college tutor about my problems and things started to improve. But the most valuable service was offered, a 24-hour free advice and help service which was always a great relief to me and other dyslexics. After starting my second term at college things greatly improved and my work improved to a standard where I could hide in the middle grades. The second year at college is very demanding with every work day full of lectures and practicals; this coupled with an active role in college climbing and birding clubs made it a very exhausting year both physically and mentally. I was still having to rewrite all my notes and put a lot of extra time into writing up practicals. The essays proved the most difficult tasks and I often turned to the Dyslexia Unit for help.

Near the end of the second year I decided I needed a brain rest. I had also been asked to complete some work on forest birds. So I took the opportunity and asked my tutor if I could have a year's leave. As this is very unusual it caused a few problems but with advice from the Dyslexia Unit and full understanding of the situation by my tutor I was granted a year's leave, much to the surprise of my friends who thought it was a year's holiday. The most difficult people to convince were my mother and relatives who viewed my life as one big holiday and thought I was dropping out of college.

The year off

Living on the dole and with equipment loaned from college I set up a small laboratory at home. Early winter was spent working on a remote Scottish island; spring working in a forest on birds; and summer in China; also a good spattering of climbing and bird-watching. To keep my mother happy I also did A-level geology at night-school to stop my brain from going to sleep. I kept in contact with college for advice on my work. Dyslexia laid very low that year as I had very little formal writing or reading to do. The year soon passed and with my brain fully rested I returned to college with a much more relaxed attitude and wider outlook on life in general.

The final year

Going back to college was easy as many of my old friends were still living in Bangor. But it was a different situation in my course; I was unable to hide any longer in the class, and stuck out like a sore thumb. Many of the teachers knew me on a personal basis and were very understanding and tried to help in various ways. I was even given my own room in the department to work in. The final year was much less pressured with more emphasis on development and expanding on ideas given in lectures. This suited me well and it was easy to keep up. I always listened to music while working as it helped me relax and work long periods (up to 1 hour) without a break. I returned to the dyslexic group to find it still going strong. Occasionally a student researching dyslexia (a spy) would attend the meeting and later lure us into a room and subject us to all sorts of nasty tests with lots of 'p's and 'b's and 'd's. But I didn't really mind providing data for these students. Around Easter time things hotted up with dissertation deadlines looming up, so out came the dictionary and hours of writing and rewriting, and I still had to have it checked for spellings by the dyslexia teacher. It was a big job but to see the culmination of five years' work was very satisfying. Then I settled down to my exams with a strong will to succeed. I now knew enough about exam technique from other dyslexics and teachers to devise my own method. This basically consisted of considering each teacher's exam separately and tailoring my exam essay to suit that person. I then wrote lots of practice essays and discussed them with the relevant teachers to refine the technique. This also allowed a personal contact between me and the department staff. Just before the exams the department decided to give me an extra hour for each three-hour exam if I wanted it. I took the extra hour although some people considered it unfair, but it's the result that counts, not how you obtain it. This meant I was able to do my exams in a small room which had a very relaxed atmosphere. Although it was hard work I was rewarded with a good degree (Upper Second) and a lot of surprised faces. But best of all was the inside contentment that I had done it despite having been classed as almost illiterate for most of my school life. I still had never read a book of fiction or fact and all my study was done directly from scientific papers and then I only read the summary. I consider my success at college to be due to four main factors: (1) my genuine interest in the subject; (2) my year's break; (3) the Dyslexia Unit which helped at both personal and higher levels; (4) the help from my department and especially my tutor. Without these four things I fear I would have not fared so well.

After college

After college had ended I kept working and even had some of my research published, which was very satisfying even though it was only one page. I was also learning to type, but finding it a very slow process, and half the time I was buried in the dictionary. After a trip to Nepal I had an interview for a research scholarship to Japan, which I was awarded. As part of the scholarship I had to go to a language school to learn Japanese for about four months. Learning Japanese was very difficult, mainly due to very bad teaching methods. My major problem was not dyslexia but the lack of a formal English education. I still don't know what a noun, verb, pronoun, etc. are. This is because I was always slow in English classes and could never keep up with the other kids. In my Japanese language exams I passed all courses except sentence pattern and construction. Even now, one year later, I still have difficulty in communicating, as I know a lot of words but I can't string them together. As my workload is very light I have a lot of spare time, so I have for the first time started to read books – mainly translations of famous Japanese novels, as the words are simple and in big print and the chapters are short. I even managed to read *Shogun* (a dyslexic's nightmare) and enjoyed it, although it took some two to three months to read. In Japan I work mainly on my own through the medium of English, and when I write, the dictionary and typewriter are my best friends.

Even though I am dyslexic and always have to fight against the system I have been rewarded for my determination. I take all the advice and help I can get and never let anyone look down on me.

Fellow dyslexics, remember Albert Einstein was dyslexic, and don't you wish dyslexia was an easier word to spell?

Postscript to the 1996 edition

Studying in Japan

After language college in Osaka, I was placed in a rural agricultural university deep in the mountains of central Japan. Here I was to carry out my study into high-altitude beetles. I was the first western student to attend the university and since the level of English spoken both in and around the college was low my Japanese improved vastly.

I entered an M.Sc. (by research) course. This meant no lectures, tutorials etc., but I had to submit a thesis in English of my research. Although most Japanese cannot speak English, many especially at university, read it very well. The research was mainly carried out independently high up in the Japanese Alps. During the two years I travelled extensively both in and outside Japan. During my spare time I started to study the biology of the local hornets (large wasps) with some mountain farmers. Eventually I was to spend more time collecting hornet than beetle data. During this time I achieved my first major publication but not without a major struggle. I thought I could write it without outside help and it was returned three times from the journal to be re-written. I almost didn't bother in the end which may have been the beginning of the end of my scientific career. However, I did and it was eventually accepted and reading the final printed version I released how right the referees were after all. That was the first and last manuscript I sent off without getting it checked first.

The writing of my M.Sc. thesis was a tricky job but I managed to substitute a lot of charts, graphs and tables in place of written words. None of the examiners corrected the grammar in what little I did write in my thesis since they were far too polite and after all I was English and so must be right! I left Japan after three wonderful years to return to the UK and no job.

After Japan

I continued to write up some of my hornet and beetle research that led me to a world wasp expert. He suggested that I should write up my hornet data and submit it as a Ph.D. However, the prospect of writing a several inch thick book was a nightmare; a three-hour essay was bad enough. Anyway I talked the idea over with the Zoology Department at Bangor and it was decided that I could do it part-time which has a time limit of nine years. This was my cup of tea, since I could now work at my pace. I of course had to fund it but I registered and wondered what I had let myself in for.

Falkland Islands and a book

Around this time I was fortunately offered a job in the Falklands by a climber friend as a scientific officer on the fishing boats. This would earn me some money and provided me with plenty of spare time for my next project. I flew south with a case full of notes, maps and papers and my portable Japanese word processor. In between measuring and sexing squid and fish I wrote an English hiking guide to the Japanese Alps. This was hard work but great fun.

Unfortunately the various publishers liked the guide but said it would not have big enough sales to merit printing it So it sits on a shelf at home waiting until I have some time to publish myself with the aid of computers.

Back to college

Now having the funds and renewed enthusiasm for my hornet work, since the hiking guide had been written, I returned to Bangor University to tackle my Ph.D. After many discussions and careful reading of the college rules we realized it was possible for me to submit my thesis as a series of papers, published or not, as long as they were sandwiched between an introduction, methods and a discussion. This was of great help to me since now each piece of work was a small free-standing unit. I had become better at writing papers and had built up a network of colleagues who would check them for errors. I set about writing endless papers and after about one year I had written 7 and submitted these between a 6-page introduction, 8-page methods and a 7-page discussion, all double spaced of course. Eventually all the papers in my thesis were published. It was only the continued support from my supervisors, Head of Department and Dyslexia Unit that had made it all possible. Fortunately the final exam is oral, my preferred medium.

Back to Japan

Within a week of obtaining my doctorate I was flying out to Japan funded by a Royal Society/Japan Society post-doc. research fellowship. This enabled me to continue my hornet research. This time I studied a rare species only found on the remote sub-tropical islands 1000 km south of mainland Japan. Fortunately, my Japanese girl friend, later to become my wife, accompanied me down to the island. This greatly reduced the language problem. There we spent over two years studying hornets, writing papers and diving on the coral reefs which ringed the island. During the hornet hibernation period we were married and went skiing in the USA.

Back to college, again!

Before leaving Japan I was awarded another Royal Society grant which allowed me to return to the UK and develop my ideas and write up my research. So it was another year in sunny Bangor working on my Japanese word processor (no spell-checker) churning out the papers and developing my hornet model. I still relied heavily on colleagues to check my work before submission to journals and I became hardened to the comments about my poor English.

After the funding ran out I started to apply for more funding and jobs. We had our first child now, and so, being responsible parents, with no jobs in sight we took off for a six-month trip to the Far East. Based in Singapore we visited Malaysia and Borneo where I collected hornet data, visited friends in Taiwan and relatives in Japan, and returned to our island to go diving again. When the money ran out we returned the UK and I applied for jobs and wrote up the new hornet data.

National Bee Unit

A month after returning to the UK I applied for a job doing research and development for the National Bee Unit. I was successful and they gave me the post of 'Head of Research'. A grand title for a research team consisting of one (me). The work was based in Devon, well away from the main offices, and concerned the study of the parasitic honeybee mite, Varroa. There was more paperwork in this job than any other I had done. But I also had a powerful computer with spell-checker and grammar-checker. I now never write anything without using the computer. It has speeded the whole process of writing enormously – I cannot imagine how I ever managed without it. I now have an assistant and I delegate most the writing of letters, memos etc. to him and I just read through and sign. My close colleagues know of my dyslexia and help in the spelling of words that even the spell-checker cannot pick up. I still get my work checked for grammar and incorrect words which of course the spell-checkers cannot pick up. People's awareness of dyslexia appears to be much greater now and so less of a stigma is attached to it.

I have coped largely by avoiding work which involves writing, especially in public, and attempt to keep my research field based. The papers are continuing, and now number around twenty-five.

Recently I have started a night class in 'teaching in further education'. This involves a lot of reading and assignments. Unfortunately many of the old problems are re-occurring and I am finding it very difficult to sit down and get the necessary work done on time. My basic dislike of formal reading and writing is the biggest problem but the teachers are a lot more accommodating now and I am sure we will work something out.

APPENDIX V – PROBLEMS WITH DYSLEXIA

S. Batty, B.Sc., M.Sc., Ph.D.

School

When I entered my secondary school, I was automatically put in the bottom class. This was because my work wasn't of a very high standard: I could hardly read and could hardly write. I wasn't very good at maths, so consequently I was put in the bottom streams and not expected to do well. When I got to the fourth year, with it being a secondary school, most people went and did CSEs, and very few did O-levels; the ones that weren't considered up to CSE standard were helped with remedial lessons, especially in English. I was immediately put into these remedial English lessons, and this is really where I learned to read, although it wasn't an awful lot of help apart from learning to read. I was put in for most of the CSEs, which I didn't work for, one reason being that I was told I was so stupid anyhow that I wouldn't get any qualifications. So thinking that, I believed there was no point in doing any work anyway.

When I was 16 I got five CSEs. All of them were very low grades, fours and fives. I decided to carry on into the sixth form, at which point I was told I was so stupid I would never get any higher than CSEs and there was no point in staying on. But my mother forced the school to get in touch with the educational psychologist who then tested me and found that I was dyslexic. Apart from then getting one or two extra English lessons with help from somebody who wasn't trained really in special English – and certainly not dyslexia – I got no other help from them at all. I proceeded to work through my sixth form doing O-levels and one A-level. I left the school with one O-level pass in biology.

College

On leaving school, I went to a College of Further Education. Here the staff were a lot more helpful. I was immediately put on a course of five O-levels. Whether they expected me to pass or not they weren't sure at the time. They certainly didn't expect me to pass my maths or English. By the end of the year I had proved them wrong: I got my O-level maths, though my English was proving very difficult to get, and it meant hard work. I didn't get very much help in the O-level years, except that the college was very strict anyway, and you had to work. Then I set about doing three A-levels and the General Studies A-level. This involved an awful lot of hard work (except for general studies where very little was required), but I did manage to get the A-levels. I got help from lecturers giving me extra work, and marking that work for me, and I was given extra English lessons as well, both inside the college and outside the college. Inside the college the lessons really consisted of remedial English on one evening per week.

When I started my second year of A-levels, I went to Lilian Hartley who was also in Northwich and who is a specialist dyslexia teacher. She helped very greatly indeed. And finally in the second year, that's the year I got my A-levels, I got my O-level English; this was after seven attempts; every summer and every November since I left school! The work needed to get the A-levels was specifically designed so that I could understand what I was doing; it wasn't designed just to learn the work, but to be learned in such a fashion that it had to be fully understood. This meant going over and over and over the work many many times so that you got a full understanding of it.

The reason behind this was that if I was doing a section of work for the exams then I would be less liable to make a mistake because I understood what was happening; and, for it to work, all the parts you were doing would have to tie up, and, if it didn't in the end, then you knew that you had made a mistake somewhere and you would go back and recheck it. I think that this did help quite considerably, but it did mean an awful lot of extra work for me to do. It meant many many hours of revision; it meant no holidays for two years; it meant not going out for two years. But it was, in fact, the only way to get the work out. From here, and all the way through university, of course, the problem was that I knew the work orally well enough, but unfortunately I couldn't write it down, and this is a great handicap. I was supposed to get dispensation from the Examining Boards for my O-levels and A-levels but I'm not very sure that this happened, as I believe they only give you dispensation if you fail your exams. As I probably passed them, just, I believe they weren't remarked; and I would have hoped to have got higher marks than I did.

University

The problems involved at university (Bangor) were similar to those found with the A-levels, with a few exceptions. First of all, you couldn't work quite in the same style as you could for your A-levels, or O-levels. Instead of being able to go away and learn and learn the work until you knew it backwards, the work had to be analysed and I found this very slow going. Not only that; note taking was erratic, or I could not get notes down, and I was finding I was having to go home and re-write my entire set of notes in the evening. But, unfortunately, this just wasn't possible and, when I did my revision, time had to be taken up in re-writing the notes, so that they were readable and legible. Overall, the problems were similar to those of the A-levels in that I could do the oral work very easily indeed, yet the written work was very hard and I used to get very low grades for written work. This in the end led me to get a very low grade of degree indeed. If I hadn't been dyslexic I would have wished to have got a much higher grade. At the same time I had involvements with the dyslexic department in Bangor, going to the odd meeting and doing tests for psychology students; and I had a number of chats, with Professor Miles especially, when I had great problems, which I certainly had near the end of the third year. This was because I was finding it impossible in many ways to get down the work that they wanted, yet I had an understanding of what they were doing. In the end I managed to get a Third Class Honours degree, which I'm still not very happy about.

Conclusions

Overall, I have found, over the last few years, that the way to get my exam passes is to work extremely hard for them, to put in many many hours' overtime. One short cut that I have found is to use symbols to represent phrases or long words. This cuts the time used for note taking and revising considerably, and by the end of my degree I had got quite a set of symbols which meant groups of phrases strung together; this helped quite a lot. Another thing I did which helped improve the readability of my work was to use word processors to write up projects and coursework. The problem I found here was that, unfortunately, there were very few word processors that had scientific symbols on them, so it meant very involved work just to get scientific symbols out. And unfortunately, in the degree I did, I wasn't given much dispensation because the people concerned felt it very important that my writing skills were up to standard, with chemistry being a profession.

Even in looking for a job the most important thing seems to be writing skills. But of course nobody ever tells you that your dyslexia is the reason why you won't even get an interview, but I suspect that in a lot of the cases where I have been, or seemed to have been, ideal for the job, this is why they do not want to give you the job – because they suspect your reading and writing. Just as passing exams involved a large amount of extra work so also looking for jobs is going to be a problem. And it's debatable whether you admit that you are dyslexic or not when you go for a job interview. It will be interesting to see how many more interviews I will get if I didn't admit I was dyslexic on my CV. However, overall, I have found that if I want to get anywhere I have got to work very hard, but it's also been very satisfying knowing that I can, and knowing that to a certain extent my hard work has paid off.

Postscript to the 1996 edition

My M.Sc. was a two-year course, the first being a general materials course to bring me to Upper Second standard, with the second year being the M.Sc. proper. These two years involved a lot of hard work, including an intensive mathematics course; however it was a happy time. Cranfield had a good attitude towards dyslexia in that once they realized I had ability, they then helped all they could to make the best use of that ability. This was especially good in that Cranfield demands a lot from its students, so having their confidence coupled with success in exams was a great confidence boost. I successfully completed my M.Sc. in molecular electronics in 1987, although writing my thesis was difficult as I did not have access to a word processor.

I was then employed by Sheffield City Polytechnic (now Sheffield Hallam University) as a research assistant working for my Ph.D. The first thing I did was buy a computer to enable me to use a word processor. I successfully obtained my Ph.D. in 1990. My thesis write-up took me six months using my word processor. This was probably the hardest thing I have had to do – I worked in excess of twelve hours a day six or seven days a week over that time. My mother spent many hours checking spellings (spell-checkers cannot tell the difference between 'there' and 'their' for example) and ordering paragraphs for which I cannot thank her enough. This was backed up by my supervisors who were very supportive throughout my Ph.D.

I was unemployed for a year after completing the research for my Ph.D., although my six-month writing-up period was within that year. One can never be sure of the reasons for this period of unemployment. I believe that my supervisors thought I was a very competent person, and I think they thought that my dyslexia was a contributing factor to my lack of job success. Eventually I gained a post-doctoral Research Assistantship at the University of Sheffield, and I am now on my third contract for the university. I have worked in three departments, engineering, materials, and electronics and I now work in the physics department, where I not only undertake research but also do some teaching.

I have obtained a great variety of experience; although I was originally a chemist, these days I am now a physicist. In my area of specialization (smart materials) there is a great need for people like me who have a broad experience. One might think that I would not have a problem getting a job, but this is not really true. Amongst people who are aware of my abilities then there appears to be little problem in getting new contracts as long as the money is available. Unfortunately, whenever I apply for jobs outside Sheffield I rarely get an interview and have never got one for a permanent job. One gets the impression that people still see my dyslexia as a handicap to doing a job, rather than seeing the quality of someone who has gained the required skills despite having dyslexia, and who may have a different/alternate viewpoint on a subject.

APPENDIX VI – A DYSLEXIC'S PROGRESS

Fiona Zinovieff, BA

I graduated from Bangor in 1994 with a first class honours degree in psychology. I am writing this in the hope that others will read this and realize that dyslexic students are at least as good as other students and with a little help we might do even better!

Although my school career was filled with disparaging remarks such as 'Fiona must make more effort with the presentation of her work', 'Fiona's writing and spelling need attention', 'Her work lacks organization', or 'She is careless'. I was not diagnosed as dyslexic until I started university as a mature student. It took fourteen years for me to decide to return to education, having decided that my problems at school were probably motivational. Once at college I began to notice that other people could read a page two or three times faster than me (a problem when sharing hand-outs or computer monitors). I also began to realize that my spelling was a problem. One lecturer told me that she just couldn't read work that was misspelled. A sympathetic tutor referred me to the Dyslexia Unit, where a formal assessment was arranged for me, and I was given information and help.

After I discovered that I was dyslexic, I felt the need to re-evaluate my situation. The good side was that I was to be given an extra grant to purchase a computer for word processing and spell-checking, the down side was that I realized that there were specific limitations on my abilities when I compared myself to others. I had already realized that I did not have the time to copy my lecture notes out in a more legible form, and I was struggling to keep up with the recommended reading and this was only the first term of a three-year course. Obviously I needed a survival plan to keep my head above water. The methods that I used to cope with the course are a rationalization of my limitations and more importantly my capabilities.

The most important thing to remember is that there are benefits that stem from being dyslexic. This might not seem immediately obvious so I shall explain. I read very slowly and frequently misread words, so I am constantly checking that what I am reading makes sense. Learning comes with understanding, so by having tried to understand what I am reading I have also been learning. I might read more slowly than non-dyslexic students, but I also read more efficiently. When I am thinking about an essay or a project, I find that my mind races around the problem as I try to relate ideas to what I already know about a subject. By imposing a structure on this and firmly abandoning ideas that are irrelevant to the question, I have often come up with a novel approach to an answer. I think that many dyslexics are good at lateral thinking, whereas the majority of people tend to think linearly. Without mechanically imposing a rigorous structure on a piece of work, this rush of associated ideas can result in confused and disorganized work, because writing is a strictly linear activity. With structure these ideas can be harnessed to create original answers to old questions.

This is an asset in university and can transform a competent answer into a first class piece of work. In common with many other dyslexics, I find it easy to visualize ideas, and to remember diagrams and pictures. This is an advantage when making mind-maps for essay writing, or learning them for revision.

I have described the advantages first, as it is easy to despair on the bad days when the white spaces on the page dominate and the words won't come. It is important to remember that as a dyslexic my thoughts and ideas are as valid as the next person's and the majority of my problems are focused on communicating through the written word. Although these problems cannot be solved, strategies for coping can be employed that minimize the workload and produce maximum benefit from the work that is done. I realize that the methods that I found useful might not help everyone, but I would recommend trying them out as they certainly worked for me.

I find it very difficult to scan a page for relevant information. I cannot judge how useful a text or journal paper might be until I have read a lot of it. How to select the most relevant material is a problem, but there are solutions. When faced with a list of recommended books and papers recommended with a course, I found many of the lecturers would help me prioritize the texts. I asked which reading the lecturer would most recommend for each different aspect of their course; this helped me to reduce the list. When purchasing textbooks, I favoured those with good chapter summaries and introductions – I found these very helpful when trying to navigate through a sea of unfamiliar vocabulary and complex ideas. If I could anticipate what I was about to read, I found the process much easier. I found it easier to read and absorb information for writing essays than when I was just reading background material. This is because I was reading with a specific question in mind. This led me to conclude that past exam scripts might hold the key to improving my ability to focus on the background reading. Thus, as I read, I started to see how information could be used to answer certain aspects of different questions. This helped me to pick out the key themes of the courses and led me to appreciate how different ideas can be interlinked. I also found it beneficial to work in a small group with people reading alternative texts; we could then compare the information from different sources and select the most appropriate evidence for our arguments.

A good way of getting a broad and general understanding is to go to lectures – just think how many hours of reading has gone into preparing an hour's talk. Often lecturers provide an opportunity to ask questions, so try to think about the information that is being presented, and then ask specific questions if you are having difficulties applying the new information to what you already know. But however good a lecture might have been on the day, without notes much of it will probably fade or become confused. Initially, I found note taking a nightmare, and I was trying to copy up my notes into a more presentable form. Within days I realized that this was far too time consuming, and I should concentrate on making useful notes. After some trial and error, this is the system that evolved. During the lectures I made an effort to try to print out names and terminology in capital letters, then if my notes were unintelligible I knew what or who I needed to look up in my textbooks. I find acronyms very hard to learn and easy to forget, and so I was wary of using a lot of abbreviations, although I shortened some words by omitting vowels. I used arrows to stand for phrases such as 'developing from this . . .' and I tried to lay out any comparisons schematically but often this was impossible in the race to keep up with what is being said. I found it hard to listen and to attend to what I was writing, so I sometimes left gaps that I filled in from someone else's notes at the end of the lecture, or instructions to myself to read about a certain study.

At a later date, often at the end of a block of lectures on a certain subject, I would read through my notes, then insert headings and underline key words and names, then highlight definitive terms. When taking notes, I used broad lined, wide margined paper and I only used one side of each page. The margin is useful for adding comments or clarifications, and the wide lines make it easier to add underlining and still read what has been written. Often lecturers give strong hints about topics that are likely to come up in the exams – I noted these in the margin, and this often proved very useful! When I've put the notes into a ring file there is a blank page beside each page of lecture notes. This has several advantages: brief notes about background reading can be juxtaposed to the related lecture material; the key points and names from each page of notes can be listed clearly, and if during revision these points have lost their meaning, there is a full explanation on the facing page.

When doing my background reading I made extensive use of the photocopier, partly due to the time limits imposed by the library short loan system, but also because photocopying saved note taking! A useful feature of photocopiers is that print can be enlarged, also it is possible to copy on to coloured paper, both can help improve the readability of the text. When reading photocopies I use a highlight pen to mark the key points, so that I can remind myself of the contents without having to re-read it. I did make notes from journal articles that I found very difficult to understand as putting ideas into my own words sometimes helps me to understand.

Brain storming is a technique that I found particularly useful for imposing structure on a piece of writing. I start the exercise after having done the reading, by writing the title of the work at the top of a large sheet of paper. I then dissected the title carefully, to check that I had included the right information and that I could use it to answer the question! Then starting in the middle of the page I wrote down the key points, each in its own bubble. Some points have closely associated ideas which form 'satellite bubbles'. I would then draw arrows between bubbles to link ideas, or use coloured lines to indicate contradictions in the evidence. Usually I found that the links between the ideas gave me a logical sequence to the paragraphs, and allowed me to group related ideas in a more coherent fashion, transforming the explosion of ideas into a logical linear format.

I then write using the word processor. I cannot overstate the value of this machine to me, despite being unable to type when I started the course and being completely computer illiterate. I still can't type properly, but then I get a huge satisfaction from producing legible, well presented work without the agonies of copying, correcting, recopying, recorrecting etc. Having entered a piece of writing, it is so easy to alter a sentence or move a paragraph. The spell-check is invaluable, but not infallible. I have inadvertently added a few of my own spellings to the dictionary, or inserted the wrong word in the place of my misspelt words. I find it very hard to read from the screen, so I always print up a rough draft. It is best to let some time elapse before reading it, as this reduces the chances of reading what you think you've written, as opposed to reading what you have really written. At this point I worked with a friend who would read what I had written and correct my spellings and also query any points that were not clearly expressed, and I would do the same for her (bar the spellings). This was a reciprocal arrangement and we both benefited from it. Not only did it improve our writing skills, but we also learned from reading another point of view. I would strongly recommend finding a work partner or a small group of like minded individuals.

The period before exams is a time of extreme anxiety and stress, which seems to make the dyslexia worse! Despite the advice, relaxation often seems impossible. Although it is necessary to impose some self-discipline and some sort of timetable, it is also important to recognize the times when some tasks seem impossible and to be flexible and try a different task. Before starting to revise, I read through all my notes for each course. I then decided which areas I really did not want to revise. By reading through the past exam questions and any specimen questions that were available, I made lists of the questions related to each specific topic. I then chose the areas that I intended to revise. I only revised one topic more than the number of answers that I would have to answer; for example, if I had to write three answers, I would revise four topics. This might sound risky but the way that I revised allowed me to write answers for a variety of possible questions that may be set on any topic. When selecting the topics for revision it is important to consider how likely questions are to come up and to be realistic in this guesswork. For example, if three lectures have been devoted to one topic and two other topics have been covered in another lecture, it would be foolish to revise one of the short topics and not the one covered in more detail. It is important to remember that often an exam question might reflect a theme that has run through a course rather than the content of two or three lectures. Having selected the topics, I then found a work partner for each topic.

I started revision by reading through my lecture notes and extracting all the key points, which I listed on the facing page. I took a very big piece of paper and wrote all the relevant exam questions at the top of the page. I put the most important issues relating to that topic into bubbles in the middle of the paper, I tried to restrict myself to only one idea, or definition per bubble. I then tried to see a shape formed by the relationships between the central ideas, for example, three core issues might make a triangle, or two opposing theories might have evolved from one phenomenon, forming a seesaw shape with the observed phenomenon as the fulcrum. It is important that it is the relationships between the ideas that guide the shape, as it is the understanding of how the ideas relate to each other that give the flexibility to allow an answer to almost any question set. I then worked through my lecture notes and added in all of the key points and evidence presented. Each idea is put into a bubble close to the central issues to which it is related. It is often useful to discuss this with somebody else when trying to establish which are the most important issues, and whereabouts to place subsidiary issues. Often these bubbles are related to more than one idea, or have more than one interpretation. These are the links that will give an answer structure, leading neatly from one paragraph to the next.

Then I worked through the highlights of my background reading and added further bubbles to the plan, I tried to find alternative examples to the ones given in the lectures. As I often worked with somebody else, I would explain my examples to them and listen to them describe the points that they thought most worthy of inclusion. With hindsight I can now see that this was one of the most useful exercises of the process. Teaching somebody else is a very good way of learning; it helps you not only to understand the issues, but also gives you a lot of practice in expressing them clearly. Your friend will let you know if you have failed to get the message across giving you the chance to try a different way of explaining. Similarly when listening to your friend's examples, do so actively, and make sure that you understand why they are important and how they fit with the other issues.

At this point the page was usually a mess with loads of

annotations and small paragraphs that were included in case of forgetting. The next stage was to rewrite the mind-map to allow the examples and related ideas to be linked as easily as possible to the key issues. I would then re-write the map using only one word for each bubble and excluding all of the paragraphs. Sometimes I drew the bubbles as a shape that might help to remind me of their content; for example, the shape of a rabbit's head reminded me of a demonstration of the effect of language on perception. This might sound very laborious, but each time the plan is reorganized it reflects a deeper understanding of the issues, and understanding is necessary for learning. The links between the bubbles also serve as cues to the memory. I used colours to make different types of link; for example, some links serve to illustrate a point whereas others are linked because they give contradictory evidence. I often made up mnemonics to help me to remember the subsidiary ideas surrounding the central issues. I would take the initials or, if possible, the first syllable, and use them to make up a sentence. I found it helpful to go for a walk without any of my notes and to try remember all the mnemonics; it isn't possible to cheat and have a quick look!

Having constructed a mind-map, I would then try to answer each question using the contents of the map. Different types of question demand different contents and it is important to decide which 'route' through the map best answers each question. Not all of the information will be pertinent to all of the questions. Doing this with a workmate is again a useful exercise, as often there is more than one way to approach an issue. I made a mind-map for each topic that I revised. I must confess that I tried to select topics that had areas of overlap, so that the same background reading could be used!

When sitting exams, I was allowed extra time on account of my slow reading and writing. I tried to make as good use of this as possible. At the start of the exam I carefully read every question twice before deciding which ones to answer. I then wrote out all of my mind-maps and mnemonics for all of the answers before I started writing. This takes time but it helped me to write organized answers, and it gives a bit of time to fill in any elusive memories. I then divided the remaining time equally between the questions, and started on my second best answer. I used a highlight pen to pick out the important parts of the question, taking care to check that I had found any 'either/or' instructions. I then worked out a 'route' through the map that I had written down, and wrote an introduction to my answer, then systematically worked through the points until I was running out of time; I would then put a brief conclusion and leave that question. I then answered my strongest question, saving my least favourite until last. I have rarely finished any exam answer, and I have always come away knowing that I left out a lot of information, and to my surprise I have obtained several first class papers. I was very worried about my writing and spelling on my exam scripts. I felt very vulnerable without the protection of the word processor. However, I think that writing an introduction to an answer helps the examiner anticipate what is written. I was worried that my spelling would give the impression that I was confused about the terminology I employed, and so I tried to give a definition for each piece of 'jargon' that I employed; then even if I had the word wrong the examiner would know that I had grasped the issues. At the end of the exam I put a note to the marker into each answer book explaining that I was dyslexic, and that I wished the work was better presented and spelled too.

I don't know which of the above techniques was the most useful, but I have shared them with non-dyslexic students who also benefited from them. I think that the most important thing is to direct yourself to the key issues. It is easy to be drawn into interesting side issues that are irrelevant to the course content. This is of course not a problem if you are doing a degree course to further an interest rather than to obtain a qualification. This all makes me sound like a naturally very methodical and organized person – one look at my desk would alter that opinion. I had to work very hard to impose this discipline on myself, but I was encouraged as the results were rewarding. At times you might find it all very hard going. Don't suffer in silence. Ask for help, then help somebody in return. Remember you too have a lot to offer.

Notes

CHAPTER 1

1.1 For a brief account of the present position see Miles (1995) and for a fuller account of recent research, Thomson (1991).

1.2 The claim that there are nearly as many dyslexic girls as boys has been made by various recent researchers, for example Shaywitz et al. (1990). It is possible, however, that not all the children in this study were dyslexic in the strict sense. When dyslexics were picked out by different criteria a ratio of more than 4 boys to 1 girl was found (Miles and Haslum, 1986).

1.3 The evidence, particularly with regard to slowness, is extensive. For sources see, for example, Miles and Miles (1990) and for a sample of the experimental evidence, Miles (1986).

1.4 An adult business man who was diagnosed as dyslexic at the age of 38 said that if he was handed a balance sheet and asked for his opinion he would either stall by saying that he would rather read it later or, in as casual a voice as he could produce, ask his questioner to tell him what was in it. He also mentioned his embarrassment when, as newly appointed president of a guild, he was asked, without notice, to read to the members the rules of the guild. Further particulars of this case will be found in Miles (1993a, pp. 52 and 61).

1.5 Interestingly, some years ago a written report of this finding was given to a (non-dyslexic) typist in London for retyping. According to her version the student had put 'corelated' for *correlated* – a much less spectacular error. The typist's mistake is, of course, a striking example of the way in which most readers automatically correct misprints and misspellings.

On one occasion this student had elected to dictate his examination answers to a typist so as to save him any worries over spelling. Many years later he told one of us (TRM) that he had wanted to use the word 'neuropsychological'. This completely defeated the typist who, in standard non-dyslexic fashion, asked him how to spell it! Not surprisingly, he replied, 'That's *your* job, not mine!'

1.6 For further details of this dyslexic adult and his son see Griffiths (1980, pp. 51–3).

1.7 For an account of how things can go wrong on a 'bad day' see in particular Hampshire (1981). Susan Hampshire is, of course, a particularly striking example of a dyslexic person who has achieved success.

1.8 In a checklist for dyslexic adults Michael Vinegrad found that the best two discriminators were: 'When writing cheques do you frequently find yourself making mistakes?' and 'When using the telephone do you get the numbers mixed up when you dial?' See Vinegrad (1994).

1.9 This research has been reported in various places. See, for example, Galaburda et al. (1987).

1.10 See Springer and Deutsch (1984, p. 45).

1.11 See Pennington (1991).

1.12 An important consequence of West's book has been to encourage dyslexics not to underestimate their distinctive abilities. See West (1991).

1.13 It is now established that the visual system in primates contains two separate sub-systems, the *magnocellular* and the *parvocellular*. The magno system carries fast-moving, low contrast information and the parvo system carries slow-moving high contrast information. When Dr Galaburda carried out post-mortem examinations on the brains of five dyslexics he found that in all cases there were abnormalities in the magno system. It is possible that there may be a similar subdivision of pathways in the auditory system and that here, too, dyslexics have a deficit in the magno pathways. For further details of the research in this area see Livingstone et al. (1991). Related work has also been carried out by Paula Tallal and her colleagues. See Tallal *et al.* (1993).

1.14 For a review of the evidence suggesting that dyslexics have a phonological difficulty see Catts (1989) and Rack (1994).

1.15 For research in the area of 'automaticity' see R.I. Nicolson and A.J. Fawcett (1990).

1.16 This account makes sense of the difficulties reported by dyslexic adults even when reading and spelling have ceased to be major problems. For example, the student mentioned earlier, who sent a 'denotation' to the Dyslexia Unit, was successfully completing a course in palaeography – successfully except for one major difficulty, that of deciphering and copying totally unfamiliar script in a limited time. There is also a case of a 14-year-old girl who had tried out of interest to take up bell ringing but had had to give it up because she could not count other people's sounds at a fast enough rate (Miles, 1993a, p. 143). There are also occasional reports of difficulties with morse and shorthand, which again is not surprising if automatic and rapid processing of symbols is the problem – though, indeed, few dyslexics attempt either of these activities.

1.17 If there is any difficulty in arranging an assessment, advice can be obtained by telephoning or writing to the British Dyslexia Association, 98 London Road, Reading RG1 5AU, tel. 01234 668271. Enquiries can also be directed to The Adult Dyslexia Organization, 336 Brixton Road, London SW9 7AA, tel. 0171 737 7646. In the USA enquiries should be made to the Orton Dyslexia Society, Chester Building, Suite 382, 8600 LaSalle Road, Baltimore, MD 21286–2044, tel. (410) 296–0232. The headquarters of the European Dyslexia Association is Avenue Charles Woeste Bt.7, 1090 Brussels, Belgium, tel. 01234 261897. Those living in Australia should write to SPELD, PO Box 94, Mosman 2088, NSW, tel. (02) 906 2977; those living in New Zealand should write to SPELD, 313 Riccarton Road, Upric 4, Christchurch, tel. 03 3666 430.

CHAPTER 2

2.1 Margaret Rawson has spoken of a 'diversity' model for dyslexia. After describing some eminent individuals with dyslexic problems she writes: 'People of their kind of constitution, whatever difficulties they may have, are not to be thought of as victims of pathology, I believe, but as examples of the diversity that is to be expected in the present state of the evolution of the human species'. See Rawson (1981, p. 32). Her chapter is entitled 'A diversity model for dyslexia'.

2.2 For more detailed information on this grant see Gilroy (1994), *Dyslexia and Higher Education*. Obtainable from Dyslexia Unit, University of Wales, Bangor, Gwynedd LL57 2DG.

2.3 Part of the controversy is political – or rather, there may have been individuals who tried to use the scientific evidence for political purposes. A possible argument is that if intelligence is something innate then races whose members on average have lower IQs are less suited for high office – a conclusion which on social grounds appears wholly unacceptable. Claims of this kind, however, imply value judgements which as a matter of logic, cannot follow from the scientific evidence (compare Miles, 1976).

2.4 Interested readers are referred in particular to the writings of B.F. Skinner. For an account of the many improvements in skilled performance which can be brought about by suitable training along Skinnerian lines see Platt (1973, pp. 22–56). To say that a particular skill is *impossible* for a dyslexic is very rash and in our view savours of defeatism.

2.5 Not long ago one of us (TRM) was asked to test a dyslexic who had recently graduated. She had been devastated by the fact that someone had told her that her IQ was 85. It is not clear what kind of testing had led to this strange result – though in an unsympathetic environment dyslexics can fail to do themselves justice in an intelligence test just as they can when given other tests. In this case it was possible to reassure her that, since she was a graduate, she had already established her high ability.

2.6 There may, however, be difficulties in obtaining a grant to 'start again' if a student stays on a course for more than twenty weeks.

2.7 If you come on a reference to the 'ACID' profile, this refers to four sub-tests that are used – or used to be used – in the Wechsler Intelligence Scales. Some of the items in these tests have been found to be difficult for dyslexics, and when traditional scoring is used this has meant a lowering of their IQ figure. ACID is an acronym: A = Arithmetic; C = Coding; I = Information, and D = Digit Span. (A mother in the USA was recently told, without explanation, that her son had an ACID profile – and immediately assumed this meant that he was on drugs!)

2.8 *The Bangor Dyslexia Test*, Miles (1982), obtainable from Learning Development Aids, Wisbech, Cambridgeshire.

2.9 Some years ago one of us (TRM) had occasion to test a girl whose mother was also dyslexic. A well-meaning psychologist had advised the mother to 'keep the landing light on at night' as a way of boosting her daughter's confidence. The mother made clear to us, however, that she regarded this advice as wholly irrelevant to her daughter's dyslexia!

CHAPTER 3

3.1 The following is an example of a report which, however well meant, seems to us to show lack of understanding and to be insufficiently constructive:

> I have just read . . .'s first essay written for my seminar in Tudor and Early Stuart Economic and Social History. I have given the essay a mark of DF and the 'D' element is mainly for trying very hard. I am bound to say that I am very worried by this case; so worried that I asked . . . whether she really considered that she ought to continue at university. My concern relates not to the historical material in the essay but to the almost total inability to express herself in intelligible terms. Sometimes this is clearly a matter of dyslexia but more often it is simply inability to put a straightforward proposition on

paper. I simply cannot see that she has any chance of taking a degree unless there is a spectacular improvement. She has gone away to rewrite the worst and most obscure passages in the essay and she is seeing the woman who will help her with her dyslexia, in the near future, but I am bound to say that I take a very gloomy view of her prospects.

3.2 Over the years we have met large numbers of dyslexics who have been successful at college despite having been 'written off' as mediocre or stupid at an earlier age. For example, in the case of John (Miles, 1993b, p. 21), a school report written when he was aged fifteen described him as 'probably an average CSE prospect'; yet a few years later he was offered a place at university. Lilian Hartley, formerly secretary of the Cheshire and North Wales Dyslexia Association, has given us the following information about two boys assessed by TRM many years earlier (Miles, 1993a, case nos. 30 and 97): 'got a first at Loughborough and . . . a lower second at Portsmouth Polytechnic. Considering they were both classified by [name of county] at the age of nine as not being 11 + or Grammar School material their achievements are truly remarkable'.

In addition we should like to quote some extracts from a confidential report made since that time on a dyslexic applicant to university:

This boy's application is being made at the insistence of his parents and against the advice of the school. In spite of considerable help in school and a good deal of private tuition, he remains severely affected by the inability to express himself clearly, fluently and accurately in writing. How far the dyslexia on which both . . . and his parents lay such stress is a genuine medical condition is not for me to judge. The School has approached this with an open mind.

The School was never confident about . . .'s potential to reach 'A' level standard' and it was only the strong parental support which he obviously enjoys which persuaded us to allow him to begin the course. His progress so far seems to bear out our misgivings . . . He works slowly and performs badly under test conditions.

He finds concentration difficult, but attributes this to his dyslexia.

Perhaps unfortunately he has been conditioned from an early age to pay great attention to this condition from which he believes he suffers . . . His parents have high expectations of . . . and are confident that in a higher education institution which will understand his condition and allow for his difficulties he could achieve degree status.

This student was admitted to university, despite weak A-levels, on the basis of a high score on the Advanced Raven Matrices intelligence test. At the end of his course he came very near to First Class Honours and has now achieved a Ph.D.

3.3 The FEFC (Further Education Funding Council) has, in 1994–5, put a considerable amount of money into these colleges to support students with special needs.

3.4 For further information see *The New Qualifications Framework* (1994). London: Department for Education.

3.5 Most colleges will have a TEC (Training and Enterprise Council) Unit which offers a range of educational and training opportunities to the unemployed. There are sometimes special courses for women returners.

3.6 Particulars are available from the Open University, PO Box 49, Milton Keynes MK7 6AD.

3.7 There are many guides to degree courses which are revised annually. Among these may be mentioned: (1) B. Heap, *How to Choose your Degree Course*. Richmond: Trotman & Co.; (2) *Which Degree?* Hertford: Consumers' Association; (3) D.E. Gilroy (1995) *Applying to Higher Education for Dyslexic Students*. Available from 21, Brynteg, Llandegfan, Anglesey. Information is also available from SKILL, The National Bureau for Students with Disabilities, 336 Brixton Road, London SW9 7AA.

3.8 For an account of a dyslexic who has become a university lecturer in mathematics see Jansons (1988).

3.9 For a personal account of this distinctive skill see Aitken (1995).

3.10 There may, however, be risks for a dyslexic teacher in an environment where spelling errors meet with severe disapproval.

3.11 Video – *A Two Way Success*. Richmond: Trotman & Co.

3.12 See McLoughlin et al. (1994). We regard this as an excellent book.

3.13 Information is obtainable from GAP, 44 Queen's Road, Reading, Berks, RG1 4BB. See also *Taking a Year Off*, obtainable from Trotman & Co., Richmond.

3.14 See Kershaw (1974), especially sections 178–81 and recommendation 23, p. 122. Copies of the Kershaw Report, *People with Dyslexia*, are obtainable from the Royal Association for Disability and Rehabilitation, 25 Mortimer St, London W1N 8AB.

3.15 UCAS Research and Statistics Office (Disability and Special Needs Section) indicated that 1803 declared dyslexics were admitted into Higher Education in 1993 through UCCA/PCAS and that 2003 were admitted in 1994 through UCAS.

3.16 SKILL and ADO operate from the same address, 336 Brixton Road, London SW9 7AA (see notes 1.17 and 3.7).

CHAPTER 4

4.1 We are grateful to Michael Newby, himself a dyslexic and retired schoolteacher, for making this point clear to us.

4.2 From *Now We Are Six* (A.A. Milne, 1926, pp. 36–41).

4.3 See Robinson and Power (1984) and Ashley et al., (1993) *Core Skills GNVQ*. Sunderland: Business Education Publishers.

4.4 For examples of errors in spoken English on the part of dyslexic adolescents see Stirling (1985, p. 57). This book is obtainable from 114 Westbourne Road, Sheffield S10 2QT. For a report of some experimental studies in this area see Stirling and Miles (1988) and for some practical suggestions based on the studies see Stirling and Miles (1986).

4.5 See, for instance, *Open Learning Resources for Education and Training* (1994/5), National Extension College, Cambridge.

4.6 See Barrass (1982), Burton (1983) and Moss (1985).

CHAPTER 5

5.1 Some dramatic reports of these scars have been published in Janice Edwards's book, *The Scars of Dyslexia* (1994).

5.2 For an account of the 'stress conundrum' ('anxiety creates mistakes; mistakes make me more anxious') see Hales, Stress and dyslexia in the workplace (1995). A good general book on stress management is Konalski (1987).

5.3 For further suggestions in this area see Gilroy, Stress factors in the college student (1995).

5.4 A catalogue of tapes dealing with stress and relaxation is available from Life Tools, Macclesfield, Freepost SK 1852. A 'relaxation and confidence' tape is available from Dr Gwyn Lewis, Flat 3, The Paddock, Martlesham Heath, Ipswich.

5.5 The following report recently came into our possession:

> I would pass . . . [non-dyslexic student] for 1 question reasonably attempted and she knew when she had gone wrong by saying so. As for . . . [dyslexic student] – forget it, is he simple or something?

This 'simple' student went on to obtain Lower Second Class Honours.

5.6 We do, however, issue our students with 'tags' which they can clip on to their written work: 'This is the work of a dyslexic student who would be grateful if you would take this into consideration'. See also the tactful approach of Fiona Zinovieff which she mentions in Appendix VI.

CHAPTER 6

6.1 For evidence, see note 3.15.

6.2 For advice on this point see Gilroy (1994), *Dyslexia and Higher Education*. Available from Dyslexia Unit, University of Wales, Bangor, Gwynedd LL57 2DG.

6.3 The following is a striking indication of the sensitivity felt by some dyslexic students: two of them had met at one of these meetings and afterwards recognized each other at a sports club. Both were worried in case it became necessary to reveal to their friends how they came to know each other.

From time to time, though very infrequently, we have met dyslexic students who themselves found it difficult to be sensitive to the needs of fellow dyslexics. On one occasion some half dozen dyslexic students were attending a study group when a seventh student, known to very few of them, but himself dyslexic, entered the room and said, 'Ah! Here are all the thickies.' No harm was intended by this quip, but the speaker had clearly not appreciated that any reference, even a joking one, to being 'thick' was likely to reopen old wounds.

6.4 See, in this connection, Morgan (1994).

6.5 Stephen Martin, who contributed Appendix IV to the present book, has given us permission to reproduce a typed letter which he wrote to DEG shortly after his graduation. We have left it unedited.

Dear Mrs Gilroy,

I hope this letter finds you and your family in good health. This letter has got a duel purpose;

– firstly find enclosed some copies of the project which you so kindly corrected along with a corrected copy and a typed copy for copmarasion. l hope you will find them of use, sorry about the delay in sending them but resonly I've been very busy.

– the reason for been busy is that on the 9th of April I am leaveing for Japan to start a 2 year scholarship which I have been awarded. It is with the Japanese Government (Monbusho). Basicaly they are giving me money about 168,000 yen per month to do anythink I want to, so I've decided to do high altitude entomology thats looking at bugs on top of mountains in Japan, not bad eh.

They is only one snag thats a promblem, for the first six months l leam Japanese at a language school. So a bought a learn

Japanese book but as let I've not got past lesson one. The main promblem is the english its all nouns and verbs etc etc and I can'T rember what is the diffrence. Still it should be interesting. I'm going with two other people both Oxford graduates and both with firsts so it looks like I'm going to be with some pretty brainy people but no-dout I'll soon bring them down to my level.

Since arriving back from Nepal & Northen India where I had a brilliant time, hope you got the card' I've been all over the country Aberdeen–Southamton and every where in between. I've just finished typing and compiling three reports; Chinese Entomological' High Stand Natural History, and Fluted Peak thats the mountain we whent to climb in Nepal. Its been a long struggle but now its all finished it feels good. l also had to turn down an interview with the B.B.C at Bristol but I've got to go back in two years time' also I've been offered a part-time job at a new field center near use' so there's been plenty going on. Well its about time I was going' I hope to see you on my return with lots of new tales to tell. Keep the good work up and give my best whishes to the dsyelixia group. Thery is still hope for use let. Dsyelixics rule O.K.

P.S. the only problem with typing is the mistakes are much more easy to spot as you can't cover them up with bad handwriting.

6.6 For further discussion of this distinction, see Miles (1988).

CHAPTER 7

7.1 Hales (1994, p. 183).

7.2 For further discussion see Palinscar and Klenk (1992).

7.3 Some educators have spoken in this connection of 'neurolinguistic programming' (see, for instance, O'Connor and Seymour, 1990).

7.4 For discussion and references see Hales (1990).

7.5 For an interesting paper on this subject see Freire (1970).

7.6 See Stacey (1994b).

7.7 See Stacey (1994a).

CHAPTER 8

8.1 See *Higher Quality and Choice: The Charter for Higher Education.* Department of Further Education, 1994.

8.2 For more details on this point see Gilroy (1994).

8.3 Further details will be found in Lane and Chinn (1986).

8.4 For some useful advice in this area see Baker and Brown (1984).

8.5 See Meredeen (1988).

8.6 *Talking Books for the Handicapped* is available from the National Listening Library, 12 Lant St, London SE1.

8.7 Lewis Carroll, *Alice's Adventures in Wonderland* Chapter 12.

8.8 See De Leeuw and De Leeuw (1965) and Buzan (1971, revised and updated 1989).

8.9 Buzan, (1971, revised and updated 1989, pp. 58–9).

8.10 You may sometimes meet the description 'scotopic sensitivity syndrome' which was coined by Irlen (1983). There is controversy, however, as to whether this term is theoretically justified (see note 8.12, below).

8.11 Such a pack is obtainable from I.O.O. Marketing Ltd, 56–62 Newington Causeway, London SE1 6DS. The introduction to this pack, *Intuitive Overlays for Use by Teachers and Optometrists*, written by Dr Arnold Wilkins of the MRC Applied Psychology Unit, Cambridge, seems to us extremely helpful.

8.12 Exactly *why* coloured filters and coloured lenses should sometimes be beneficial is not clear. For critical discussions see, for instance, Evans and Drasdo (1991); Evans (1993).

CHAPTER 9

9.1 See Meredeen (1988) Chapters 7 and 9.

9.2 See Burton (1976), section 4.1.

9.3 See Buzan (1974, revised 1989). The video tape, *Get Ahead*, is available from the Buzan Centre, 37 Waterloo Road, Bournemouth BH9 1BD.

CHAPTER 10

10.1 For a useful list of such words see Casey (1985, pp. 50–3).

10.2 See Main (1980).

10.3 We recommend *Roget's Thesaurus of English Words and Phrases* (1987). London: Longman.

10.4 Many examples of good paragraphing will be found in Imhoof and Hudson (1975).

10.5 In this connection we recommend in particular Fabb and Durant (1993); Berry (1994); and Day (1989).

10.6 See also Fabb and Durant (1993) 'Putting together a bibliography' (pp.134–6); Berry (1994) 'Preparing a bibliography' (pp. 19–30); and Day (1989) 'How to cite the references' (pp.49–55).

CHAPTER 11

11.1 Some simple exercises will be found in Burt (1982); Evans (1986) has more detailed exercises at the end of each chapter.

11.2 These examples are drawn from Kirkman (1992, p. 177). In the appendix he presents six different versions of three scientific topics which are then analysed for clarity and simplicity.

11.3 These are set out clearly in Dykes (1992).

11.4 Spelling dictionaries are useful here as they indicate the spellings of verbs when they are extended from the root. See

Chambers Spell Well!, compiled by Kirkpatrick and Schwartz (1990).

11.5 If there are any dyslexic readers who have failed to detect the differences between the last three sentences they should look carefully at the placing of commas. Shortly before the publication of the first edition of this book we came on the following passage in *The Times* (4 January 1986): 'The ashes of J.B. Priestley . . . are to be buried in the Yorkshire Dales parish of Hubberholme, where he had many friends on April 19.' As written, this implies that he had no friends on other days; a comma after 'friends' was essential!

11.6 These will be found in Kirkman (1992).

11.7 For example, Day (1989, pp. 160–1) writes: 'Do not be afraid to name the agent of the action in a sentence, even when it is "I" or "we".

CHAPTER 12

12.1 See O'Connor and Seymour (1990, pp. 182–3).

12.2 Mnemonics are of course possible; for example the letters of the name JASON are also the first letters of the months from July to November.

12.3 The main exceptions are *much, such, rich, which, attach*, and the tiresomely irregular word *touch*.

12.4 A very interesting book in this connection is Brown and Brown (1990).

12.5 Burt (1982) has spelling rules set out clearly in boxes. Books on spelling written specifically with the needs of dyslexics in mind include: Hornsby and Shear (1975); Miles and Miles (1983); Brand (1985); E.Miles (1992); Thomson and Watkins (1990); and Cooke (1993).

12.6 A useful desk-top dictionary is Collins (1982); as a paperback we recommend *Oxford Word Power Dictionary* (Oxford: Oxford University Press 1993).

12.7 For example, the *Penguin Reference Dictionary of Geography* (Harmondsworth: Penguin, 1985) and the *Pocket Dictionary for Nurses* (Oxford: Oxford University Press, 1984).

12.8 We recommend in particular *Chambers Spell Well*, compiled by Kirkpatrick and Schwarz (1990); *Pergamon Dictionary of Perfect Spelling* (Leeds: Pergamon, 1978); *Cassell's Spelling Dictionary* London: Cassell, 1993); and *Harrap's Dictionary of English Spelling* (Bromley: Harrap).

12.9 In particular, there is a range of Franklin spellmasters and wordmasters. Details are available from Franklin Educational Distributor's Association, Bingham-Gurney, Old Commerce House, Pontwelly, Llandysul, Dyfed, Wales SA44 4AJ.

CHAPTER 13

13.1 For documentation see, in particular, Miles (1993a).

13.2 Some initial research in this area has been reported by Pritchard et al. (1989).

13.3 For an account of how these procedures can be put to good use see M. Kibel's paper, 'Linking language to action' (Kibel, 1992).

13.4 Research on a multimedia calculator for dyslexics is at present being carried out by Sue Flynn at Coventry University. The intention is that the operations (addition etc.) should be *demonstrated visually*. The user can therefore *see what is happening*, and the risk of pressing the wrong button is therefore very much lessened.

13.5 Some useful help with the basics of mathematics will be found in Henderson (1989). For further suggestions see also Miles and Miles (1992).

CHAPTER 14

14.1 The following are useful addresses:

• Adult Dyslexia Computer Interest Group, c/o Computer Committee, 13 Hurstleigh Drive, Redhill, Surrey RH1 2AA.

- Dyslexia Computer Resource Centre, Department of Psychology, University of Hull, Hull HU6 7RX.
- NCET – National Council for Educational Technology, Sir William Lyons Road, Coventry CV4 7EZ.
- BCS – British Computer Society Disabled Specialist Group, Geoff Busby, GEC Computer Services Ltd, West Hanningfield Road, Great Baddow, Chelmsford CM2 8HN.

Ability (the journal of the BCS Disabled Specialist Group), Issue 11, Spring 1994, dealt with dyslexia.

14.2 Information is available from National Federation of Access Centres, Hereward College of Further Education, Bramston Crescent, Tile Hill Lane, Coventry CV4 9SW.

14.3 These are available from Intertan UK Ltd, Tandy Centre, Leamore Lane, Walsall WS2 7PS.

14.4 LM600 A, Speaking Language Master.

14.5 Que Quick Reference Series (a portable resource of easily accessible microcomputer knowledge), e.g. Que (1992), *Word for Windows* 2, Carmel: Que.

14.6 In this connection see Bray (1994) *Buyer's Guide to Notebook PC's.* (Sevenoaks: O'Connell Read). Also Salisbury (1994) Laptop computers: avoiding the pitfalls. *Skill, Notes and Queries* 9, Jan. 1994, 4–5.

14.7 See Laycock (1994).

14.8 See Morgan (1994).

14.9 West (1991).

14.10 Dr Chris Singleton, Department of Psychology, University of Hull, is currently doing research in this area.

CHAPTER 15

15.1 See, for example, *Regulations Governing Special Assessment Arrangements for Students with Disability or Injury.* Oxford: Brookes University (1994).

15.2 Guidelines on the use of an amanuensis are available from SKILL, 336 Brixton Road, London SW9 7AA.

CHAPTER 16

16.1 Psychologists have traditionally distinguished 'long-term memory' from 'short-term memory'. However, there is no simple theory as to how our memories work. According to Baddeley (1982, p. 160) 'there are probably *more* than two memory systems. Short-term memory is not a single unitary system; rather it is an amalgam or alliance of several temporary memory systems working together'.

16.2 In an early experiment on mental imagery, Galton (1883) asked a number of eminent contemporaries to 'think of some definite object – suppose it is your breakfast table as you sat down to it this morning – and consider carefully the picture that rises before your mind's eye' (p.255). There were 100 replies, some of the subjects reporting that they had very vivid mental imagery, others virtually none. This appears to be an area where there are wide individual differences.

16.3 See Baddeley (1982, pp. 95–6).

16.4 See Buzan (1989, p. 51).

CHAPTER 17

17.1 In this connection see Shone (1984), *Creative Visualisation* and Davies (1986) *Maximising Examination Performance*.

CHAPTER 18

18.1 The word 'provision' is now used in preference to 'concession', although some institutions prefer 'accommodation'.

18.2 In its booklet, *Dyslexia: Policy and Code of Practice*, the University of North London says of its arrangements for dyslexics, 'In both examinations and coursework submissions, dyslexic students are disadvantaged by the nature of their disability. The above arrangements are an attempt to *equalise*, not to unfairly advantage the dyslexic student.'

18.3 For details of this case see Miles (1993b, pp. 30–9).

18.4 While it is true that any examination candidate may have an 'off-day' there is reason to think that because of their disabilities in the area of language dyslexics are particularly vulnerable.

18.5 National policy, however, at least in Great Britain, seems to reflect some uncertainty on this matter, since most grant-giving bodies do not make awards to students who have not obtained First or Upper Second Class Honours. This is, in effect, to use the student's degree class not as a certificate of achievement but as a means of predicting her future performance.

18.6 See West (1991).

Recommended books on study skills

Although the reference section which follows contains details of all the books mentioned in the chapter notes, we thought it would be helpful if in addition we provided a separate list of *recommended books on study skills*. This will enable readers to pick out immediately the books which are most relevant to their needs. The list includes some books not referred to in the main text.

Bailey, R.F. (1977) *A Survival Kit for Writing English*. Melbourne: Longman.

Barrass, R. (1982) *Students Must Write*. London: Methuen.

Berry, R. (1994) *The Research Project: How to Write it*. London: Routledge.

Burt, A. (1982) *A Guide to Better Punctuation*. Cheltenham: Stanley Thorne.

Burt, A. (1985) *A Guide to Better Grammar*. Cheltenham: Thorne.

Buzan, T. (1971) *Speed Reading*. Newton Abbot: David & Charles.

Buzan, T. (1989) *Use Your Head*. London: BBC.

Buzan, T. (1989) *Use Your Memory*. London: BBC.

Casey, F. (1993) *How to Study: A Practical Guide*. Basingstoke: Macmillan.

Clanchy, J. and Ballard, B. (1992) *How to Write Essays*. Melbourne: Longman Cheshire.

Davies, D. (1986) *Maximising Examination Performance: A Psychological Approach*. London: Jessica Kingsley.

Day, R.A. (1989) *How to Write and Publish a Scientific Paper*. Cambridge: Cambridge University Press.

Dykes, B. (1992) *Grammar Made Easy*. Sydney, NSW: Hale & Iremonger.

Evans, D.W. (1986) *Improving English Skills*. London: Longman.
Imhoof, M. and Hudson, H. (1975) *From Paragraph to Essay*. London: Longman.
Leader, D. (1990) *How to Pass Exams*. Cheltenham: Thorne.
Lindsay, D. (1984) *A Guide to Scientific Writing*. Melbourne: Longman Cheshire.
Meredeen, S. (1988) *Study for Survival and Success: Guide Notes for College Students*. London: Chapman.
Pechenik, J. and Lamb, B. (1994) *How to Write about Biology*. London: Harper Collins.
Peelo, M. (1994) *Helping Students with Study Problems*. Buckingham: SRHE & Open University.

As a general guide for dyslexic adults we recommend *Dyslexia: Signposts to Success. A Guide for Dyslexic Adults*. Compiled by Matty, J. Reading: British Dyslexia Association.

References

Aitken, G. (1995) in *Dyslexia: An International Journal of Research and Practice*, 1, 1, 55.

Ashley, K., Ellison, J. Hind, Knott, D.G., Morton, J. and Waites, N. (1993) *Core Skills GNVQ*. Sunderland: Business Education Publishers.

Baddeley, A.D. (1982) *Your Memory: A User's Guide*. Harmondsworth: Penguin.

Bailey, R.F. (1977) *A Survival Kit for Writing English*. Melbourne: Longman.

Baker, L. and Brown, A.L. (1984) Metacognitive skills and reading. In Pearson, P.D. (ed.) *Handbook of Reading Research*. New York: Longman.

Barrass, R. (1982) *Students Must Write*. London: Methuen.

Berry, R. (1994) *The Research Project: How to Write It*. London: Routledge.

Brand, V. (1985) *Remedial Spelling*. Baldock: Egon.

Bray, P. (1994) *Buyer's Guide to Notebook PC's*. Sevenoaks: O'Connell Read.

Brown, H. and Brown, M. (1990) *A Speller's Companion*. Wigton: Brown and Brown. (Available: Brown & Brown, Keeper's Cottage, Westward, Wigton, Cumbria CA7 8NQ.)

Burt, A. (1982) *A Guide to Better Punctuation*. Cheltenham: Stanley Thorne.

Burton, S.H. (1976) *Using English*. London: Longman.

Burton, S.H. (1983) *Writing Letters*. London: Longman.

Buzan, T. (1971) *Speed Reading*. Newton Abbot: David & Charles.

Buzan, T. (1989) *Use Your Head*. London: BBC.

Casey, F. (1985) *How to Study: A Practical Guide*. Basingstoke: Macmillan Education.

Casey, F. (1993) *How to Study: A Practical Guide*. Basingstoke: Macmillan.

Catts, H.W. (1989) Phonological processing deficits and reading disabilities. In A.G. Kamhi, and H.W. Catts (eds) *Reading Disabilities: A Developmental Language Perspective*. Boston, Mass.: Little Brown.

Cooke, A. (1993) *Tackling Dyslexia the Bangor Way*. London: Whurr.

Davies, D. (1986) *Maximising Examination Performance: A Psychological Approach*. London: Jessica Kingsley.

Day, R.A. (1989) *How to Write and Publish a Scientific Paper*. Cambridge: Cambridge University Press.

De Leeuw, M. and De Leeuw, E. (1965) *Read Better, Read Faster*. London: Penguin.

Dykes, B. (1992) *Grammar Made Easy*. Sydney, NSW: Hale & Iremonger.

Edwards, J. (1994) *The Scars of Dyslexia*. London: Cassell.

Evans, B.J.W. (1993) Dyslexia: the Dunlop test and tinted lenses. *Optometry Today*, 33, 13, 26–30.

Evans, B.J.W. and Drasdo, N. (1991) Tinted lenses and related therapies for learning disabilities – a review. *Ophthalmic and Physiological Optics*, 11, 206–17.

Evans, D.W. (1986) *Improving English Skills*. London: Longman.

Fabb, N. and Durant, A. (1993) *How to Write Essays, Dissertations and Theses in Literary Studies*. Harlow: Longman.

Freire, P. (1970) *Ideology and Adult Education in Latin America*. Hull: University of Hull Department of Education.

Galaburda, A.M., Corsiglia, J., Rosen, G.D. and Sherman, G.F. (1987) Planum temporale asymmetry: reappraisal since Geshwind and Levitsky. *Neuropsychologia*, 25, 6, 853–68.

Galton, F. (1883) *Inquiries into Human Faculty and its Development*. London: Dent.

Gilroy, D.E. (1994), *Dyslexia and Higher Education*. Obtainable from Dyslexia Unit, University of Wales, Bangor, Gwynedd LL57 2DG.

Gilroy, D.E. (1995) Stress factors in the college student. In T.R. Miles and V.P. Varma (eds) *Dyslexia and Stress*. London: Whurr.

Griffiths, J.M. (1980) Basic arithmetic processes in the dyslexic child. M.Ed. dissertation, University of Wales.

Hales, G. (1994) The human aspects of dyslexia. In G. Hales (ed.) *Dyslexia Matters*. London: Whurr.

Hales, G. (1990) Personality aspects of dyslexia. In G. Hales (ed.) *Meeting Points in Dyslexia*. Reading: British Dyslexia Association.

Hales, G. (1995) Stress factors in the workplace. In Miles, T.R. and Varma, V.P. (eds) *Dyslexia and Stress*. London: Whurr.

Hampshire, S. (1981) *Susan's Story*. London: Sidgwick & Jackson.

Henderson, A. (1989) *Maths and Dyslexics*. Llandudno: St David's College.

Hornsby, B. and Shear, F. (1975) *Alpha to Omega*. London: Heinemann.

Imhoof, M. and Hudson, H. (1975) *From Paragraph to Essay*. London: Longman.

Irlen, H. (1983) Successful treatment of learning difficulties. Paper presented at the annual convention of the American Psychological Association. Anaheim, California.

Jansons, K.M. (1988) A personal view of dyslexia and of thought without language. In L. Weiskrantz (ed.) *Thought without Language*. Oxford: Oxford University Press.

Kershaw, J. (1974) *People with Dyslexia*. London: British Council for the Rehabilitation of the Disabled.

Kibel, M. (1992) Linking language to action. In T.R. Miles and E. Miles (eds) *Dyslexia and Mathematics*. London: Routledge.

Kirkman, J. (1992) *Good Style: Writing for Science and Technology*. London: Spon.

Kirkpatrick, E.M. and Schwarz, C.M. (1990) *Chambers Spell Well!* Edinburgh: Chambers.

Konalski, R. (1987) *Over the Top*. Bicester: Winslow.

Lane, C. and Chinn, S.J. (1986) Learning by self-voice echo. *Academic Therapy*, 21, 4, 477–81.

Laycock, D. (1994) The technology needs of the dyslexic adult. *Ability*, 11, 7–9.

Livingstone, M.S., Rosen, G.D., Drislane, F.W. and Galaburda, A.M. (1991) Physiological and anatomical evidence for a magnocellular defect in developmental dyslexia. *Proceedings of the National Academy of Science of the USA*, 88, 7943–7.

McLoughlin, D., Fitzgibbon, G. and Young, V. (1994) *Adult Dyslexia: Assessment, Counselling, and Training*. London: Whurr.

Main, A. (1980) *Encouraging Effective Learning*. Edinburgh: Scottish Academic Press.

Meredeen, S. (1988) *Study for Survival and Success: Guide Notes for College Students*. London: Chapman.

Miles, E. (1992) *The Bangor Dyslexia Teaching System*. 2nd Edn. London: Whurr.

Miles, T.R. (1976) The Jensen debate. *Philosophy*, 51, 216–18.

Miles, T.R. (1986) On the persistence of dyslexic difficulties into adulthood. In G.Th. Pavlidis and D.F. Fisher (eds) *Dyslexia: Its Neuropsychology and Treatment*. Chichester: Wiley.

Miles, T.R. (1988) Counselling in dyslexia. *Counselling Psychology Quarterly*, 1, 97–107.

Miles, T.R. (1993a) *Dyslexia: The Pattern of Difficulties*. London: Whurr.

Miles, T.R. (1993b) *Understanding Dyslexia*. Bath: Amethyst Books.

Miles, T.R. (1995) Dyslexia: the current status of the term II. *Child Language Teaching and Therapy*, 11, 1, 23–33.

Miles, T.R. and Haslum, M.N. (1986) Dyslexia: anomaly or normal variation? *Annals of Dyslexia*, 36, 103–17.

Miles, T.R. and Miles, E. (1983) *Help for Dyslexic Children*. London: Routledge.

Miles, T.R. and Miles, E. (1990) *Dyslexia: A Hundred Years On*. Milton Keynes: Open University Press.

Miles, T.R. and Miles, E. (1992)(eds) *Dyslexia and Mathematics*. London: Routledge.

Milne, A.A. (1926) *Now We Are Six*. London: Methuen.

Morgan, E. (1994) Can dreams come true? *Dyslexia Contact*, 13, 1, 8.

Moss, W. (1985) *Writing Letters*. National Extension College, Cambridge.

Nicolson, R.I. and Fawcett, A.J. (1990) 'Automaticity: a new framework for dyslexia research'. *Cognition*, 35, 159–82.

O'Connor, J. and Seymour, J. (1990) *Introducing Neurolinguistic Programming*. London: Mandala.

Palinscar, A. and Klenk, L. (1992) Fostering literacy learning in supportive contexts. *Journal of Learning Disabilities*, 25, 211–25.

Pennington, B.F. (1991) (ed.) *Reading Disabilities: Genetic and Neurological Influences*. Dordrecht: Kluwer Academic Publishers.

Platt, J.R. (1973) The Skinnerian revolution. In H. Wheeler (ed.) *Beyond the Punitive Society*. London: Wildwood House.

Pritchard, R.A., Miles, T.R., Chinn, S.J. and Taggart, A.T. (1989) Dyslexia and knowledge of number facts. *Links*, 14, 3, 17–20.

Rack, J. (1994) Dyslexia: the phonological deficit hypothesis. In A.J. Fawcett and R.I. Nicolson (eds) *Dyslexia in Children: Multidisciplinary Perspectives*. Hemel Hempstead: Harvester Wheatsheaf.

Rawson, M.B. (1981) A diversity model for dyslexia. In G.Th. Pavlidis and T.R. Miles (eds) *Dyslexia Research and Its Applications to Education*. Chichester: Wiley.

Robinson, D. and Power, R. (1984) *Spotlight on Communication*. London: Pitman.

Roget, P.M. (1987) *Roget's Thesaurus of English Words and Phrases*. (prepared by Kirkpatrick). London: Longman.

Salisbury, J. (1994) Laptop computers: avoiding the pitfalls. *Skill: Notes and Queries*, 9, 4–5.

Shaywitz, S.E., Shaywitz, B.A., Fletcher, J.M. and Escobar M.D. (1990) Prevalence of reading disability in boys and girls – results of the Connecticut longitudinal study. *Journal of the American Medical Association*, 264, 998–1002.

Shone, R. (1984) *Creative Visualisation*. London: Aquarian.

Springer, S.P. and Deutsch, G. (1984) *Left Brain, Right Brain*. New York: W.H. Freeman.

Stacey, G. (1994a) Dyslexia from the inside: or some ways to make the most of your dyslexic mind. *Dyslexia Contact*, 13, 1, 12–13.

Stacey, G. (1994b) My brain is wired differently. *Dyslexia Contact*, 13, 2, 18–19.

Stirling, E.G. (1985) *Help for the Dyslexic Adolescent*. Obtainable from 114 Westbourne Road, Sheffield S10 2QT.

Stirling, E.G. and Miles, T.R. (1986) Oral language of dyslexic adolescents. *Child Language Teaching and Therapy*, 2, 143–53.

Stirling, E.G. and Miles, T.R. (1988) Naming ability and oral fluency in dyslexic adolescents. *Annals of Dyslexia*, 38, 50–72.

Tallal, P., Miller, S. and Fitch, R.H. (1993) Neurobiological basis of speech: a case for the pre-eminence of temporal processing. In P. Tallal, (ed.) *Annals of the New York Academy of Sciences*, 70–81.

Thomson, M.E. (1991) *Developmental Dyslexia*. London: Whurr.Thomson, M.E. and Watkins, E.J. (1990) *Dyslexia: A Teaching Handbook*. London: Whurr.

Vinegrad, M. (1994) A revised adult dyslexia check list. *Educare*, 48, 21–3.

West, T.G. (1991) *In the Mind's Eye: Visual Thinkers, Gifted People with Learning Difficulties, Computer Images, and the Ironies of Creativity*. Buffalo, New York: Prometheus Books.

Name index

Subject index

draft 101–3; writing introduction
and conclusion 107
examinations 4, 22; anxiety 171;
discussion points for moderators
and Examining Boards 180–9;
examination techniques 171–9,
204–6, 209–10, 227–8; obtaining
provisions 153–5; oral
examinations 157, 179; provision
for examinations in general 11,
22, 155–9, 244–5; use of word
processors 158–9

familial incidence of dyslexia 2
finance 36–7
form filling 29, 30; *see also* UCAS
form

GCSE 18
GNVQ x, 18, 19, 69
grammar 109–11; common
grammatical errors 117–19

hemispheres of the brain 6, 64
HEFC (Higher Education Funding
Council) x
HND courses 18

intelligence 14, 15
interviews 25, 26

Kershaw Report 25, 236

lateral thinking 61
lenses, coloured 11, 79, 240
Local Education Authority
12

magnocellular system 230–1
mathematics 137–42, 197; difficulties
137; statistics 140–2; symbols
138–42
mind-maps 82–3, 85, 94, 224, 226–7
mnemonics 103, 125, 134, 163–5
194, 195
modular courses 22
morse, difficulties with 231
multimedia calculator 243
multisensory learning 132, 194

National Curriculum 21, 109
neurolinguistic programming 239
norm based tests 13
note-taking 80, 81; in lectures
81–5, 223–4; taped notes 84; from
texts 86
NVQ courses 18

Open University 18, 39, 235
oral examinations 155, 157, 179
oral language *see* spoken
language
organizing works 28, 29, 31–8, 46,
201–3

paragraphing 103, 241
parvocellular system 230–1
'pegging' 164
percentiles 12
phonological difficulties 7
planum temporale 6
punctuation 88, 90, 112–15

reading 3, 12 13, 74–8; aloud 38,
75; rapid reading 78